Worship TEAM HandBOOK

WRITTEN BY URBANA WORSHIP TEAM MEMBERS

Alison Siewert (editor), Andy Crouch,
Matt Frazier & Sundee Frazier

InterVarsity Press
Downers Grove, Illinois

To the mentors, teammates and students who have led us,

followed us and joined us in worship, not only

by singing but by living out the gospel together. Thanks be to God.

InterVarsity Press
P.O. Box 1400, Downers Grove, IL 60515
World Wide Web: www.ivpress.com
E-mail: mail@ivpress.com

InterVarsity Press® *is the book-publishing division of InterVarsity Christian Fellowship/USA*®*, a student movement active on campus at hundreds of universities, colleges and schools of nursing in the United States of America, and a member movement of the International Fellowship of Evangelical Students. For information about local and regional activities, write Public Relations Dept., InterVarsity Christian Fellowship/USA, 6400 Schroeder Rd., P.O. Box 7895, Madison, WI 53707-7895.*

All Scripture quotations, unless otherwise noted, are from the New Revised Standard Version of the Bible, copyright 1989 by the Division of Christian Education of the National Council of the Churches of Christ in the USA. Used by permission. All rights reserved.

Chapter 20 is used by permission of Phil Bowling-Dyer.

Chapter 22 is used by permission of Dan Siewert.

Chapter 26 is used by permission of Jun Ohnuki.

The Perfect Relationship and Electronic Breakup in chapter 36 are used by permission of Scott Brill.

Chapters 38 and 39 and the sidebar and art in chapter 40 are used by permission of Scott Wilson.

Permission is granted to reprint-photocopy the skits in chapter 36 for members of a drama team. Requests for other uses should be directed to the publisher.

Cover photographs: courtesy of 2100 Productions

ISBN 0-8308-1943-6

Printed in the United States of America ♾

Library of Congress Cataloging-in-Publication Data

Urbana Worship Team.
    Worship team handbook / written by Urbana Worship Team members.
    Alison Siewert (editor) . . . [et al.].
       p.   cm.
    Includes bibliographical references.
    ISBN 0-8308-1943-6   (pbk.: alk. paper)
    1. Public worship.   2. Liturgy committees.   I. Siewert, Alison.
    II. Title.
    BV10.2.U73   1998
    264—dc21
                                           98-34177
                                              CIP

| 26 | 25 | 24 | 23 | 22 | 21 | 20 | 19 | 18 | 17 | 16 | 15 | 14 | 13 | 12 | 11 | 10 | 9 | 8 | 7 | 6 | 5 | 4 | 3 | 2 |

| 19 | 18 | 17 | 16 | 15 | 14 | 13 | 12 | 11 | 10 | 09 | 08 | 08 | 07 | 06 | 05 | 04 | 03 | 02 | 01 | 00 | 99 |

Part 1: First Things First

Part 2: Follow the Leader

Part 3: Go, Teams

Part 4: Making Music: The Musicians

Part 5: Making Music: The Music

Part 1
First Things First

1
Who We Are and Why We Wrote This

Alison Siewert

This book grew out of an invitation to redesign worship for a major conference. Every three years the Urbana Missions Convention brings together about eighteen thousand college students, pastors, missionaries and other Christians at the University of Illinois in Champaign/Urbana (thus the title—you couldn't really call it Champaign!) to think about and respond to God's call to love the whole world with the good news of the gospel. The conference is hosted by InterVarsity Christian Fellowship, an interdenominational ministry to students on college campuses across the United States and Canada. In 1988 Dan Harrison, then the new director of Urbana conferences, asked Phil Bowling-Dyer and me to help rework worship for the 1990 conference.

For over forty years Urbana conventions had enjoyed worship with a gifted hymn leader accompanied by organ and piano. But musical and student cultures had changed, and it was time for a shift in worship style and format. As we worked on Urbana 90, we gained some understanding of the issues and challenges that come with the new. Changing from an individual leader to a team moved the whole of worship at Urbana in a new direction and gave us enormous new potential.

Andy Crouch joined us in 1993, and by the time we were planning for the 1996 conference, we had worked on three Urbana conferences. We recognized how unique this experience had been in our lives as worship leaders: As we studied Scripture, prayed for vision, rehearsed music and led worship, we were challenged and stretched in ways we never had been before. We came to deeply value each other and our

work together as a team because we realized how much God was teaching us through one another. We saw that Urbana's move from individual to team leadership was a gift and a challenge to us as much as it was to the conference. We also recognized how little specific training for team leadership most of us have had, and how little is available. We decided we wanted to pass on some of what we've gleaned.

We write this book knowing that it will be read from many angles: as an opportunity to renew your team and its ministry, out of general interest, as a way to start thinking about new ways of worship, and for help in working with a worship team for the first time. We hope it's helpful in every situation, though we recognize our reflections are far from everything you could say about worship. For instance, we don't cover the topic of children in worship, and we focus more on new forms of worship than on traditional liturgies. But hey, we had to stop somewhere or this handbook would never move from our computers and into your hands.

We set out to offer something of our own experience to others attempting to lead together. We wanted to create something that would speak to diverse worship settings. And we wanted to build a practical tool that would help and encourage worship leaders like ourselves, week to week, meeting to meeting. We hope that, now in your hands, this book will be even more. We hope it will be a stream for dry places and a plow for hard ground.

Most of all, we hope for your growth in faith and skill as you lead others in worship. We pray your worship will witness to people around you of a God who knows and loves us, who died for us yet lives, who calls us to declare his worth-ship by staking our lives on his promises. We've had a good time writing this together, and we hope you'll enjoy reading it.

Oh, by the Way, We Are . . .

Alison Siewert, editor. Alison lives in Lancaster, Pennsylvania, with her husband and two sons. Formerly Associate Director of Worship at the First Presbyterian Church of Bethlehem, she now pastors a community of young adults and consults with churches on the development and design of worship. Alison also does staff training with InterVarsity.

Andy Crouch. Andy lives in Cambridge, Massachusetts, where he ministers to students with InterVarsity and enjoys his wife and son. Andy leads worship at conferences, writes music and edits *re:generation quarterly*, a magazine for Christians in community.

Matt Frazier. Matt is on InterVarsity staff in Madison, Wisconsin, where he and his wife, Sundee, are planning worship for the Urbana 2000 convention. He has written many worship songs, including some used at Urbana 93 and 96, when he played drums with the team.

Sundee Frazier. Sundee works in worship development for Urbana and leads worship extensively. She has worked on campus with InterVarsity with her husband, Matt, whom she got to know while preparing for Urbana 93. She has written on ethnicity and culture as they relate to faith.

A Few Other People Pitched In Too. They Are . . .

Phil Bowling-Dyer. Phil is InterVarsity area director for Black Campus Ministry in Oakland, California and led worship at Urbanas 93 and 96.

Scott Brill. Scott works with InterVarsity at the University of Rhode Island.

Jun Ohnuki. Jun works as a researcher in Pasadena, California, but he's really a visual artist. He played bass on the teams for Urbana 93 and 96.

Dan Siewert. Dan is InterVarsity area director for central and northeast Pennsylvania, where he plays loads of guitar.

Scott Wilson. Scott directs InterVarsity's Twentyonehundred Productions, which creates multimedia tools for use in ministry.

A Note about Copyrights

This book is copyrighted. That means if you want to copy parts of it (in any way—photocopy, chalkboard, skywriting) you need to contact InterVarsity Press (don't be afraid—they're really nice) for permission. *We'll make one exception:* You can copy the dramatic sketches for use in your worship without contacting IVP first. But please, only copy the number you need for the cast, and tear them up when you're done. If you want to use the book or parts of it with your worship team (like the Bible studies at the back), please get each of them a copy of the book rather than photocopying. We think that's pretty fair, and we hope you do too.

2   Why Worship in a New Way?

Andy Crouch

At the turn of the century a tremendous tide of change—part renaissance, part revolution—is flooding the worship lives of North American Protestants. If you are reading this book, you are probably part of the wave. Churches and fellowships are making new forms of worship a priority in their schedules, budgets and attention. Often these new forms are characterized by two key features: the presence of pop culture (including current popular music, language, forms of humor and dress) and the absence of the conventional liturgical forms that used to go along with "church." Whether on Sunday morning or Saturday night, these services are growing, generating—and requiring—lots of energy.

But as leaders of worship we ought to ask ourselves, why? Why are we worshiping this way? What are the roots of what we're doing, and where are we going? The question isn't really, why do we *worship?* The answers for that are plain in Scripture, theology and our own experience. For Christians, worship has always been an openhearted response to the incredible grace and love of God. It still is. The question is, Why are we choosing to worship *in a new way*: embracing popular culture and setting aside traditional orders of service? The way we answer this question will say a lot about whether we are just following a trend or following Jesus.

One of the most common reasons given for worshiping in a new way is that we want to grow, or we want to reach more people. But a moment's reflection suggests

that even if new worship is a way to grow, that isn't necessarily enough. Lots of organizations are growing in North America. One of the most spectacularly successful growth stories in history is an organization that has reached more "people groups" in one hundred years than Christian missionaries have in two thousand. This organization's members are marked by incredible zeal for growth, crosscultural sophistication and a very deep understanding of popular culture. The mission of this organization? To bring a particular kind of flavored fizzy water called Coca-Cola to the ends of the earth. Another great growth story is a company that wraps leaves in small paper cylinders. Unfortunately they happen to cause cancer, but that hasn't stopped Philip Morris from growing like crazy by selling cigarettes.

All sorts of things grow. Many of them are useless or worse. And it's not just consumer products—other religions are growing, around the world and around the corner. What makes church growth any different from these other kinds of growth? The reality is that the answer to the question Why worship in a new way? will have to come from some deeper source than our desire to grow, or even to "reach people." The reason for our worship needs to be *evangelical*—rooted in the gospel (the "evangel"), not in the culture of growth and pragmatism that surrounds us. Anything as central as worship should go to the heart of our faith. When we talk about the way we worship, we should be unable

> *The Word, the Son of God, moved into our neighborhood.*

to keep ourselves from talking about Jesus.

He Moved into the Neighborhood

The deepest and best reason for embracing new ways of worship comes from one of the New Testament's pivotal statements about Jesus Christ. In introducing his Gospel, John says that "the Word became flesh and lived among us" (John 1:14). The word translated "lived" comes from the Greek word for pitching a tent and carries the meaning of taking up residence in a place. Eugene H. Peterson puts this phrase in vivid contemporary language in his version of the New Testament, *The Message:* "The Word became flesh and blood, and moved into the neighborhood."

This central belief for Christians is usually summed up in the word *incarnation.* When John wrote his Gospel, the idea that God would move into a human neighborhood was scandalous to both Jews and Greeks, and it still is to many people today. When God's Son was most present on earth, he was not blazing with otherworldly glory (though he could have been, as a few disciples found out!)—he was an extraordinarily *ordinary* person. He looked like most everyone else; he ate, drank and bathed like us; and he spoke the same language as his friends. The Word spoke ordinary human words.

The incarnation can help us understand why we worship the way we do. In particular, the fact that Jesus spoke the "vernacular"—the plain language of his time—has potential implications for those who would follow Jesus today. What is our ordinary language? What are the normal features of our culture that Christians might tend to ignore? What do we see as we look around our neighborhood?

A Trip Through the Neighborhood

It doesn't take long to realize that one dominant feature of our neighborhood is that it is changing fast. Not that long ago, children grew up in basically the same world as their parents. When they were children, they dressed the way their parents and grandparents had dressed as children; when they grew up, they dressed like their parents and grandparents, and probably dozens of generations before, dressed. Language, occupations, economic status—all were relatively stable, changing little over even hundreds of years. Today, for a host of reasons, culture changes dramatically from decade to decade. Fashions change rapidly as the media transmit the latest styles at the speed of light. Jobs and careers are not the same from one generation to the next. Language and music are constantly evolving.

To speak the language of this neighborhood, Christians have to be more agile than they used to be. At the time of the hymnwriter Charles Wesley, for example, there were only a few musical styles available to English Christians: what we would now call "classical" music, influenced by court and church music on the European continent, and the flowing folk melodies of England and the Celtic isles. A hymn writer could write in one of these styles and be fairly certain that everyone in his or her potential congregation would be familiar with them. Today on the other hand, any given group of North Americans will be familiar with a dizzying variety of musical styles (each featured by at least one radio station) from classical to country to hip-hop—and not many people like both country and hip-hop! If our worship is locked into one style of music, we almost certainly will not be speaking the language of many people in the neighborhood.

Our neighborhood is also much more culturally diverse than it used to be. North America is largely a land of immigrants who brought their own diverse cultures, but most immigrant groups assimilated rapidly to the dominant, Anglo-American culture. (A significant exception, of course, was African-Americans, who did not emigrate voluntarily and who were not allowed to assimilate.) Today, people from every part of the world are present in every North American city, and increasingly in suburbs and rural areas. While they want to be part of American life, they see less need to abandon their cultural heritage to do so.

This ethnic diversity poses real challenges to forms of worship that draw exclusively from one culture. Ethnically homogenous worship may indeed lead to growth, but as we saw earlier, growth itself is not a sign of faithfulness. To "move into the neighborhood" is to make very different choices from those who try to move away to someplace homogenous and "safe." More and more, incarnation in North America will have to be multiethnic.

In our neighborhood, people tend to talk and think in shorter, more impressionistic ways than they used to. Take a look at print advertisements from the 1920s and 1930s—you'll see pages filled with paragraphs describing a product. Then look at an ad in last week's magazine—you're likely to see three-page gatefold ads with one sentence at most: "Just do it," "Absolut Moscow" and so forth. We value short, penetrating phrases over long, discursive paragraphs. Fifteen-second commercials are the norm and people are used to being busy. Even *60 Minutes* breaks up its hour into short segments. Speaking the language of this neighborhood will mean learning to use shorter, more evocative forms of communication.

Our neighborhood is also one that values intimacy—or at least the appearance of it. Consider the changes in the forms of entertainment in the twentieth century. We have progressed from stage, to film, to television. On stage, actors are life-size, and unless you have expensive seats they are difficult to see. Their voices are often unamplified and so they speak and sing in spe-

cial, "theatrical" ways. On screen, the actors are larger than life and the director can choose close-ups that give us access to subtle expressions of emotion. On television, which has a relatively low resolution, almost all the shots are of faces. Television producers have learned to exploit the intimacy of the medium by giving us shows that trade on the most personal of human experiences, from *Oprah* to *Seinfeld*. In the course of a century we have moved from a very distant medium to a very intimate one. Worship in this neighborhood will need to provide a place for intimacy, or else it will seem unreal. Worship leaders will need to learn to be more transparent in order to gain the attention of people who distrust theatrics.

Finding Our Way

What will it mean for Christians to move into this neighborhood? The new forms of worship are attempts to address these questions.

The answer certainly is not to imitate the culture around us in every way. Jesus moved into the neighborhood, but he also made many of his neighbors very uncomfortable (Luke 4:16–30). He even redefined who one's "neighbor" was—the poor and needy (Luke 10:25-37). If we simply accommodate all the preferences of the media-savvy, affluent consumer culture, we will be assimilating, not incarnating. Our presence in the neighborhood should cause some uneasiness! But if we don't speak the language, no one will ever be engaged, or disturbed, by our message.

So we need to keep asking, Why worship this way? constantly paying attention to our neighbors and to the example of Jesus. With that question in mind, we can grow into communities that reflect the wonder of incarnation.

3 The Power in Worship

Alison Siewert

As a college student I attended our cam-pus worship service (a remnant of the college's Christian founding) on Sundays in the chapel. The beautiful building, great classical music—often sung in Latin—and magnificent organ music combined to produce a formal, objective expression of traditional worship. The upstairs service could be characterized by the chapel choir's robes: affectionately called "the kidney beans," they were hooded, deep-red cassocks tied monastery-style with thick white ropes at the waist. When they donned the robes, the choir members looked nothing like anything or anyone else on campus. They became other-than-us, set-apart, Latin-speaking. But the upstairs people found meaning there: to them, it was powerful worship.

I also attended a midweek meeting downstairs in the same chapel. The undecorated room, guitar-led singalongs and ice-breaker games created a friendly, warm, if not particularly substantive, opportunity for worship. The downstairs service was characterized by its opportunities to build relationships, its campy songs ("Scratch another back, scratch the back next to ya") and its silly skits full of insider jokes—aimed at a group who really wanted to love one another. Gathered for this meeting, the fellowship looked even goofier than the rest of the campus. It was so imbued with zippy fun that it struggled to dwell deeply on the real issues of faith. But to the downstairs people, it was awesome worship.

Upstairs we had beauty; downstairs we had laughter. Upstairs we saw truths about God; downstairs we had to find the hidden meaning. Upstairs felt like a museum; downstairs felt like a youth retreat. Upstairs we had the power of aesthetic and articulate expression; downstairs we had the power of familiar and caring relationships.

There's no question in my mind that the downstairs meeting was onto something important: It met, if shallowly, our need for fellowship, connection and experience. It took seriously that Jesus shows up in our neighborhood. But the upstairs service also had something important to offer: It reflected, if impersonally, some of the splendor, depth and holiness of God. The reality is that both services were powerful and both were incomplete, at the same time.

A Time for Reflection

As we consider new forms of worship, there must be not only a why? but also a what? and a how? in our discussion. This is an important time for exploring questions and for interpreting experience. The church in the United States has seen renewed interest in the experience of worship. In the last ten years more worship music has been published than in the previous twenty. No longer is worship only the domain of the church choir director and the occasional, specially gathered band. Worship leaders have made recordings and gone on tours that accord them the status of popular concert artists. ("One night only! Bring your church and come worship with Famous Worship Leader and his amazing world-class band at the Big Arena!") Worship leading has its own magazines, its own conferences, its own professional networks. In short, an entire industry has sprung up around worship.

Activity zings all around the realm of worship. But the church is in danger of spending less energy than ever doing substantive reflection on it. The proliferation of music and products and personalities around worship makes it more and more difficult to evaluate the meaning and usefulness of all the options available. This is a problem, but not one that need overwhelm us. Rather, it should motivate us to begin to do some deeper thinking about worship as we see it in Scripture, as we experience it, as we live it out together in Christian community. Looking back through history, we can see that others have gone before us in this task of reflection. The Wesleys, for just one example, spent a great deal of time and energy thinking about worship and writing songs and prayers for their communities. They and others, then and now, have demonstrated the church's need to pause in the midst of new works of God to reflect, to understand and to learn from what's happening.

Reflection is crucial because it's possible to travel down fruitless paths in response to new developments in worship. Some, repulsed by the shallowness of much of what they hear and concerned for the loss of history, repair to tradition. They hold on to the liturgies and music in the books they grew up with and reject the new music and methods that represent for them the loss of what is old and valuable. Others grab everything they can get off the new releases shelf in the hope of being as up-to-date as possible, as hip and attractive as they can. They pursue the new—the downstairs—while presuming traditional forms—the upstairs—are old and dead.

To take either of these paths is a mistake. The traditions of the past are full of beauty, meaning and depth that we should take care not to lose in the glut of newly available options. But traditions grew out of the efforts of leaders to create expressions of deep worship that were accessible to their congregations. More than one historical Christian movement used popular tunes gleaned from pubs as musical settings for some of the most theologically profound hymns ever written. High liturgical traditions set their prayers and responses to music to help people—even those who could not read—remember and participate in meaningful worship. The power of worship was found in the congregation's experience of comprehending and responding to God and his Word, not only in the forms used to help the congregation. To hang on to the material produced by these movements as *the way to worship* is not actually true to the practice of the traditions. For the traditions themselves were about making worship accessible and meaningful in specific contexts and to particular people. They were not about choosing one set of expressions and canonizing them as "worship."

Neither is it right to throw out all the riches of history and use only what's been devised in the last ten years, calling old things categorically musty. Some things are musty, but others retain a kind of beauty and clarity that has stood through hundreds of years and may continue to resound at the throne of the Lamb. It is true we have a more diverse, more accessible range of music available to us now than ever before. But not all of what's out there is deep. The power of new forms of worship is not their funky grooves. Some music reduces worship to the experience of a TV show theme song: It grabs your ear long enough to make an identity for itself and to hold your attention for the sermon. We have to ask, is our approach to worship helping people come to God, or is it merely catchy?

The Measure of True Worship
Neither style nor history nor expertise makes for powerful worship. Finally, in all our thinking about worship, we must concede that it is not worship itself that is powerful. The *power* in worship is not worship, but God. I have often heard people talk about "the power of prayer" as though

prayer itself has some strength. Applied to worship too, this is often meant as a figure of speech; but we know from Scripture that God himself is the point and power of worship. Nothing we do, no tradition we keep, no new thing we discover has any actual power to produce worship. Nothing celebrates God that does not issue from him and help us move toward him. In fact, to think and act as though worship (or anything other than God) has power—to appeal to a song or team or person or place as "powerful for worship"—is to enter into idolatry. Nothing and no one but God either possesses or empowers worship. So the ultimate standard for the measure of our worship is, does it reflect and glorify God?

Does our worship reflect and glorify God? Now that's a lofty theological question! But we know our worship reflects and glorifies God very practically when it is lived out not just in our one-hour service but from day to day in the lives of worshipers. Worship does its job—attributing worth to God (from the Old English *weorthscipe,* worth + ship)—when it brings the truth and reality of God to light in a community of people in a time and place where they can encounter and enjoy him, and where their lives are changed because of their deepening relationship with the living Christ. Just believing more interesting things about God is not worship: "Even the demons believe—and shudder" (James 2:19). Real worship permeates life in the way any really significant relationship does. If you want to know whether your congregation is really worshiping, look at other people's lives and your own. To worship is to live out a relationship with Jesus. It is

not a one-hour meeting; it is neither upstairs nor down; it is a whole life's progress in loving God.

Worship is about relating deeply and affectionately to a profound and loving God. To think that any particular song or any one style carries power for worship leads us directly into trouble. The reason we can express love toward God is that he first expressed love toward us, and to the fullest extent. God is always the initiator of relationship. Without God's work in Jesus, we would be unable to relate to him at all. When we come to worship we must do it acknowledging that we have no power, our songs have no power, our skills have no power in and of themselves to invoke worship. *God actually provides for our worship of him.* Now *that's* power!

Worship is God's party. That may sound strange, but it's true. God is our host, and we are his guests. As guests at a wedding reception, you celebrate and honor the bride and groom by enjoying all the food, drink, music and interaction they have prepared. You wouldn't go as a guest carrying your own portable stereo and a sack lunch. That would insult the bride and groom, as though they didn't plan enough or wouldn't provide for their guests' enjoyment. To worship God, to attribute him worth, is to know God well enough to relate to who he really is—the amazing and complete provider—and to know ourselves well enough to be satisfied with our guest—our *creature*—status. We needn't think we must perform for God or think of ourselves as God's needed resources. God himself *is* the resource, the focus, the power of all right worship.

Worship is God's party.

---

4 Worship Through History

Andy Crouch

Consider the following scenes:

☐ In a candlelit sanctuary an entire congregation sings elaborate songs of praise and worship in perfect unison. The monks are beginning their day. It's five o'clock in the morning.

☐ Spread out through the cramped rooms of a private home, a church gathers to celebrate the Lord's Supper. Everyone has brought their own dinner, and the worship leaders try valiantly to get everyone to start supper at the same time. They're hoping to prevent a repeat of last week, when several members got drunk and a fight broke out over who had the best food.

☐ In a massive cathedral a priest and choir celebrate the Mass antiphonally, singing the words of the liturgy back and forth to one another. The congregation of several thousand is silent through the whole service, except at two points: they recite the Lord's Prayer together and, at the time of the Eucharist, they all surge forward to receive the Host.

☐ A series of preachers and song leaders alternate in leading a crowd of rough-living, self-reliant immigrants, most of whom have not bathed in at least a week, in a meeting at an impromptu camp in a forest clearing. At the center, emotions run high and the sobbing sometimes drowns out the person who is speaking. At the outskirts, teenagers flirt shamelessly.

☐ A preacher in a severe black robe approaches the plainly designed pulpit and delivers a meticulously prepared sermon to an attentive congregation—for nearly two hours.

What is worship? If you had asked Christians in Europe and North America at different times over the last nineteen centuries, they would describe all these scenes and many more. (By the way, do you know which of the above scenes is from the New Testament? For a hint, check out 1 Corinthians 11.) Because worship is a form of human culture, as culture changes, forms of worship change along with it. This is true not only for different ethnic cultures (see chapter 5) but for the same culture through time. Current innovations in worship are just the latest in a series of adaptations. As a worship leader you should know something of this history. Being historically informed will help you understand the strengths and limitations of your own worship tradition, and draw fruitfully on the resources of the past.

Innovative Worship Traditions

The incredible variety in worship over the centuries is a result of many different factors. Often innovations in worship accompany renewal within the church. The emotional songs of camp meetings and the meditative music of monasteries both grew out of people rediscovering the presence of God and committing themselves to prayer. The Reformation in the sixteenth century, which emphasized the Word of God and often gave less weight to the presence of Christ in communion, led to a preaching-centered service that is still typical in many Protestant churches today. Vatican II, where the Roman Catholic Church reexamined its assumptions about how God is at work in the world and the church, led to sweeping changes in Catholic worship, including the celebration of the Mass in the language of the people. When people are rediscovering truths about God that have lain dormant within the established forms of worship, they often invent new ways of worshiping that emphasize those truths.

Because worship is about communication with one another and with God, new forms of worship often reflect changes in the way people communicate. Worship in the Middle Ages, when most people were illiterate, was accompanied by numerous images and rituals that made the gospel visible and tangible. The Reformation, with its emphasis on preaching and reading Scripture, accompanied the invention of the printing press which made books, especially the Bible, available to many more people. Two key preachers of the eighteenth century, John Wesley and George Whitefield, originated the practice of preaching outdoors and without notes, bypassing official churches where formal sermons had become stale and irrelevant to most of their members.

Since worship is intimately tied with human culture, changes in worship often reflect human, not just "spiritual," realities. Social and economic class are powerful forces in shaping choices about worship. Methodists and Baptists had their greatest success on the American frontier. Pioneers, who had already made dramatic, life-changing decisions to leave their former lives in the east, could easily relate to tent revival meetings that culminated in a plea for a "decision." However, as they settled in towns and established more secure ways of life, the pioneers' children and grandchildren often wanted church services that resembled those of the prosperous east. They built impressive church buildings, employed professional ministers and musicians, and created a "three-hymns-and-a-sermon" liturgy that reflected the increased security and stability of their lives.

As culture changes, the meaning of a particular form of worship can change dramatically. Consider the use of the word *thou* to refer to God. In sixteenth-century English *thou* was universally used to address a friend or family member intimately. In more formal situations (such as, addressing royalty), the word *you* was used instead. So when the translators of the King James version used *thou* to refer to God, they were making an important and biblically grounded statement: God was not to be addressed as a distant ruler, but in the way one would address a parent or a friend. However, over time the word *thou* dropped out of general use in English and (largely because of the continuing use of the King James version) came to be associated only with God and with religious situations. Today, the use of *thou* to refer to God seems distant and formal to most people—exactly the opposite of what it used to mean!

What Does This Mean for Worship Today?

Understanding the complex history of Christian worship can enrich our own worship in several ways. We can gain a certain humility about our worship. All forms of worship were new—and usually controversial—at one time. By the same token, anything and everything we do in worship will one day seem dated and "traditional." On earth, at least, there is no single right way to worship. The choices we make about what songs to sing, what language to use or what instruments to play reflect not just our beliefs about and experience of God, but much more mundane and even doubtful influences: the values and habits of our culture and our own place, socially and economically, in that culture. Future generations will probably find our forms of worship as strange and inadequate as we sometimes find those of previous generations. We will do well to be humble in the presence of our spiritual descendants as well as our ancestors.

On the other hand, while all forms may ultimately be limited by their place in history, we can also learn something valuable from the past. Rather than reinventing worship from scratch, we can learn from the many faithful people who have gone before us. For example, knowing the original meaning of the word *thou* can make it possible to appreciate, rather than neglect, hymns that speak to God in that intimate way.

Consider again the scenes at the beginning of this chapter. Each historical form of worship has something to offer us today. Monastic worship (popularized in recent years by the CD *Chant*) can teach us about contemplation, simplicity and unity. The Lord's supper as practiced by the very earliest Christians models the down-to-earth, household-based community that so much of the North American church lacks. The grandeur of a high Holy Mass

reveals something of the wonder of heaven and the mystery of grace. Frontier revival services set the pace for a faith that is willing to completely surrender—emotionally, physically and spiritually—to God. And the Puritans' two-hour sermons put our puny attention spans and laziness in Bible study to shame.

Each of these scenes comes from a particular moment in time, moments very different from our own. But their moments and our moment have something in common: God is moving and people are responding. The wise worship leader will lead people to respond in the present by building on the faithful responses of the past.

5   Worship & Culture

....

Alison Siewert

Our InterVarsity chapter in Los Angeles always had a large number of students who were not able to travel home—which in many cases was overseas—for Thanksgiving. One of my housemates suggested we create a giant Thanksgiving feast for them and ourselves. We invited people to bring a festival food from their home culture and to join us for the traditional turkey too. What emerged was a wonderful, wild celebration of God's love and provision for us across many cultures and experiences. (Mashed potatoes and curry anyone?) And it was somehow much more complete a celebration than I had ever taken part in. We continued this tradition over several years, growing to include seventy-five students, homeless people, administrators, parents and neighbors. What a great picture of God's kingdom!

Worship is not so unlike our Thanksgiv-

ing food fest. Scripture is clear in its description of God's house as "a house of prayer for all peoples" (*peoples* here means people groups or nations) and of the purpose of God's people, beginning with Abraham, as the nation through whom "all the families of the earth shall be blessed" (Genesis 12:3; Isaiah 56:7). It's a common misconception that worship and its music must be either monocultural—culturally specific or even exclusive—or multicultural. True worship is really both. It is culturally specific because God comes to us as we are and makes himself accessible to us according to our experience and background. God relates to each of us in the deepest parts of our being. Musical and artistic worship, however, is also multicultural because God is the God of all cultures and all peoples. As leaders of worship we need to guide people in worship styles so they can immediately relate to and also in styles that will help them grow and stretch their picture of how great God is. Our worship and our life together as congregations need to reflect these realities: God is interested in humanity in all its diversity, and he is interested in every individual uniquely; his people are also called to these interests.

God is interested in humanity in all its diversity, and he is interested in every individual uniquely.

From a biblical perspective cultures are relative. That is, no one culture possesses all knowledge of God, and no one culture reflects God perfectly. Every culture contains partial understanding of God, and every culture contains sin. Some cultures have obviously been influenced by the gospel, and we can celebrate this. But since cultures are human and express human rebellion against our Creator, we must count every culture as fundamentally fallen. No one culture, then, adequately celebrates God's glory. Our worship awaits the perfecting force of Jesus' kingdom coming in fullness.

Breaching Crosscultural Boundaries
Until that time, we can expand our worship of God and our picture of his glory by appreciating what other cultures highlight about him. Hearing God's Word and about his works in another language or in a different cultural form can draw our attention to what we hadn't seen clearly through our own cultural lens. Just as Guatemalan chuchitos and Korean pulgogi afforded our community new delight and more reason for thanksgiving, expressions of worship from cultures other than our own can build whole new avenues for enjoying God together.

To worship transculturally reflects what God's kingdom will be like. We must remember that our worship, no matter how inspired, is couched in culture—it *has* to be, because we are. Every human lives within a culture. But there is no hint in the Bible that our worship around the throne of the Lamb will be in English, in Western tonalities or in 4/4 time. We can trust that we will worship with full understanding not only of what we are doing and why, but of who God is. Remember that when the Holy Spirit came in many different tongues, each people group heard a different language but all understood the same message. How much greater will heaven be!

As we learn to stretch across boundaries in worship, we also prepare to be called by God across boundaries in mission. If you read through Acts, you will see a God who is deeply committed to sending his people over every kind of cultural hurdle to get the good news out. Even if you don't know for certain that God will call you to a foreign place, nearly every Christian can be assured of an opportunity to share the gospel crossculturally. Your neighbor, a classmate or a coworker may be as culturally different from you as someone you'd sail the seas to meet. Training our hearts to welcome the ways and words of others is wise and may be fruitful in ways we never imagined. And we must not only hope to send missionaries out but, especially on campuses and in cities, to welcome the nations in as well: "for my house shall be called a house of prayer for all peoples," says God (Isaiah 56:7). How can you welcome all peoples into God's house in your context?

As a worship team you have an unusual opportunity to practice and demonstrate working together across cultures. Not many up-front leadership tasks, such as preaching and choral conducting, can be done in teams. But leading worship can rely on teamwork in visible, tangible ways. You have opportunities to share leadership, to honor one another, to listen to each other's "native tongues." My friend and worship teammate JJ Hansen can play great gospel piano, and she can teach a whole song, in parts, straight out of her head without written music. She amazes me, and I appreciate the way her musical, church and cultural backgrounds come to light as she blesses people with her leadership. The coolest thing is getting to lead alongside her, and to share together with a congregation the music that we have worked on together. I see and hear the gospel differently through JJ's experience and music than I do my own (JJ's black; I'm white), and my life and faith are richer for it. And every congregation we've led together has gotten to see us in action: a live demonstration of how God blesses us across cultures and traditions.

Five Steps for Crossing Cultural Boundaries

1. *Examine your home culture.* How does it, or how do you, see God? Are you aware of any perspective on the gospel that is missing or incomplete in your culture? What do you like about your culture and its expressions of worship?

2. *Get to know people from other cultures.* Develop real friendships in which you grow to appreciate people's strengths and struggles. If you can, spend some time in another culture—in another country or even in an ethnic community within your own borders. Short-term missions are a good point of entry. If you do participate in a cross-cultural project, work at developing relationships. Otherwise it's easy to arrogantly assume that since we've seen a culture, we know all about it when in fact we have only begun to comprehend it.

3. *Ask questions.* Be a learner. Look especially for how people worship differently, how they experience and express the gospel, how they celebrate. Participate in as many different-culture worship and celebration experiences as you can. Write down or record what you are learning, and try to talk about it. If you can, get people from other cultures to help you teach new songs and explain worship elements to your home congregation. The more people understand, the more they will enjoy and receive from God in transcultural worship.

4. *Welcome "all peoples" into your house of prayer.* If you have crosscultural people in your midst who already follow Jesus, ask them to teach you a way of worship from their home culture. What a great opportunity to understand our brothers' and sisters' perspective on the gospel and to invite them to contribute to the building up of the body.

5. *Prepare your heart to receive.* Prepare your heart as you enter into other people's cultures and their worship. You may not understand things to the degree you do in your home culture. But it's important to receive what's new to you with patience, trusting that while things may seem really strange, they are not at all odd to the culture. I once took a group of mostly suburban college students from mainline churches to visit the inner-city Pentecostal church of some friends. The service was true to its heritage, lively and loud. Several of the students were offended by what they called the preacher's "yelling" during the sermon, as well as the service's longer length (two and a half hours).

My friend, on the other hand, took another group of students to a service at an African-American church. Before they went, she reviewed with them some of the differences between the students' previous experiences and what they were about to see. She talked about the custom of shouting "Amen!"—a way to agree with God's Word and say, "This is worth hearing." She also explained details about the offering, Bible translation choices and length of sermon—several traditions that might have been difficult for them to comprehend. The whole group enjoyed and appreciated the service, in part because they had been prepared to receive it within the framework of its own cultural context, rather than their own limited perspective. Preparation helps you receive and learn across cultures.

6 Multiethnic Windows on Worship

Sundee Frazier

"Contemporary worship" is being led in churches of every cultural group in the United States. In each place it means something different because it is being defined and done by people with different values, needs, views of God and ways of expressing themselves. With this in mind, I interviewed people of different ethnic backgrounds (some of whom are making these services happen in their churches) to see worship through a variety of windows, and to help us celebrate the diversity of God's people. It's a gift that "our way" is not the only way! There is much for us to learn from one another.

As authors we are coming from a particular perspective when we discuss worship, because we are particular people (mostly Anglo, InterVarsity-trained and university-educated). If you are someone who is coming from a different cultural background than the majority of contributors to this book, we want you to know that this book is for you too. Please adapt its material to fit your context.

Here are the ten people I interviewed for this chapter:

Tony Begay, campus pastor at University of New Mexico and Southwestern Indian Polytechnic Institute, working primarily with Native American students; member of Fellowship Christian Reformed Church in Albuquerque, New Mexico.

Marilyn Begay, assistant to her husband in campus ministry and member of Fellowship Christian Reformed Church.

Mark Charles, InterVarsity alumnus and member of the Navajo tribe.

James Choung, worship leader at Cambridge Community Fellowship Church in Massachusetts, a predominantly Asian church (40 percent Chinese-American, 30 percent Korean-American) striving to be multiethnic.

Orlando Crespo, InterVarsity area director in the greater New York City division.

Julie Freeman and Oscar Huertas, worship leaders at Shiloh Baptist Church in Easton, Pennsylvania.

Melvin Fujikawa, associate pastor of worship, Evergreen Baptist Church in Rosemead, California.

Joanne Geiger, former missionary to Costa Rica, and member of El Templo de Refugio Church in Bethlehem, Pennsyvania.

Jeanette Yep, InterVarsity divisional director in the Midwest and leader at Parkwood Community Church in Glen Ellyn, Illinois (55 percent Korean-American, 40 percent Chinese-American, 5 percent other Asians and Caucasians).

To underscore the diversity of styles and values that are represented, and to provide cohesiveness, this chapter is formatted so that responses to the same question are put together, even though the interviews were done independently.

Sundee Frazier: *What does worship mean to people from your culture?*

Orlando Crespo: It's hard to say because in the Latino community there's so much diversity—not only because of the different ethnicities but also because of different denominations. Generally, worship is not a means to an end. You're not trying to prepare your heart for a message. Worship in itself has incredible value. There have been times I've been at services and we've felt God's Spirit moving in our midst, and so we decided to spend the whole time worshiping. There was no message. What I've found in the Hispanic community is a high level of expectation for meeting God in worship. It's a place where burdens can be lifted as we lose ourselves and enter into loving him.

Melvin Fujikawa: The key word is *relationship*—this is connected to being Asian-American. Relationship with God is what Asians are striving for in worship. There's a longing, a desire for relationship, especially with a father.

James Choung: For Korean-Americans musical worship is an important and emphasized time. Earnestness and expressiveness are valued. The Korean people have been an oppressed people group in Asia and perhaps this has led to such expressiveness in musical worship and prayer. A friend of mine made a comparison to the African-American experience, calling Koreans the African-Americans of Asia. It seems that true worship hits the heart and not just the head for Koreans, and it seems to have spilled over to Korean-Americans as well.

Jeanette Yep: Worship styles have developed among the Chinese and Koreans along denominational lines, according to the missionaries who were sent to them.

The Chinese are more staid and hold it back more. They are a Bible church kind of people, which reflects the European and North American missionaries who were in China before communism in 1949. It's been the same worship styles in yellow skin. There is now a counterwave of folks who are experiencing "contemporary" worship.

Mark Charles: There is a strong sense (on the reservation) that you need to do things the way the missionaries did them. For a long time, becoming Christian on the reservation meant becoming "white," for all practical purposes. And so there was, and still is, a strong sense that you can't be traditionally Navajo and be a Christian. Just these past few years there's been more people grappling with the issue of "can I be Navajo and be a Christian? What does that mean?"

Julie Freeman: Worship is a breakthrough. A lot of us are looking for something we can't find by going to work every day. The joy and peace we find in worship separates us from everything that pulls us down. For a while you're free just to be free. For African-Americans, to come together at church and be of one accord and worship one God means a lot, especially when there are still a lot of struggles out there for us, depending on where you are economically.

Sundee Frazier: *What characteristic or aspect of God is most often emphasized in your culture's worship times?*

Joanne Geiger: The power of the Holy Spirit (particularly for the Pentecostals) enabling us to use the gifts of the Spirit, such as intercession, tongues, healing, prophetic messages. I think this is a result of the Catholic church being ritualistic and more centered on the do-and-don't list as opposed to the freedom of God and the power that he gives us in our relationship with him. Another thing is the second coming of Jesus. This is more across the board—not just Pentecostals. This may be a result of poverty. And that God chooses the underdog, the fishermen, uneducated, ordinary . . . you don't have to be intelligent or powerful. When Jesus comes back, it's like justice will reign.

Orlando Crespo: In the Pentecostal tradition it's that the Holy Spirit is real. As you enter into worship, God will meet you and do great things in your life, such as bring healing, a word of knowledge or discernment for something.

Melvin Fujikawa: The relational character of God. This comes from people lacking intimacy with their parents, especially their fathers. Parents would basically cut off their right arm to get their kids through school and anything else that would enhance their lives. Parents are very sacrificial, and the value of the family is very high in that sense. But from the relational side of it, there isn't as much communication of support, love and care. And so people want this with God.

Jeanette Yep: The fatherhood of God almost to the exclusion of anything else. The mercy and grace of God.

James Choung: In the 1980s Korean-Americans seemed to emphasize God's holiness and subsequently our unworthiness. These worship times were often motivated with much guilt and shame, and it wouldn't be unusual for a Korean-American worship leader to remark, "Since God bled and died for us, how can we not worship him with everything we have?" Nowadays, this emphasis does not seem as strong, and loving God and enjoying his presence seem to be emphasized more—possibly due to the influence of the Vineyard Christian Fellowship on Christian praise music today.

The sense of duty is strong in Korean culture, and often that will spill over into our expression of worship—it is our duty to worship God, since he's done so much for us.

Tony Begay: The concept of harmony, or being one, through God. In Navajo thinking we are one with nature. If we disobey or do something to harm nature, then we develop disharmony with nature and have to suffer the consequences. We need to be reconciled back to nature, and we have to do different kinds of performance for this to happen. This parallels the Bible's teaching that we are separated from God because of our sin. And the person that brings us back to harmony is Jesus. He shed his blood, and through belief in him we are back in harmony with God.

Marilyn Begay: Native Americans emphasize unity. Denominationalism is very confusing to Navajo and other Native American people. They don't make those fine distinctions like we do in the larger church. For Navajos, to become a Christian in the early years was to separate yourself from parts of your culture. It was a very lonely thing, and so wherever other Christians were found there was a bond regardless of denomination.

Julie Freeman: God is the answer to struggles. God is the breakthrough. With God, you're no longer in bondage but have a sense of freedom.

Oscar Huertas: Being Hispanic in a black church, and being married to a black woman, I know that they are a people familiar with struggle. They have to work 110 percent to get a raise on their job or a promotion. They might get broken up if they eat lunch with other African-Americans because people don't want a clique to start. It seems that they have this burden. The wondrous thing about the way African-Americans worship is they have this tremendous faith in God as their deliverer.

Sundee Frazier: *What's the highest value in a worship service?*

Joanne Geiger: There are a couple different styles, but I'd say the preaching. Services can go from two to four hours, and often they will preach very long. They're trying to lead up to what the Word says and what it means for their lives.

Orlando Crespo: There's not as strong an emphasis on worship being this perfectly run and led thing, but that it's something that God leads. Worship is often a place to be trained. It's not uncommon to have someone lead worship who isn't very experienced. But if their heart is right before God and they have some skills, people will give them opportunities to lead others. It's a training ground for developing people in ministry.

Melvin Fujikawa: That the whole service would be worship. We've been very intentional to help people understand that from the moment they come into the service they are worshiping. Worship is not the message or the music by themselves—it's life. The totality of the worship service is a microcosm of life—the meeting of people, the songs as they're being sung, the passing of the plate, afterward when they're sitting around talking—all those are aspects of worship.

James Choung: It seems that Korean-Americans hold on strongly to the Word and good expositional teaching. Many Korean-Americans want to be *challenged* and *convicted* and may feel that a worship service falls short if this doesn't happen.

Expressiveness and openness is most highly valued during the musical part of worship, and often the worship service falls short if a vibrant, heartfelt expression of worship is missing.

Jeanette Yep: What we say is that meeting God through the Word is most important. But fellowship and worship is actually what's most valued by people today. They want to be a family in Christ, together, and experience God as bigger than themselves through musical worship. The first generation Chinese-American church doesn't understand this hunger; they tend to want cognitive truth, Bible teaching.

Mark Charles: It's being together. That's what's given the most time. The sermon is what's being built up to, but going to church is not just about hearing the sermon or worshiping. It's about being with the people. People will stay a long time afterward. There are, more than in most churches, potlucks and times for the church to come together.

Sundee Frazier: *What are the signs that true worship is happening?*

Joanne Geiger: This could be slanted by my experience, but I think people are looking for God to do something and for them to experience it in a tangible way (an emotion, a prophetic word, someone prays over them and says something no one else knew). If they cry before the Lord in repentance, or go to the altar and experience healing—that almost seems like what they're looking for in a church experience.

Orlando Crespo: Being bilingual and bicultural, there are times that I'm having trouble worshiping God in English, and I switch to Spanish and there's something about it. I've heard other Hispanics say this as well. There's something about communicating with God in Spanish that's different from doing it in English. So there are times, in terms of being intimate with God, if I can't do it in English, I turn to Spanish and something breaks.

Melvin Fujikawa: People have been more responsive in our church lately. The key word would be *anticipation*—when people walk in there's a higher energy level. People are wanting and waiting for something to happen. We've been soliciting more verbal responses. People need permission. *Permission* is a key word for Asian-Americans at this point, especially in the corporate setting, where you don't want to be singled out or be an individual. It's better to be corporate in the Asian-American mindset.

James Choung: Worship leaders often look for vibrant expression as an indication of true worship. If people are clapping loudly or singing loudly or waving their hands in the air, they may feel that true worship is happening. But I think true worship happens if it glorifies God and God alone. If the words of the song speak the truth about God and his character and praise him, and the leader is worshiping him, then it's true worship.

Jeanette Yep: The philosophical roots of Asian cultures are contemplative; our cultures value silence. People are eating this up, especially in prayer.

Mark Charles: There's some clapping—is that true worship? I don't know. If a person is really touched by a song, they would probably say something or exhort the church or ask to sing the song again (right then).

Julie Freeman: I look for posture, crying, smiling, excitement, quietness. I look to see what people are doing, to see if they're being blessed. I don't want to cut them off too soon because sometimes people are really caught up in worship, and so you have to know within your spirit how long to keep going. You don't want to lose that person.

Oscar Huertas: If I don't see tears, sometimes I think I haven't done my job. There's nothing like a good cry, a good release. I want to see hands in the air. I want to see brokenness because a broken and contrite heart the Lord will not despise. And we've got to get that guard down; people are so angry. God would have you hot or cold. I'd rather see people doing cartwheels and back flips or on the ground prostrate, crying.

Sundee Frazier: *What role does the worship leader play? What is he or she striving for in worship?*

Joanne Geiger: The worship leader is a seamstress sewing themes together, responding to God and what he's saying to you in the moment, moving people along, responding to what the Spirit is doing. Between songs they keep the music going, and speak to the people using words of the songs that have been sung. It's about getting people to think about what they're singing.

Orlando Crespo: There's a strong call for people to forget the problems and burdens they brought into church and enter into worship. Part of the worship leader's role is to motivate and inspire people to let go and to really enter in. At times I've seen the worship leader stop and ask someone to come up and share what God's been doing in their life. So part of the worship experience is everyone coming prepared, whether it's a word of encouragement or a song in their

heart. It's very participatory, and you don't always know what turn it's going to take.

Melvin Fujikawa: I'm intentional about finding ways to help them be released from the bounds of what Asians would consider propriety—maybe too much propriety to the point of not wanting to stand out. The other side of the coin, however, is that I'm aware of the fact that there is a quietness, a spirit of solitude, the aspect of needing to have a time of centering. It's a quietness that is very key to our culture. So I try to balance helping people be released but also have times of quiet and monastic kinds of responses.

Mark Charles: If you walk into a Navajo church for their worship session, at least in the Christian Reformed tradition, you'll have a Navajo couple up front leading it. They will sing several hymns translated into Navajo as well as hymns in English. There will be a lot of taking requests from the congregation. Most of the time, because you're taking requests, you're not structuring the songs around the sermon. People will lead worship, and there is no regard given to talent. Most often, families are asked to lead worship. And if you had a few lessons as a child you will probably be asked to play the piano. Occasionally you'll have a solo, and once again there's no regard given to talent.

Julie Freeman: My desire is that all of me will be to the side, and that God will be able to use me as a vessel. I say, "Lord, what is it that you want me to say to your people?" One of my biggest desires is that everyone who has a need will receive an answer. Even if it's just that one person, touching that one heart, with one prick—I want to be the prick to open up their mind, eyes and ears. You are a messenger with a very important message to speak, like a torch bearer. So we have to be ready to speak that word.

Oscar Huertas: Whether we have ten or fifteen minutes, our job is to somehow break through the silence, to make something invisible, visible. Life-changing experiences are what we need desperately to bring back to the church, because people have lost their zeal and faith.

It's an awesome responsibility [to lead worship] because if you tell them to turn to their neighbor or touch three people and tell them "God loves you," that's an amazing power you have over people. You really have to be careful where you take them. Confessing with our mouth is very important, and I try to get people to make a statement of faith during worship.

Sundee Frazier: *How do worship leaders plan the worship time?*

Orlando Crespo: It depends on the denomination and tradition. But generally my impression is that a lot of prayer goes into leading worship. There's more an emphasis on praying than on what songs you're going to sing, or how exactly they're going to be done or exactly what order. I've been to many services where there was a song that the leader felt we had to sing, and they hadn't prepared it and there was no overhead for it, but there was a sense of really listening to God's voice and where he was leading.

Melvin Fujikawa: I spend a lot of time working with the head pastor to organize and plan the worship service. We are looking for an "organicness" for our services. So there is a pre-service planning aspect and then the aspect of being aware of what the Spirit is doing during the service and altering our plans as necessary. We want to have a balance between planning and preparation, and at the same time be aware that all those things might at one moment not be important at all.

Mark Charles: It's very impromptu. The people who lead it often times will go up there not knowing fully what they're going to sing. And so they'll ask people for their favorites, what they want to sing.

Julie Freeman: I may know what songs we're going to do, but I'll always tell the pianist, "Just flow with me; I don't know where I'm going, but you just flow." And that's how we work. The thing about it is, the Holy Spirit is the one who is directing this whole thing. God is in control, and if he says we're going to go this way, that's the way you go. So again, you have to remember that there are certain songs picked, but you may have this one planned and he'll say, "No, do that." And it's because you saw someone's face or you saw the pastor in the pulpit. You prepare for worship by living your life for God. You have to be real and legit. I try to live my life as legit as possible. You better live it because you can't get up there and talk unless you live it.

Oscar Huertas: I usually start planning on Monday. I will make an attempt to talk to the leadership the first few days of the week. I ask what they're going to be teaching. If my pastor is not preaching a particular series, I will find out what's happening in the church on a more personal level. I try to find a theme, and I ask, "Where are you leading us, Lord?" On Saturday our team gets together, and through experience—by getting together and worshiping—we prepare. This is not choir ministry. With that, music mastery is the key. The praise team is a good thermometer for what's going to be happening in the congregation. If it's working with the team, then it will probably work with the congregation. If a breakthrough's not coming for the team, then you need to stop and find out what's happening. Our practice is open to anyone, so twenty people might come and worship together with the team. It doesn't matter whether we get through one song or ten [during rehearsal], because what's important is that God is there.

Sundee Frazier: *What does your culture's expression and experience of worship contribute to the larger body of Christ's understanding of worship?*

Joanne Geiger: Freedom and joy. The freedom to express how you feel about someone. North American culture is stifled in its freedom to express love and joy openly. Even our sadness and suffering—we close off and don't want anyone to know our pain. But the Latins are able to add that "we are real, we have these feelings and we're going to express them because God's given us the freedom to do that. He understands us."

Orlando Crespo: One of the things is a genuine expectation that God is alive and in our midst. Worship isn't just us telling God what we love about him, but also God responding back to us in love as well. So that's where I think the sense of expectation that God's Spirit is going to do something in our midst comes from. We contribute the sense that God may decide to lead us into things that we didn't have planned.

Melvin Fujikawa: We are people who value control, which can be both negative and positive. The positive aspects are waiting for your turn, listening, being gracious. The negative is being so controlled that you can't say what you want to say. We like to listen, and listening can be used well if we steer it toward teaching people how to hear God. It's a value of our culture to want to have time to sit and to center, to listen, waiting. My hope and dream is that we would find expressions and liturgies to help the larger church to understand that quiet intensity that God desires for us [which is a part of Asian culture], and to help [the church] understand how even deep within us God speaks some incredible truths.

James Choung: Korean-Americans add vibrancy of expression, in musical praise and especially in prayer. Korean-Americans have much to learn from the previous generation about the power of prayer.

Jeanette Yep: Family-ness. We bring a sense of community and family identity—an appreciation and enjoyment of that. Also a sense of solidarity: we're in this together and will stay together through thick-and-thin. There is a respect of authority in our culture—a sense that God is *Other,* not hu-

man. We are not as cynical toward authorities, and if you're an authority you don't have to prove to me why you're talking to me. In Chinese-American culture specifically, there is a thoughtfulness about the faith. Chinese people count the cost upfront and then go for the long haul, which is probably the result of there not being as many Chinese Christians as there are Korean. It's a serious matter for a Chinese person to become a Christian.

Tony Begay: The concept of *now,* the present. *Now* we are the people of God—not yesterday or tomorrow, but today we are God's people. We're to live our Christian lives and our faith now, we are to love one another now, we are to share with people we know, that we live with, we are to visit and help the sick now, not tomorrow.

Marilyn Begay: Along with that, sharing is one of the concepts that is typical of Native Americans across the broader community. There's quite a bit of sharing testimonies. There's more openness to sharing burdens and experiences, and finding time to do that in the service. There's also a lack of concern about time. Traditionally, time wasn't that important on the reservation. They were more task-oriented than time-oriented.

Julie Freeman: We have freedom, basically. If you listen to the sound of our music, there is harmony and spontaneity. It just happens and there's no fear to be free. I guess what's in us is music, singing, movement, rhythm, and this adds spice to worship.

Oscar Huertas: There's something very earthy and spicy about how African-Americans worship God. I've been to storefront churches where the only instruments were a lot of high heels and a hard wood floor. I've been to churches where they took clapping to another level. They use senses that other cultures just don't use. It's not just worshiping with their minds, but their whole bodies. They're probably the closest you're going to find to David's people.

Part 2
Follow the Leader

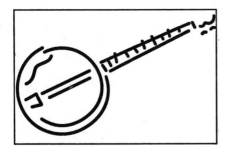

7   God-Needing Worship Leading

....

Alison Siewert

The psalmist said, "These things I re-member, as I pour out my soul: how I went with the throng, and led them in procession to the house of God, with glad shouts and songs of thanksgiving, a multitude keeping festival" (Psalm 42:4). That's what he used to do. By the time he writes the psalm, he is in a different place: "My soul thirsts for God, for the living God. When shall I come and behold the face of God? My tears have been my food day and night" (Psalm 42:2-3).

Have you ever felt like this guy? I have! Leading worship can be thrilling. To see God's people gathered to sing and pray, to be in touch with God's Spirit so you can lead others to him is an exciting process—most of the time. Then there are those occasions when I have a headache or a sore throat, when I've lived most of the week struggling with sin or feeling ugly, so that the last thing I want to do is get up in front of a bunch of people and worship enthusiastically. In those times I wonder, *How can I call people to worship with integrity? How will I worship God authentically in this situation? Why do I have to lead worship at all?*

The reasons people get involved in leading worship are as diverse as the reasons people worship. You have, by whatever means, gotten involved in leading worship. But perhaps you're wondering, *Why me?* On the surface it may appear that you were chosen to lead because you have a great voice, or because, even though you just started learning to play, your church or fellowship is low on guitarists. But God has much

greater reasons for your involvement, and it's important for you to see what Jesus is doing in this process.

Why Does God Call People to Be Leaders?

In God's Word we see many stories of people called to lead in all kinds of situations. But one basic goal undergirds all God's leadership choices. God calls people to lead as a way of calling them to himself. In other words, God calls you into leadership for your blessing, healing and growth. The call to leadership is about what God wants to do *in* you as much as it is about what he wants to do *through* you.

Look at Peter, who was called to lead before anyone could see a good reason why! He was impetuous, impulsive and constantly sticking his foot in his mouth. He was anything but solid and steady—yet Jesus renamed him "Rock." Why? Because Jesus knew that as Peter gave himself to the gospel and to leading others to God, he would become someone very different. Leadership was the particular path along which God called Peter to travel in order to receive all God had to offer him. Certainly leadership is not always the call. Many people who would never consider themselves leaders are called by God into other forms of ministry that function as growth roads for them. But if you have truly been called to lead worship, be assured that it is because God wants to do good things for you and make you more like Jesus.

When you view leading worship through

> *God calls people to lead as a way of calling them to himself.*

this frame, you'll more easily accept the glitches, the attention, the failures and the challenges worship leading presents as opportunities for your growth and blessing. You'll see how well God has crafted a path for you and how expert he is at calling you to grow and giving you all you need to get there.

It's important to approach leading worship knowing that you lead because God wants to bless you—not as though he's your employer who has a job for you to do. Psalm 50 finds God correcting the people of Israel who are sacrificing as though they're doing God a favor, providing him with something he needs. God says,

> Not for your sacrifices do I rebuke you; your burnt offerings are continually before me. I will not accept a bull from your house, or goats from your folds. For every wild animal of the forest is mine, the cattle on a thousand hills. I know all the birds of the air, and all that moves in the field is mine. If I were hungry, I would not tell you, for the world and all that is in it is mine. Do I eat the flesh of bulls, or drink the blood of goats? (Psalm 50:8-13)

Clearly God doesn't eat bull meat or drink goat blood! But his people evidently had come to think that he needed these things from them. They were wrong—God has access to all resources and needs nothing from us. This is an important way that he is distinguished as Creator, and we as creatures.

What Makes a Good Leader?

Asaph, the psalmist, continues to quote God as he outlines what the Israelites are to do differently: "Offer to God a sacrifice of thanksgiving, and pay your vows to the Most High. Call on me in the day of trouble; I will deliver you, and you shall glorify me" (Psalm 50:14-15).

God wants his people to relate to him as provider *to whom we give thanks* and as deliverer *on whom we call in the day of trouble.* God doesn't need us, but *we need God!* And

we glorify and honor God not in our ability to do things impressively but in our willingness to ask and receive help and blessing from him. One good reason to lead worship is that it gives you the opportunity to call on God and to offer thanksgiving. You will honor God as a worship leader when you *need him.*

Living in need of God can be difficult because most of us are trained to be self-sufficient in every way. Isn't this, after all, why you're so proficient at what you do? Or why you've so often been a leader? We honor those who can do the most work, get the best grades, romance the most beautiful people, make the most money, achieve the greatest athletic feats. All of human culture is geared toward exalting human accomplishment. It's easy to approach leadership—especially of a potentially "flashy" event like a well-attended worship service—with your mind trained on success, accomplishment, looking good, making it powerful or doing it right. But if you give yourself to this thinking, you will actually distance yourself and anyone who follows you from God and his goals.

When you think about Peter, which of his life events come to mind? Indeed he led the Christian community on the day of Pentecost, took the gospel across cultures, and saw countless conversions in the course of his ministry. But Peter is probably more immediately remembered for his *denial* of Jesus. Peter was a person who needed God's help! And we know that because it showed. His shortcomings were obvious. Perhaps this is why Jesus picked him. Perhaps you'll find too that it's through the cracked and weak places in you that God's Spirit flows most freely.

Knowing this, you can lead worship because God calls you to, not because he or anyone else needs you to. If you live and lead as a God-needer, you will honor God in ways that deeply, definitely help others worship.

8
Spiritual Disciplines for Worship Leaders

●●●

Andy Crouch

Much of the information in this book is practical. But the most practical part of worship leading is developing a deep and faithful spiritual life, since without that any worship we lead will be empty at best and hypocritical at worst. Though we are just ordinary people called to the same ordinary faithfulness as any follower of Jesus, our position of leadership should encourage us to pursue faithfulness with extra care. Who knows, maybe one reason God called you into leadership was to jump-start you into a more faithful life!

Faithfulness is largely pursued through *disciplines*: day-to-day, undramatic practices that shape our characters into Christlikeness. Many spiritual disciplines are helpful, even essential, for every Christian. But here are a few that are especially crucial for worship leaders.

Practice the Presence of God

We cannot lead people into something we have not experienced. Worship leaders need to be people who practice God's presence. This means cultivating our awareness that God really is here now, seeking relationship with us. Most of us fall short of this awareness in two ways. First, we tend to think that God is only present in particularly religious or holy times and places, and we reserve our awareness of his presence for those settings: our morning prayer time, a weekly worship service. The rest of the week, as far as our heart and thoughts are concerned, we're on our own, living as if we had left God behind. Instead we need actively to practice seeing God in the times and places where we have assumed he was

absent or irrelevant. A good starting point for learning about this is the book *The Practice of the Presence of God,* by Brother Lawrence, a seventeenth-century monk who discovered that one could experience God's presence even while peeling potatoes!

Second, we think that God will only be present if we work ourselves into a spiritually aware state. Spiritual squinting—straining to make out some sense of God—is worse than useless. Far from leading us into a deep sense of God's reality, it tends to make us frustrated with his elusiveness. Instead of effort, we need simplicity and relaxation. God will show himself to us if we will cease striving to make him show up. A good contemporary guide to this aspect of practicing God's presence is Leanne Payne's book *Listening Prayer.*

Consider the effect this kind of practice might have on our worship leading. If we are practicing the presence of God, we are much less likely to think or communicate that the goal of worship is to "invoke" the Holy Spirit. Instead, we will begin our worship already aware that God is near. We will begin with thanksgiving rather than having to spend most of the worship service trying to stir up our hearts! As we model this for those we lead, we will see a real change in the depth and quality of worship.

Practice Confession and Repentance

There are two reasons that worship leaders, even more than other Christians, ought to have a regular discipline of confession and repentance in their lives. First, any leadership brings the temptation of seeing ourselves, often in exceedingly subtle ways, as like God. Association with holy moments can lead us to think that we ourselves are holy! A discipline of self-examination, confession and repentance gets rid of that illusion very quickly and prevents pride from accumulating over time.

Practicing also involves going up to and just beyond the limit of our abilities and working at what doesn't come naturally to us.

Second, precisely because repentance humbles us, it leads us much more deeply into worship. We become aware of the immensity of grace. Our thankfulness grows. As our hearts soften they inevitably become more willing to praise. It is no accident that one of the great songs of praise, "Amazing Grace," grew out of John Newton's own encounter with his profound sin as a slave-trader and his subsequent renunciation of that lifestyle. The more we understand how much we have been forgiven, the more worship will flow naturally out of our lives. Forgiven sinners are the best worship leaders.

Find a small group who will commit with you to regular, candid confession and prayer for forgiveness. If that's your worship team, all the better! You may want to read Dietrich Bonhoeffer's chapter on confession and communion in his classic book *Life Together* for more insights on the role of confession in the Christian life.

Practice Your Instrument

This point may be a surprise—you thought this chapter was about spiritual disciplines! Well, it is. Practicing your instrument can be as important a spiritual discipline as any other. We're not talking here about *playing*—which is all that many people do once they have gained a certain level of proficiency. *Practicing* involves concentration on the basics: for pianists, scales and arpeggios; for singers, vocalizing; for drummers, rudiments and time keeping. Practicing

also involves going up to and just beyond the limit of our abilities and working at what doesn't come naturally to us.

Both in its focus on basics and its focus on limits, musical practice is a very humbling activity. When we're playing, we may feel pretty good about ourselves: when we go back to the basics, find it impossible to play something or discover how easily we give up on things that are difficult, we are brought up against our humanness and limitedness. The humility that results is absolutely essential for spiritual maturity.

Vocalists particularly need to learn to practice. Most singers on worship teams have never studied singing, since unlike playing an instrument singing is a fairly natural human ability. One of the most humbling (and, if you stick with it, exhilarating) experiences you can have is to take voice lessons with a good teacher. Not only will your singing improve dramatically but in the course of discovering how to properly use your voice, you will undoubtedly be led into some unexpected and important emotional growth. That may sound bizarre, but believe it! Don't miss out on the growth that can come through developing, not just using, your gifts.

Immerse Yourself in Scripture, Especially the Psalms

The Psalms are the worship book of Scripture and have been used by the people of God for several thousand years. They cover nearly every possible human situation and emotion: thanksgiving, loneliness, disappointment, awe, anger and hope. One of the best things you can do for your own prayer life is to pray the psalms, reading them and letting their words pray for you. As you do this, you will soak up the worldview of the writers of the Bible, and you'll find that their ways of thinking and praying will come to mind in the most unlikely situations.

For several years I have read several psalms every morning, reading through all 150 in the course of two months. I don't think I'll ever stop. They provide an ever-fresh source of ways to say what I needed to say to God. They also are a good source of ideas for new songs!

Spend Time with People in Need

If worship is a declaration of dependence on God, we naturally independent people need to learn about what it means to trust God for everything in life. Children, who are too small to depend on themselves, and the materially poor, who are prevented by powerful social forces from providing for themselves, know a lot about trusting God, and they have something to teach you about worship. Spend some time in a church in a poor urban neighborhood or overseas—your view of worship, prayer and faith will be revolutionized.

By the same principle, seek out any experience you can that takes you out of your secure comfort zone and makes you depend more on God. Crosscultural mission trips are valuable not so much for what you may have to give as for what you have to learn

about being weak and out of control—just make sure you don't go with such a large group of fellow citizens that you're sheltered from the experience! You don't have to leave home, either, to make yourself dependent on God: sacrificial giving is a great way to learn more about faith. The more you depend on God in very practical, tangible ways, the more God will show you his goodness and the better you will become at leading worship.

And Don't Just Lead—*Be Led* in Worship

If you lead worship every Sunday morning, seek out another church in your area that has a Sunday evening or weekday service. Go out of your way to be a member of the flock, not always a shepherd. From personal experience I'd say that a ratio of two to one—two times of leadership to one time being led—is the outer limit for spiritual health. Unfortunately, many, many pastors and worship leaders have a ratio of twenty-five to one or worse! Churches are discovering the value of having multiple worship teams so that no one is leading all the time; in the long run, a team approach will benefit everyone, including the congregation. God has no intention of burning you out in leadership; allow other worship leaders to lead you in worship.

9

Dancing in Your Underwear
A Biblical Model

· ·

Sundee Frazier

"When the Spirit of the Lord comes upon my heart, I will dance like David danced. . . . I will dance, I will dance, I will dance like David danced!" The melody of the song was infectious. People shouted, "Sing!" to

the choir. But the moment the soloist broke into the chorus about dancing like David, he was no longer a soloist but a worship leader, and this was no longer a performance but a worship time. Seated bodies with heads that had been bobbing up and down to the beat (including mine) became standing bodies, swaying and moving in rhythm with the Hebrew-style music. One voice multiplied into hundreds of voices as we sang along—carried away by the vision of a royal king dancing with all the energy of a warrior's body, and becoming like that vision as we sang and danced and clapped and shouted with all our energy.

My husband, Matt, and I are members of what might be called a "lively" predominantly African-American church. What amazes me continually about our church is that people never grow tired of worshiping with all their might. The scenario I just described is the norm and not a rare occurrence. Sure, the atmosphere is more sober sometimes: when we are confessing sin, asking God to meet needs or waiting for people to come forward during an altar call. During these times, however, the place is no less full of a sense of unapologetic adoration and exaltation of God as the one and only true and great God. The atmosphere is produced by the focus and zeal of the people leading worship—ministers of music and the Word alike, and even those who make announcements. They allow the Spirit of God to work through them to draw themselves and others into authentic worship.

I am learning through the leaders and members of my church not only how to dance as David danced but how to worship as David worshiped. As a man after God's own heart (Acts 13:22) and as the one who danced before the Lord with all his might, David is certainly a model worshiper and worship leader.

Dancing As David Danced

The story of King David dancing before the Lord in linen drawers is just one snapshot of this worshiper of God (see 2 Samuel 6:12-23 and 1 Chronicles 15). To learn from David about worshiping and leading

others to worship, it's helpful to look at his life from beginning to end (1 Samuel 16—1 Kings 2:12), and to reflect on the many worship songs he wrote, recorded in the Psalms. However, we can glean a great deal from the one snapshot. Let's look at it more closely.

The ark of God (2 Samuel 6:2) had been neglected by Israel for some twenty years by the time David came into power (1 Samuel 7:2). To Israel the ark was symbolic of God's presence with his people. It had accompanied them throughout their wanderings in the wilderness and had reminded them whose side they were on as they encountered opposition. It was also a constant reminder of their need to obey the God whose commandments it housed. Neglecting the ark of God was tantamount to neglecting God himself.

When David retrieves the ark from its marginalized location, bringing it to the new capital at the heart of the nation, Jerusalem, he is doing much more than moving an expensive piece of furniture for his own personal enjoyment (2 Samuel 5:6-12). He goes to welcome God back into his rightful place at the center of the nation's focus, attention and corporate life. He takes thirty thousand men with him to do this. In essence, he becomes a worship leader of thirty thousand.

David and those with him bungle the first attempt to retrieve the ark because they fail to obey God when they transport the ark not on the shoulders of priests (as God instructed) but on a "new and improved" cart pulled by oxen instead. Their outward disobedience is a sign of an inward problem with their hearts' loyalty to God. When David successfully retrieves the ark on his second attempt, he is much more conscientious. He comes into Jerusalem rejoicing and with the ark carried in the way God had commanded (2 Samuel 6:12). He is careful to give God all the honor he deserves, and he is willing to take as much time as necessary to this end. Just think, every six paces on his way to Jerusalem with the ark, David would stop and sacrifice two animals. This was a time-consuming procedure, but God was (and is) that worthy of our time and focus.

This image of David taking his time to give God due honor reminds me again of our church. There is an appropriate time-consciousness, and the leaders don't keep people there forever for the sake of keeping them there or because they want more attention. For the two-plus hours church is in session, however, people are wholly focused on the worship of God, as David was while leading the procession to Jerusalem.

Here are two questions to consider in response to David's model:

Are you giving enough time to musical worship? Are you using music and other forms of worship to allow people to respond to and interact with God for themselves? Do you give people a good chance to get focused on God?

Do you handle the time you do have with care? Are you conscious of who you are worshiping? Are you incorporating elements that move worship from being simply an act of "going through the motions" to being a time of meaningful interaction with and adoration of God? Do you focus on the condition of your heart as primary in your acts of "sacrifice"? God wants to move back into the center of your attention. Consider if through worship you lead people in welcoming him back into the center of their lives.

How to Dance in Your Underwear

Not only does David take as much time as is necessary to give God all the honor he deserves and to welcome him back to the center of Israel's life, he also expresses his heartfelt love to God without shame and with wild abandon. In 2 Samuel 6:14 we see David dancing before the Lord with all his might in a linen undergarment. There are a few things to notice here. First, he is

using all his energy to worship God; second, he is exposed and vulnerable (in what he's wearing and doing) before people; and third, he is exposed and vulnerable before the Lord.

As I said before, our church is full of people who worship God unapologetically because they know who he is and what he's done for them. The leaders, who worship with the most abandon and energy, set this atmosphere. They don't care that there might be some present who aren't that excited about God, who are in church because it's what they were always taught to do or who think it's childish to get as loud or be as enthusiastic as they are. The leaders just let go, and the whole church follows their lead, worshiping with enthusiasm.

Worshiping in public and with this sort of energy exposes you and places you in a vulnerable position. You might do something that looks silly. People could laugh. You may find that it's harder than it should be to locate in yourself genuine excitement about God. To worship with real abandon is to let yourself express how you really feel and what you really think deep down inside, and this can be uncomfortable for those of us who only do that behind closed doors, if we do it at all.

I remember one time in particular I found myself unable to contain my joy over who the Lord is and what he was doing for me. This joy overflowed into ecstatic dancing and singing in the living room of one of my friends. It was a spontaneous worship time, aided by a CD of Urbana tunes, and one song in particular, "You're the Source." I was using *all* my energy to worship the Lord. I was exposing my true feelings and thoughts before him. It was before him and him alone that I was dancing and singing—making myself vulnerable, as David did. No one else was home at the time! The difference between David and me is that if someone had come into the room at that point, I surely would have clammed up, frozen up and reddened up!

David worshiped as he did in front of thirty thousand men, but he was able to be shameless because he knew ultimately it was only before the Lord that he worshiped. David adhered to the principle that we worship before God, not people, even when we lead worship in front of thousands.

David also knew how worthy of worship his God was. He knew what the Lord had done and continued to do for him, and kept that at the forefront of his mind. This made it impossible for him not to worship God with all his energy. He didn't have a self-conscious bone in his body because he was only God-conscious.

How do you need to become more God-conscious and less self-conscious? How can you be free to worship the Lord unapologetically and with all your might when you are leading a group of people?

What has the Lord done for you? How can you cultivate your awareness that he is constantly demonstrating his lovingkindness toward you, that he is constantly acting on your behalf? How can you keep this in the forefront of your mind as you lead worship?

10 You Are a Leader

. . . .

Matt Frazier

Worship is big. Worship is really big. It's what is happening in heaven right now, and it's on the agenda for the rest of eternity. Being a worship leader is a high calling. It's a thrilling opportunity with lots of chances for joy and failure, rewards and difficulties. Anything that will last as long as worship will should be taken quite seriously. Anyone who will lead something that is so everlasting should take their leadership quite seriously too.

Leadership is an odd thing these days. We have so many bad examples of leaders that few of us are all that excited about being leaders ourselves. It seems almost impossible to conceive of a leader with real integrity. It's easy to believe that anyone who aspires to lead must be out for power, attention or some other selfish and dishonorable gain. If we lead, we know others might think that about us. So it's tempting not to lead at all, even in a position of leadership! In spite of all the mistakes that parents, pastors, politicians and others have made, however, we are still in search of leaders we can trust—and we need them. People are looking for leadership in worship too, and if God has called you to lead in this way, then you are whom they seek.

As a worship leader you're worshiping God, and you're helping others to do same. It can take some practice to find the balance between giving yourself to worship and leading others in it simultaneously, but there is a balance! If you are worshiping God yourself, then your words and actions in front of a congregation should say, "Follow me; do what I'm doing; come, worship God." This can happen in various ways.

Leading with What You've Got
Use your eyes and your body to lead. Making eye contact is a great way to connect and communicate with those you are leading. Your eyes should speak to your congregation, "Isn't it great to worship God to-

gether!" Your body movements should also serve to lead people into worship. Usually this simply means being comfortable and not doing anything that is particularly distracting. Most people possess at least a couple of odd physical habits. If you have any that might draw attention to you, try to lose them in order to serve your followers.

Use your voice. The best of all tools to lead others in worship may be your voice. What kind of voice helps a worship setting? Probably one that is excited and pleasant. A voice that is harsh, bored or awkward will not help anyone worship God. I've noticed that sometimes when worship leaders call out a verse or a chorus in the middle of a song as a way of giving direction to the group, they can switch into a totally different voice. They're singing along worshiping God when all of a sudden they switch into "information" voice and yell out the first line of a song in a way that breaks the entire mood of a worship time. Your voice should fit the feeling of a song or set of songs and lead people more fully into the worship of God through that particular music.

Be aware of the people you're leading. It's easy to believe that when we lead worship we should forget about those we're leading and just focus on our own experience. There's a way in which this is true: If others don't follow us in worshiping God, that shouldn't stop us from worshiping anyway. But you cannot simply be in your own world, having an experience that ignores everyone around you. Can you imagine if other spiritual leaders, like Bible-study leaders or preachers, took this approach?

Believe it or not, it's also easy to simply forget your congregation. I can recall ending a set of worship songs, turning around to unplug my guitar and preparing to walk off to my seat when I suddenly realized that the entire congregation was still standing! I hadn't invited them to sit, so they didn't know what was going on. This was an awkward (but now humorous) breakdown in leadership. They were following me, but I hadn't led them well—I had lost my awareness of them. Now I always remember to ask people to be seated when the time comes.

> *Leading worship with integrity involves calling others to follow you to where you are going.*

Tune in to your congregation's current needs. Make sure your group knows where you're headed next. If they don't know a song very well, you'll need to lead them more strongly until they become comfortable with it. If your group isn't sure what verse of a song comes next, help them. Try to be aware of what your congregation is experiencing from the beginning to the end of every worship time. What will help them worship God at any given moment? What cultural, social or holiday events might influence the congregation's focus on God? The beginning of a service at one point in the calendar year should not necessarily be like the beginning of a worship service during another part of the year. What will help people to respond to one spoken message will not be particularly useful after every spoken message. You are a leader, and to know how to guide others to a new destination, you usually need to know something about their point of departure.

Plan in specific ways how you will lead each worship time. As a worship leader you'll have many wonderful opportunities to help others reach new destinations in their worship of God. Make sure you think through how to do that most effectively in every situation. If you want your fellowship or church to reflect on a particular attribute of God, for example, give them Scripture, a story or an illustration to help get them thinking. In other words, don't just say something like, "Reflect for a few minutes about how holy God is." Instead, tell those who you're leading what holiness is about. Give them a specific analogy or metaphor that they can relate to. Read Scripture that illustrates God's holiness in fresh way (it doesn't even have to use the word *holy* as long as that's what it's about). Help people move physically into worship. If you want them to respond in excitement to God, ask them to stand. If you want them to experience God's rest, give them the option to sit.

To lead worship, we must worship—we can't take others where we're not going. It is crucial, however, that we develop the skill of focusing on God while also being aware of the experience of those we lead. We must then respond to that awareness by creating a situation that facilitates others' worship experience. Leading worship is for us, but it's not just for us. Like so much of God's surprising gospel, it is also true that in the act of leading worship, we receive by giving.

11 Leading Versus Performing
The Lens

• •

Andy Crouch

Nearsightedness runs in my family, and since I was eight years old I have worn glasses. The first thing I do in the morning is put them on. I'm not blind without them, but I certainly can't do much. Glasses make it possible for me to see where I'm headed, recognize my family and friends, and see beyond the tip of my nose—in short, they help me know the truth about the world around me rather than just seeing a colorful haze.

I've come to the conclusion that leading worship is like being a pair of glasses—or, let's say, a lens—for a group of people. The fact is that spiritual nearsightedness runs in the human family. All of us, without exception, have a hard time focusing on anything past the tip of our noses, let alone on God. Everything that is not directly related to our own self-interest is fuzzy at best, indistinguishable at worst. Consequently, left to ourselves we will worship only that which is very near at hand—ourselves and other creatures. The Creator, on the other hand,

is much bigger than ourselves and much harder to perceive, even though his presence is everywhere. In order to worship him, we need some help. We need a lens that can focus our attention on his presence, and that's where worship leaders come in.

If you lead worship in your church or fellowship, I bet you've experienced what I'm referring to. Have you noticed that most people don't come in suffused with an awareness of God's presence? We arrive at the time and place for worship having been out in a world that dulls our senses. It can be hard work to get a group of people to pay attention, focus and see that actually God has been present all along. That's the work of worship leading. In the songs we choose and sing, the words we say and don't say and the themes we use, we are helping a group of people focus on someone greater than themselves. We are an aid to their spiritual vision.

Just as with people, every group has a different level of nearsightedness. It also varies over time. Some weeks your group may be eager to worship, requiring only the slightest direction and leadership to be aware of the presence of God; other weeks (for whatever reasons) your group may require a massive amount of lens correction to bring true reality into focus for them. I know that on my campus the nearsightedness increases dramatically around midterm time! Whatever the amount of "correction" required, the goal of the worship leader is to redirect the people's attention.

This is where worship leading is so different from performing. Performers are effective precisely to the extent that they draw attention to themselves. Their goal is to establish a deep relationship with the audience through their performance. Think about the best concert you've attended, and you'll recognize that part of what made it outstanding was the relationship you developed with the performer, a relationship made possible by his or her extraordinary talents at communicating through music. (You can see the importance of this relationship when you consider how popular "unplugged" sets are in the middle of concerts—at a time when relationship is built.)

There is nothing intrinsically wrong with performing. Even in the context of worship services, an authentic performance can be very powerful. But when performance is confused with worship leading, the results are disastrous. Worship is not about one person's relationship with God (or even one band's or choir's) but about the *whole congregation* growing in that relationship. That can only happen as the whole congregation is led into the presence of God—and the process can quickly be derailed by a worship leader who is focusing on his or her *own* presence.

Here again the metaphor of the lens helps us understand the role of worship leading. Lenses are not the focus. I couldn't live like I do without my glasses, but I don't spend much time gazing lovingly at their curved surface. When my lenses do draw attention to themselves, it's usually because I need to clean them! Lenses aren't meant to be looked at; they're meant to be looked through. That's a good description of our role as worship leaders.

> *Lenses aren't meant to be looked at; they're meant to be looked through.*

Polishing the Lens

We can "polish the lens" in a couple of ways so that we don't distract from the real focus of worship. (For more on this subject see chapter 8.) First, we need constantly to let God reduce our ego. Most musicians and public speakers (many worship leaders are both) have an inflated sense of self-importance. God wants to gently humble us so that we no longer take over people's attention. If we are up front in order to be significant, to be recognized or to be applauded, we are like a badly scratched lens that calls all too much attention to itself. We need love and accountability in our lives—people who know us very well and who are not impressed by us. Of course, it may seem easier to get friends by showing off our musical talents, but the kind of friends we're really looking for and need are those who couldn't care less whether we "perform." Every worship leader should have some of those friends.

Another way to "polish the lens" is to practice. Sometimes it seems that worship teams conclude that since worship isn't performance, there is no need for excellence. True, we don't pursue excellence for its own sake in the way performers do, but we do pursue it for the sake of being transparent. Excellent musicians can play a song without calling any attention to its technical difficulty; excellent speakers simply communicate without making you notice their fine pronunciation or well-thought-out sentences; excellent musical teams know how to work together seamlessly. Only practice can get us to the point where the technical aspects of our leadership—from the musical techniques to finding the next slide—are completely transparent, leaving the group we're leading free to focus through us rather than on us.

Even worse than a scratched lens, though, is no lens at all. Some people say humbly, "I don't lead worship, I just get out of the way." Well, I want my glasses to be in the way—I can't see without them! God has always used people to make himself known. From Moses to Deborah to Isaiah—and ultimately Jesus—God has used people who were willing to be very much in the way of others who had an inadequate understanding of God. God wants to use you to clarify who he is to other people. That will require you to take the risk of "getting in the way," being up front helping the group to focus. Don't be afraid to lead!

All of us, of course, are scratched lenses. We'll always distract somewhat from the presence of God. But as we pray and as we practice, we become more and more able to lead others into the real presence of God, where we all can see him clearly. There's no greater calling than to be a well-crafted lens.

12   Becoming a Guide to the Throne Room

....

Sundee Frazier

Getting to our destination in worship is like getting to the Holy of Holies through the tabernacle. As worship leaders we guide people from outside the tabernacle, through the court and the Holy Place and into the Most Holy Place, where they actually connect with God, become open to hearing his voice and to being transformed by him. If we are to help people find this place, we need to think like leaders all along the way.

In the tabernacle metaphor, outside the tabernacle is where we're either oblivious or hardened to our need for God, wrapped up in our problems or distracted by our busyness. We may also be so overwhelmed by a problem that we are desperate for God's help. In any case, we're not experiencing his peace. We are not neces-sarily confident of his deliverance.

Our Destination: The Holy of Holies

We need to get to the Holy of Holies! This is where we can experience the presence of our Father, approach the throne of grace boldly to receive mercy from him and be awed by who he is now that we can see him clearly (Hebrews 4:16). At this, our ultimate destination, we are transfixed by God's goodness and aware of nothing but the meaningfulness of doing that for which we were ultimately created—worshiping Jesus. Our problems melt into peace as we realize that he holds the universe in his hand. While there are no formulas for getting others to worship God, there are some things we can do to guide them nearer if they are willing.

How to Become a Guide

Find times to worship when you're not leading, and experience what it's like to go from where your heart is walled in and pent up to the place where it is bowed down in worship of your God. What was that progression like? How were you helped by the leader or the songs? What action did you take to get your heart freed from the encumbrances of your day? You need to know the route to Jesus from firsthand experience. The more you travel there yourself, the better you'll guide others there. (For more on this topic read chapter 8.)

Each time you are going to lead worship, you need to pray specifically for guidance. Ask God to help you know people's needs, how they might be encouraged, what he wants them to hear. Only God can read the hearts of humans; only God knows all the struggles and fears each has faced in the week leading up to this worship time. He alone knows the song, the words, the promise from his Word that will break through to the person who really needs a breakthrough. So ask the Lord before starting worship (and throughout the time too) to be your guide as you lead his people to him.

In order to hear from God, you need to learn how to listen to him. It's the only way you can know how God wants to meet people in worship. What this means, practically, is asking God a question and waiting in focused and expectant silence for him to respond. The response might come in a word or words you "hear" (like the voice in our heads), a picture you see in your mind's eye, a sense or intuition you get, or a rational idea.

If either listening to God or leading people is new to you, try listening as you prepare for the service and discuss what you are hearing with another leader before you lead with what you heard. As you gain experience in listening and in providing pastoral care for a group, you will learn to hear from God as you are leading worship. You will be able to use what you hear to minister to people through your apt words, through some Scripture God brings to your mind, through a song you add that wasn't in the original lineup. Over the years, I've found that there are certain aspects of God and his character that particularly help people draw closer to him in worship. These truths never change, and you can emphasize them in what you say and pray as you lead.

☐ God loves us and desires to be with us.
☐ God proves his love in the cross, and he always forgives us when we ask.
☐ God is the perfect Father.
☐ God is a promise-keeper—he will always do what he says.
☐ God can and wants to provide everything we need.
☐ God is a grace-giver—he doesn't give us what we deserve but what we don't deserve.
☐ God is unchanging—he's the same yesterday, today and forever.
☐ God is a redeemer—he works all things together for good, and makes a way where there appears to be none.
☐ God never forgets us or stops thinking about us.
☐ Jesus is the friend who is with us in all things.
☐ The Spirit empowers us to do things we didn't think we could.
☐ Jesus will return and take us to be with him forever where there is no more death, pain or sadness, and we need to be ready for him.

Our goal is always to help people open up to God. We participate with God in calling others to drop the guards they have up against him because they are injured, worn down, continuing in sin, believing lies or busily out-of-touch. Getting bound up, distracted worshipers to the throne room means helping them know how to respond at each juncture. Undoubtedly, some will have less trouble than others: some have more experience getting to the throne room on their own, and others' guards come down more easily.

Helping People Respond

When I toured Mammoth Cave in Kentucky, our tour guides helped us to know how to respond at various times and places to get the most out of our trip and to make it all the way to the end. They told us to hold our lamps down low so we could see the ground—a useful tip to prevent both blinding ourselves and tripping. They told us how to descend extremely steep mountainsides and climb the one hundred or more steps out of the cave. They pointed their flashlights at places where they wanted us to look so that we could see remnants of indigenous people who had used the caves as shelter. They told us not to write on the walls or move any rocks. (Apparently, guides in the 1800s didn't tell their followers this: people formed little piles of rocks into monuments to themselves, their universities and even U. S. Presidents.)

When we lead worship, we help others know how to respond at various points so that they continue to move farther into God's presence. We shine our flashlights in the direction they need to go. And we must call them to build monuments only to God—not, like the nineteenth-century cave explorers, to themselves or anyone else.

Here are some examples of what it might look like to help your congregation respond and draw closer to God in worship.

God's love. If people are having a hard time knowing God's love, have them think about Jesus on the cross in their mind's eye, with themselves kneeling below, and read to them: "God proves his love for us in that while we were still sinners Christ died for us" (Romans 5:8). Follow this with a song about the cross and God's love for us.

Thanksgiving. Ask people to pray short prayers of thanksgiving out loud in the midst of the congregation. Or ask them to think of a few things they are thankful for; then have them share one of those things; thank God silently for them or write them down. Sing an upbeat song of thanksgiving,

or for a more meditative setting, a gentle version of the doxology.

Confession. Lead a confessional prayer. You might pray out loud, asking God to help people see their sin; then have them wait silently for God to show them how they have turned from him and need forgiveness. Ask them to continue reflecting and praying while the worship team sings a song of confession or a song of God's mercy. After one verse and one chorus, you might invite the congregation to continue praying by singing the words of the song with the team.

In general, remind people who they are worshiping, using vivid word-pictures to help them grasp something true about God. Then, depending on the need, invite them to sing loudly or quietly, or to listen to the words as the worship team sings a song.

It may be important to give people permission to raise their hands, sit, stand or kneel. When necessary, give them some idea from Scripture how all of these responses to God can be appropriate. If an explanation has never been given, help your congregation know why raising hands or kneeling is a valid and helpful response. People need to know the meaning of what they're doing for it to be useful.

Always Follow the Ultimate Guide

At times you will have what you think is the perfect worship set planned and ready to go. Often you will lead according to that plan and God will work powerfully through it. Other times, something will happen that makes it clear your plan may be perfect for some other situation but not this one. The preacher may end with a heart-piercing, convicting call instead of the victorious, upbeat note around which you planned. Suddenly your response song no longer seems appropriate.

We had planned to end the midnight New Year's Eve communion service at Urbana with a very upbeat version of *Joy to the World*. But the preacher went a different direction from his original plan. He closed his sermon by sharing the moving story of the premature birth of his daughter and the vigil he and his wife had kept over her as God brought her from near death into robust life. Half the convention was in tears. *Joy to the World* really wasn't the thing for the moment. So the worship leader quickly adjusted and led us in *Jesus Loves Me* instead, followed by a time of prayer about God's love—like the preacher and his wife's love for their daughter—for every person in creation. *Then* we did *Joy to the World,* which at that point accurately reflected the progression of our hearts.

Listen to the Spirit's leading. Sometimes the Spirit speaks through common sense, using our abilities to analyze and make decisions about a situation. Sometimes he speaks through "urges" or intuitions we have. Let's say you had a quick, bouncy praise song planned for the congregation to sing immediately following the message. But you see that God has created an atmosphere of repentance; people are not yet ready to celebrate deliverance from their sin because they're still grappling with what their sin is. Give them opportunity to reflect and repent in prayer, and then sing a reflective version of Psalm 51. If there's not time for both songs, and you think it's best that people end upbeat, still give them time to pray. While they are praying, have the pianist play the Psalm 51 piece in the background (you whisper for her to do this as you're walking up to the front because you know it's something she's prepared to play). Then make a transition into the upbeat song by reminding people how thankful we can be that God has not cast us away from his presence but has taken away our sin and the punishment we deserved as well.

What exactly does it mean to be led by the Holy Spirit? There are no simple answers to this question. Do not assume, however, that a worship time that is Spirit led will always go longer than planned. Or that a leader who cuts worship short (or is concerned about time) is not being led by the Spirit.

The Holy Spirit is the Spirit of Jesus, who taught and lived servanthood. One thing we can be sure of, then, is that whenever we have an impulse to serve, we are being led by the Spirit.

Sometimes it will serve people to keep singing, even though the worship was supposed to end ten minutes ago. Sometimes it will serve better to end early (yes, *early*) because the song you just sang was the perfect ending point, and the other songs you had planned to use are no longer needed. The Spirit could even have you stop early so everyone can go live-out that which they've heard God saying! Most times it will serve best to stay within the time that you and others who are coordinating your service have agreed on.

There is no finely drawn map for getting people from outside the tabernacle into the presence of God. We must be careful not to turn any particular method into a system. To think we can create worship by our own effort is idolatry. God, in the person of the Holy Spirit, will be our guide to his throne room. Remember what he has promised us: "Draw near to me and I will draw near to you" (James 4:8 paraphrased). Be confident as you lead people to the Holy of Holies that the separating veil has been opened by Jesus (Hebrews 10:20); he wants you and all his people to worship right at the foot of his throne, not from outside the tabernacle. We can trust in him to lead us to the words to say, songs to sing and actions to take that will help people get all the way into his presence.

13 The Mechanics of Leading

Sundee Frazier

Have you ever been in a car with a driver who is lost—but won't admit he or she is lost? Have you ever been in a worship service with a leader who left you feeling like that?

There are a few mechanics to leading worship that, put into practice, will give you and those you are leading more confidence during worship times. Following these guidelines will free you and others to focus on God.

Offer a Welcome

It's important to welcome people into worship. How you create your service's atmosphere is up to you and whomever else you are working with. You can be casual or formal, have people greet each other or not, use the same basic welcome each week or change it to fit the week's theme. Whatever you do, a welcome will help people take that first step from the blustery outside (literally and metaphorically) into the presence of God. Think ahead about how to do this so you start off on a confident note.

Don't Leave People Hanging

Remember to help your congregation know when to stand, when to sit and when they can posture themselves however they want. Nothing disrupts a worshipful atmosphere more than when people realize the worship team has left the front of the room and no one said anything about what to do next.

Cues to help people know where the music is going are crucial to enable them to stay focused on God, their destination. Whenever someone isn't sure of where to go next in the music, he or she will stop focusing on God and start worrying about becoming an accidental soloist. Our goal is to give cues that are clear but not disruptive. Learning how to do this takes practice.

You'll need cues for helping people know when you are going back to the top of a song, repeating a chorus or a verse, or singing the last line multiple times to

Your Fashion Statement   Alison Siewert

Your clothes do make a statement! A useful standard for worship leaders' clothing is, choose what's not distracting and what fits your context. If you're in a shorts culture, shorts are fine—as long as they're not too short or too ripped. Clothes with writing (like T-shirts with logos or sayings) are nearly always distracting because people in the back may spend half a song trying to make out what a shirt says. Anything very revealing, either by showing skin or body form, is out. (Ask an honest friend of your own gender to help you evaluate.) Dressing neatly (as opposed to turning yesterday's sweatshirt inside out for rewearing) can help communicate that we're here to meet God. This is a deliberate exercise, not a haphazard gathering, and your appearance should reflect it.

Worship leaders do not need to look like they walked off the pages of *Vogue*, either. Dressing too hip or too formally can put off a congregation and draw attention to what you're wearing instead of the God you're worshiping. As you evaluate what to wear, consider whether your clothes might be a distraction to *you*. Self-consciousness can distort your focus and hinder your ability to lead others to worship God. Pick what you won't have to think about, adjust or otherwise pay attention to. Finally, talk about clothing as a team so that you all dress at the same level of formality. Avoid the surfer-dude-and-prom-gown mix-and-match look!

close. To get back to the beginning of a song you can say, "One more time," or "Let's sing it again" (without sounding too campy). Or you can just say the first line of the first verse to indicate that's where you are going. The instrumentalists can also cue by playing a lead-in that makes it clear you are going to sing the song again. In this case you don't necessarily need to say anything, although more clarity is preferable to less.

To repeat a chorus or verse, you can simply say the first few words of the chorus or verse you want to sing, or you can make up a musical prompt that you sing in time with the music. For both of these methods, you need to figure out the right timing for saying or singing these prompts so that they don't come too soon or too late (although too late is much more disruptive). Think about what you want to say, how much musical space there is before the transition and how much time it takes you to give the prompt. Practice giving the prompt during worship rehearsal and on your own. (Try different things while you're alone in your car, and no one can mock you.) This is the best way to work all this out and learn how to do it seamlessly.

Signal Your Team

Finally, you need to establish signals with your worship team so that they are sure of where you are going as well. If you give signals confidently and visibly, your team will go with you when you repeat the chorus for the third time, even though you only practiced doing it twice in rehearsal. (Before you start worship, always make sure that all team members can see you from wherever they're standing.) Helpful signals include back to the top, repeat, last time, end, volume up, volume down, tempo up, tempo down. Develop nondisruptive hand signals for these and any others that you need for your setting.

Becoming proficient at these mechanics isn't the key to you or anyone else having a genuine worship experience. Worship is ultimately a matter of the heart, and no amount of mechanical excellence can produce a heart change. Knowing how to welcome, direct and communicate with your congregation and team, however, will provide a more focused, less distracting, environment. You will "make people's paths straighter" on their way to having their hearts draw near to God.

Part 3
Go, Teams

14 Choosing a Team

Matt Frazier

As you begin your quest to form a musical worship team, you will no doubt ask the question, what kind of people should I invite to join me in leading worship? People often assume the answer is, good musicians. That's incomplete, however, because leading worship is spiritual leadership—not just musical leadership. To understand this, we must consider how significant worship actually is: Worship is the act of participating in supreme and ultimate truth—the truth of who God is and how we need him.

The Key Requisite
Those who lead the worship of God need much more than the ability to play chords and scales. If people are going to lead others in worship, they must be spiritually mature. They must be people who have tasted God's goodness, who have taken risks to be faithful and have seen God deliver them, who have felt great needs and experienced God meeting them. In short, to be spiritually mature they must know God and know themselves.

This spiritual maturity is also required because of the amount of attention worship team members will receive from their congregation. Admiration and acclaim, if not tempered with the wisdom of spiritual maturity, can cause worship leaders to idolize their position. Our sense of importance must come from God, and we must lead people to reflect on God's importance in worship, not our own.

Who Are Good Choices?
Some team members will be obvious choices—individuals who, along with their spiritual maturity, have musical skills and the confidence to lead others. Other choices may not be so obvious. Perhaps some in your community of faith have only modest musical backgrounds (say, piano lessons at a younger age) but would be willing to commit to musical growth if you spark their interest and give them a vision.

The odd truth is that sometimes the most talented musicians have a harder time leading worship than people with more modest skills. This is because most expert musicians have been trained to attract attention to themselves through performing. (Honestly, this is a tendency that runs deep in many of us with musical backgrounds.) Sometimes, it's the musician of unassuming skill who will lead others in worship with the most appropriate humility. So don't be afraid to consider musicians who are relatively new to their instruments. If they're willing to work hard and learn, they might be just the people you're looking for.

My wife was invited to be a part of the worship team for a large conference as a percussionist. She was a spiritually mature Christian, had lots of experience leading worship and was a good musician. But she had never played much percussion. The leaders took a risk to include her on the team, but since they offered her the time and resources to grow and she possesses natural musical gifts and was willing to practice, she eventually became a fine percussionist and an important part of several worship teams in that role.

You probably will not have an entire team of people who are spiritually mature, excellent musicians and confident leaders, so try to balance these values among your team members. For example, if you have one or two highly skilled musicians, the less-experienced musicians will do better. And if most of your team members have extensive experience in following God, less mature members might learn a lot from them (although I would not recommend putting an extremely spiritually immature person on a worship team).

If you're interested in inviting someone to join your worship team but aren't sure about his or her character, get to know the person. Be observant and ask questions about their life. (In the process of getting to know them as people, you'll probably also find out about their musical interests—he sang at a coffee bar last week or she gives piano lessons as a part-time job.) If you're not sure about their level of musical ability, give them chances to sing or play in low-pressure situations. I've taken my guitar to college students' dorm rooms to play together. I've invited others to sing or play an instrument in special situations like a prayer meeting or a low-key retreat. If you want to know more about others' vocal ability, you can simply

stand next to them in a corporate worship time.

Another way to discover musical gifts is to organize worship music afternoons and invite your entire fellowship or church to bring their instruments or just come and sing. If a lot of people turn out, divide them into smaller groups and have them learn a song, and then have them lead the rest of you in learning it. You'll learn a lot about potential team members, and everyone will gain experience in the process.

You might also consider offering lessons on particular instruments taught by your best players. Those who learn will get useful input, and those who teach can identify potential new team members.

Finally, when you invite someone to consider joining a worship team, do just that: invite them to consider it. Tell them why you think it might be good, but also give them room to make a wise decision. It will be hard work for them to be a part of the team, and they must see how it's a faithful decision for them and why it will, therefore, be worth the hard work.

> *Spiritually mature people who have some skill leading a congregation and in singing or playing instruments make the best worship team members.*

15 Developing Talent

Sundee Frazier & Alison Siewert

Developing talent for a worship team starts by helping others become more like Jesus. After all, when you ask people to join a worship team, you are inviting them to lead others in spiritual activity. First, ask

God to send people to your fellowship or church, and to show you those already there, who know him and want to become more like Jesus. These are the ones who may be most ready to lead worship.

Then take an inventory of your present team, and think about how you'd like it to grow. Develop a sense of what you want to see happen in coming years, such as adding more instruments or expanding your vocal styles. If you want to add more instruments next year, you need to start praying this year for people with talent, as well as the money to buy instruments if necessary. You can also start now to train a developing leader in a particular instrument, and to have fund raisers to build up your budget.

Ways to Deepen Your Talent Pool

After praying, assessing your resources and envisioning a goal, you are ready to take some active steps.

Encourage current and potential team members to take formal lessons. Even a few sessions with a good teacher can go a long way. Many worship leaders have never had vocal or instrumental training.

Create some training in worship leading. Do the training yourself or bring someone in. Go on a retreat, or do several sessions over a year. Or take your team to one of the many worship-leading seminars offered by various ministries. Often we confuse musicianship with worship leading, but even the best musicians need specific help to learn how to lead a congregation.

Give new leaders your time and attention. Keep in mind that the main way leaders learn to lead is by doing it with more experienced leaders. Your encouragement, prayers and willingness to let these people see both your strengths and your failures will work together to help them understand how to lead, and how to follow Jesus—which is the best of all training.

Consider inviting youth from your congregation to contribute and develop their musical talents by being a part of the worship team. At our church, a high-school student who skillfully plays trumpet in his school's band adds a regal sound to hymns and a festive touch to upbeat praise songs.

If you can, recruit people who will be around for more than one year. This way you can build momentum with your team, and you will have veterans to welcome and help train newcomers as they join. One way to keep people around (though not the only factor in a person's choice to stay or leave) is to help them have a good experience the first time around. If we pastor those who commit to our teams, they're more likely to stay. And they'll grow constantly in their experience and gifts and contribute more as time passes.

Develop a rehearsal schedule that team members agree in advance to commit to. The team could agree to a certain number of hours of personal practice each week, as well. (You might set up some sort of accountability to help people stick to this.) Practice develops talent. It's also where the rubber meets the road, because time is one of the hardest things for us to give up. But if you want to improve and not just maintain, then you have to put in time. Help your team catch a vision for what they can become if they practice. Not only will they make a more excellent contribution to the worship sound, they'll also grow more like Jesus as they develop their ability to serve others through leading well.

Other Options

One strategy for developing talent over the long run is to create rotating teams so that more people can be involved in leading. While having one team may feel ideal, having two or three that take turns may be a smarter strategy in terms of developing more people's worship gifts. This is absolutely crucial in campus fellowship groups (or any transient context) where the congregation and its leaders' turnover rate is consistently high. In a church you might want to consider developing more worship leaders instead of fewer for the sake of sparing people from burnout, encouraging people in the gifts that God has given them (a scriptural mandate) and being prepared for growth in your congregation (moving to two services, needing a second worship team for special outreach events or conferences).

Sometimes you don't need to develop talent—you need to recognize what's already there in forms that you didn't know were useful. Accordions, bagpipes, oboes and dulcimers may not be ideal on their own for leading a congregation, but they can contribute! You don't have to stick with what is considered standard instrumentation. And you don't have to have two guitarists to make worship fly. Flexibility with instrumentation will make you open to a wider variety of people and their gifts for worship.

Start with who and what you have, and build from there. Receive who God sends, and ask for more!

16 Butcher, Baker, Overheadmaker
The Creative Team

Alison Siewert

Anyone who has watched a professional football game can see that a football team is composed of many players and that each player's position contributes to winning the game.

But if you watch carefully, you will notice that the team includes more people than its players. The head coach, the assistant coaches, various managers, the support staff—trainers, statisticians, watercrew—all contribute in significant ways to the team effort. A good team is characterized by the effectiveness of its whole organization as much as by the talent of its offensive line.

When people refer to "the worship team" they often mean the instrumental and vocal musicians who lead the congregation in singing. Church members might also think of the pastor or others who give the message. But in reality a worship team, like an athletic team, includes a much larger group of people who work together to build a worship experience. Sound technicians, dancers, the person responsible for overheads or power-point presentations, all play an important role and are part of the team that leads and supports your congregation in worship. Your team will be characterized not only by its worship leader or the cool lead guitarist but by the whole team, even the people who are never seen in an "up front" capacity.

Successful team building requires thinking ahead, matching gifts with tasks and planning with people in mind. What can each person offer the process?

Remember when the people of Israel built the temple with the many offerings they contributed—so many the supply overflowed? Or remember how Nehemiah wisely divided the labor among the families of Israel as they returned from exile to rebuild Jerusalem's wall? Think inclusively about what it will take to get worship happening in your context. Then seek out gifted people who are willing to participate in the preparatory phase of worship. Here are some positions, other than the musicians and speaker, to consider.

Artists of All Sorts
Very few churches have figured out how to in-

corporate the arts, beyond music, into their worship. But you probably have people skilled in visual arts, dance, drama and poetry who will be blessed and a be blessing as they are drawn into building worship with you.

Gloria, a woman on a student worship team I worked with, had extensive training in dance. But there weren't enough students with sufficient training to form a dance team. So Gloria came up with a sort of sub-dance form we came to call "creative movement," and she taught it to several other students. It was a beautiful mix of dance, mime and natural gesture, and it communicated successfully, especially alongside Scripture reading. Once, we got two dozen students—including a few football guys—to participate in a piece Gloria had made for a reading of Hebrews 11. It was one of the most powerful visual expressions I've ever seen in worship.

Look for ways to incorporate the artists in your crowd, and see how they lead you and your fellowship into deep and fresh adoration of God.

A good team is characterized by the effectiveness of its whole organization as much as by the talent of its offensive line.

Hospitality Team

Our student fellowship at Occidental College included a half-dozen gifted students who were committed to the ministry of hospitality. Before the service they welcomed people into our meeting room, and after the service they provided food, which encouraged people to stay around. They organized their hospitality to match the theme of the service. When we focused on creation, for example, they made a huge multimedia mural covering most of the entry area, and they offered fruit (just like God made it, right off the tree!) to people. The thematic, artistic atmosphere was great. But the most important thing the students offered was

their authentic, warm welcome and their availability to people with questions, to folks who looked lost or to anyone with a need. They made our meetings "open houses" to all who came.

Overhead Artist

Bruce not only plays guitar but also makes the overheads for my worship team. He's a graphic designer, and his equipment is pretty amazing. He can make color overheads that are beyond nice—they're inspiring! Bruce takes time to find just the right layout and illustration for each song. Sometimes he does several versions of the same piece to cover the various moods in worship (mellow versus upbeat, for example). His contribution is a gift I've never before experienced on a team.

Overhead Technician or Power Point Pro

Someone has to get the lyrics up somewhere during the service. Projecting lyrics—with whatever equipment you have—is kind of an art form in itself: getting them on the screen at the right angle, focusing the image, changing in time for people to follow continuations of songs. In many settings I see teams grabbing the first willing body from the congregation to manage the lyrics, which is sort of okay. But if you have someone who is sensitive to the movement of worship and can participate on a regular basis, all the better! Running the projector might be a good ministry opportunity (it *is* ministry) for someone who has difficulty standing during worship: it puts them near the front and employs a sitting position.

Child Caregivers

In many churches, child care is provided by

paid staff. But whether the caregivers are paid or volunteer, if you have opportunity to build or influence a child-care team, you can bless both the children and the parents worshiping with you.

Make sure that you know and understand safety and liability issues clearly. If you don't, find a knowledgeable children's ministry resource person or a social worker to sort out these issues with you. The caregivers need to help parents feel confident about leaving their children with them: no one will leave a child where she or he could be neglected, easily injured, or illicitly taken. Develop and implement a plan for caregivers to contact parents in an emergency. Even when the parents are nearby in the sanctuary, if there are five hundred people worshiping it may be difficult to find little Joe's mommy! (Many churches assign vibrating pagers to parents as they sign their children in at the nursery.) Pay attention to who will work with the children in your care. You are developing little worshipers! Even for the smallest children, the demonstration of love they receive when they're with God's people may make a huge difference in their lives. Find the people in your circles who have the call and gifts to serve the least among you.

Setters-Up and Tearers-Down

Setting up and tearing down are perhaps the least glamorous tasks surrounding worship services. At my home church we have to set up a whole sanctuary every week because we meet in a gym. That means dragging out huge boxes and carts, setting up heavy stands and sound equipment, and pulling it all apart again in two hours. Locate folks who are willing to give them-

Equipment Check!   Alison Siewert

I was leading a service recently when, after the sketch, the teacher for the evening got up to begin a message and could not be heard. He checked his lavaliere microphone, and it was on. The sound technician checked the receiver unit, and it was on. Ahh . . . the batteries! The microphone had been left in the "on" position over the week, and the batteries were completely drained. He had to talk *very* loudly for a few minutes while the technician ran to another room to find batteries, install them and replace the mic on the speaker.

Check your equipment. Worship can get stalled by a burned-out overhead bulb, a cord with a short in it, a broken guitar string. Try to have replacements handy for everything. Of course you can't plan for every potential mishap, and when one happens, try to let it go with humor. But whenever good planning can help things run smoothly, it's your job to do it, or better yet, to delegate and encourage others to do it. Think through the whole service, checking for things like microphone and projector placement. Do you have someone to operate the computer projection unit for singing? Is the VCR cued up for the video clip? Will someone dim the lights at the right moment? Has the sound technician corrected last week's problem with that speaker? A thorough check of these sorts of things will help your worship be about worship rather than about that terribly loud, ringing feedback from microphone #4!

selves to this hard work; they may be people with the gift of service. If the work is very strenuous or people aren't available weekly, you might consider rotating teams, spreading the burden—and the joy— among a larger number of people.

Sound Technicians

Ah . . . the sound people. If you are using a sound system (see chapter 27, "Sound Systems") you must find at least one, preferably more, person who has a good musical ear and who is willing to pursue training in the set-up and use of your equipment. It may be helpful to send this person (or team) to a seminar for training, but you should also consider asking a consultant to come to your venue to train your sound technician(s) on-the-spot. Only by seeing your space and and using your equipment will a trainer be effective with your team.

Multimedia Technicians

With the growing availability of computer technology and audio and video options for worship, you may want to add some folks to your team who love to program electronic gadgets. Many churches have begun using computer-driven projectors, rear-projection video monitors and sophisticated stereo systems to create images and enhance their illustrations for worship. Explore who in your congregation might have gifts to use the equipment you have or to help develop the kind of set-up that fits in your context.

Prayer Ministries

What happens after the sermon? Many congregations and communities value opportunities to pray in response to what God is doing in worship and beyond. One way to encourage and facilitate prayer is to call some people to prayer as a ministry. Find people who are emotionally stable and spiritually mature, who enjoy praying for others, who possess (or are willing to learn) excellent listening skills, who have time to participate in team training and who can

stay after services to pray. Many churches offer training conferences in healing and responsive prayer; if this is new to you, look into the resources of communities who have developed ministry in this area.

For All Your Teams

How do you weave these diverse contributions into a unified vision for worship? And how do you nurture and encourage people in areas of giftedness you hardly even understand? (For instance, I'm sound-equipment challenged!) Many of the hard-working people supporting the worship service won't have the confidence-building experiences that the artistic worship teams do—spending time together reading Scripture, praying and getting the recognition of being up front. To help the support team bond, to integrate them into the whole and to give them vision, consider including them on a worship-team retreat. Some of the teams may want to meet together from time to time to discuss logistics and experience community. If team members are given adequate support and allowed to develop their gifts, they will recruit and train others over time, allowing for greater flexibility and creativity.

17 The Care & Feeding of Worship Teams

●●

Sundee Frazier

I got together with Lori, a member of my team, and through talking with her discovered she felt very self-conscious while leading worship. I could tell by watching her lead that she was struggling to assert her authority because of her self-consciousness, and I knew I could help. To address the spiritual issue first, I encouraged her to

lead with the authority that God had given her, and I prayed for her. Then I gave her some practical advice: she needed to call out transitions for the group when she was leading so that they knew where she was going next in the song. Her self-consciousness was keeping her from doing this, but with some encouragement she improved. To help Lori, it was crucial for me to *know* Lori.

Know Your Team

You need to know your team. Find out who they are as people—their personality traits, communication style, ways they want to grow in their relationship with God, their struggles. You might invite them to discuss how they feel about being a part of the worship team—what they fear or look forward to in the experience, what they hope to contribute, what helps them to worship. It will help you to know each person's gifts and skills, their weaknesses and potential.

This will take time since there's no shortcut to getting to know people. Get together one on one, and learn about each person. Have the whole team gather, and share about one of the topics from the list above. Make sure you share too! You can learn a lot about people by observing them, as well, especially as you work together and see how they express themselves in worship. You may know some about each member's skill level and potential gifts from your selection process, but you can always discover more if you're watching carefully and with love.

Getting to know the people on your team is crucial to being able to care for them well. A common phenomenon among worship teams (as with pastors and other spiritual leaders) is always to minister and never be ministered to. You have the responsibility of watching for this dynamic and looking out for your team so they have their needs (to worship, be prayed for, confess struggles, grow in their relationship with God) met as well. Since you bear the responsibility of ministering to your team, it's important to have someone else to whom *you* can go for prayer and encouragement.

Help the Team Get to Know One Another

People on a worship team need to have good relationships with each other for several reasons. First, when problems come up, they can care for one another (*you* can't do it all). Second, they will worship more freely if they trust and feel comfortable with each other. And last, they are spiritual leaders, and how they interact (how they work together or don't) sets an example for the congregation. Your team will have a more profound and useful experience if they have good enough relationships to give feedback to one another and to share what they're learning about worship leading.

Help your team build good relationships. You might ask the team to do Bible study on a weekly basis. If this isn't practical, get together periodically for times of fellowship, creating vision and sharing and praying together. Schedule regular times when members can get to know each other better. Leave time at the beginning or the end of rehearsal to share personal needs and pray for each other. Even if you must adjust your rehearsal time to do it, creating some space for relationships will benefit the whole team. If you have more than one regular team for your worship services, form rotating teams. This will allow people to get to know the others in their group.

Also, take time to worship as a team. It can be an upbuilding experience to get together to worship *only*—not rehearse but worship. Worshiping will draw people together around God himself. When a team gathers around Jesus, you'll see him compel people to resolve differences, speak honestly about their needs and tap into their deepest joys together.

Use Your Knowledge of Team Members to Serve Them

Jesus made it clear: leaders *serve*. They don't push people around, and they don't do things only to make others or themselves feel good. They follow Jesus' example by laying down their lives for others. Mature leaders realize that people are more than flesh and bone—that there is a spiritual aspect that needs to be nurtured and encouraged. This can be a difficult task to do, for it consumes time and taxes energy to extend yourself in compassion, kindness, humility and patience. It's hard work to become a person who's out for the good of others.

The good news regarding this task, however, is that it is not the team leader who accomplishes this work but the Holy Spirit ruling in the hearts of the leader and members. As Paul said, his aim was to present everyone he led "mature in Christ" (Colossians 1:28), but he didn't try to accomplish this on his own—he couldn't! "For this I toil and struggle with all the energy that he powerfully inspires within me" (Colossians 1:29). So we too must rely on the strength God gives as we seek to be servant leaders of our teams.

You'll have ample opportunity to serve your team members. Follow up occasionally on the hopes and fears you've heard people express. How have their hopes been realized? How are folks managing fears? Encourage the growth you see. Also follow up on issues that come up in practice or during worship. Review difficult interactions, tension and mistakes and what can be learned from them. Help people see that God can turn their stumbling blocks into stepping stones. Offer to pray for people on the spot when they are in need, and regularly pray for members on your own.

Occasionally it's useful to ask people how they're feeling about their contribution to the team. Do they feel like they have more to give but few opportunities to do so? Do they have ideas that haven't been heard or tried? Ask the team periodically for ideas for improvement and development. Listen carefully, and implement ideas that are feasible and fit your overall vision.

Know Your Own Strengths and Weaknesses

God is working in us so we can see him clearly. As we grow to understand who he is, we grow in understanding who we are as well. As you come to know your gifts and talents, bring these into your leadership of the team. None of us, however, is gifted in every area that is required to care for and develop a mature team of worship leaders. We will serve our teams deeply if we know not only our strengths but also our weaknesses and work to compensate for them.

First of all, just because you might not be strong in some particular area—pastoral care, teaching a group or establishing a tempo—doesn't mean you shouldn't seek to lead in these areas with your team. Trust God to give you the strength and wisdom you need, and he will develop your weak areas and work through your attempts to be faithful (2 Corinthians 12:9-10). (If you ignore or deny your weaknesses, on the other hand, you are also denying God the opportunity to work in you.) You can also learn from team members who are stronger where you're weak. For instance, I don't notice as quickly as my husband does when a team is having a hard time sticking to a tempo, so he helps by alerting me to that problem when it occurs.

You can also have someone from outside your team come and help in areas where you are deficient. If your guitarists are struggling to learn a strum pattern, and you don't play guitar, have an experienced guitarist come in and do a clinic with them. I have led worship seminars at various campuses. At one I was asked to help the vocalists learn how to harmonize and to teach them basic skills on the tambourine. I enjoyed helping the team leader in an area in which he was unskilled.

Make Scripture Study Central

We need to aim for God-shaped, not people-shaped, worship times. This will happen only as we allow Scripture to inform and shape our view of what true worship is. On our own, we're prone to shaping our work to people's responses and preferences, and to "what's hot out there." Instead, we must let God speak to us in our context and lead us where he wants us to go.

Having real experiences of God in his Word, encountering him there, will ignite our worship teams so that we worship and witness to what we have seen and heard for ourselves (1 John 1:1). It will keep our vision and goals rooted in truth, and help our teams know why we're doing what we're doing rather than just imitating others.

When the Urbana 96 worship team was preparing to lead at the convention of eighteen thousand people, we studied Scripture together; it was one of the most crucial elements of our preparation. Practice was an important part of being ready, but if we had had to make a choice between Scripture study and practice, the Scripture study would have won out. Studying the story of King Jehoshaphat and his response to an invasion of enemy nations gave us the focus we needed. It reinforced for us that the "battle" was not ours but God's (2 Chronicles 20:15). What he wanted us to do was to praise him, focus on him and call others to do the same— he would do the delivering! Through his Word, we encountered God's delivering power demonstrated in history, and came to believe his delivering power would be the same for us in the future.

Develop a Vision for Your Team
"Where there is no vision, the people perish" (Proverbs 29:18 KJV). As the primary

person responsible for the care and feeding of your worship team, you have to have a vision for your team. It's also helpful to have a vision for the congregation. What do they need next to become worshipers in spirit and truth? This vision, these hopes, will provide fuel for your prayers and keep you motivated as you strive to lead people into real worship of our God.

Organize your team so it can function well and within the range of people's abilities and resources: When and how should you rehearse? What kind of training do people need? You should also think about questions of long-term vision, such as: What do you hope for people to learn from their experience? In what one or two areas will you strive to grow as a team by the end of the year? Your goal may be as fundamental as to stay together on songs or to develop better relationships, or it could be to develop original arrangements or incorporate creative elements into your worship times. What individual goals can each member set so they will have improved in their worship leading by the end of the year?

Take time to build vision and to care for and feed your worship team. The results will be astounding as your team develops vision, maturity and depth to lead others in worship. Most exciting of all, you will grow, having accepted God's invitation to be his partner in his life-giving, eternally significant work.

18 Growing Through Conflict

Alison Siewert

One of the scariest things about team life is conflict. Most people loathe and fear it, and some of us avoid it at all costs. But the minute we set our sights on becoming like Jesus and living in Christian community, we enter into conflict, because who we want to become and who we are—well, they're not exactly in sync. A whole team full of sinful people is bound to produce some rough spots. Personalities clash; feelings get hurt; and not everyone likes every decision. Conflict is part of life together.

One way we can live together better is to consider conflict an ally rather than an enemy. Conflict can be very constructive, even life-giving, if it is welcomed and handled well. At Urbana 96 the worship team found itself embroiled in conflict over the use of a particular video. Although it was focused on an objective and specific decision rather than the personal relationships of team members, the discussion raised issues of ethnicity and tapped into some deeply felt pain for several team members. At the point the conflict arose, we had a half-hour to get back to our rooms, get ready to lead the evening session and go back to the huge assembly hall on the University of Illinois campus. There wasn't time to work through anything together or to sit down and consider a solution. We were stuck. Our trust, honor and love for one another were intact, but they were stressed. We were a team in pain. Since we had to lead worship for nearly twenty thousand delegates so soon, however, we had to make a decision. We

Conflict is part of life together.

chose not to use the video because several of our teammates couldn't in good conscience lead worship with its use—at least not without creating a context and interpretation we didn't have time to create.

Our decision not to use the video created even more conflict. The people who had made it felt hurt and judged. Other folks felt angry because they thought the worship team was being oversensitive. I was shaken. I didn't know if we had done the right thing in the first place and was afraid I had just let down my teammates along with the video team and the leaders of the conference. But we had to lead worship. Before the meeting started, we gathered to pray: "God, we have to lead worship, and we really can't. Please, do something." That was it. We looked around the circle at one another, took a collective deep breath, walked onto the platform and led. And God responded. I don't even remember what song was first that evening. But after the second song, "Joy to the World"—which was the most ironic thing I could imagine singing right then—the congregation exploded in waves of applause, in hollers, in praise to God for several minutes. Worship happened. We stood on the platform, looking up around the huge arena and laughed and cried in amazement. This had never happened to us before—even though we'd experienced many powerful worship times. I suppose we shouldn't have been surprised, but God really came through. We had nothing to offer, but somehow God had offered himself, and people really experienced "joy to the world."

After the evening session we gathered in a back room to debrief our night's events, and to work through the issues surrounding the video. For two hours we listened, questioned and spoke our minds and hearts to one another. It was a difficult time. I heard things from my African-American, Asian-American and Latin-American partners that I'd neither known nor imagined. I reckoned with their pain, with the way culture and media affect them differently because of their different experiences. Our different perspectives became clear, but our love for one another became even clearer. We ended the meeting more committed than ever to working out our stuff.

When Is Conflict Good?

To be a team, you have to work out your stuff. There's no way around the difficult practice of plowing through conflict. But if conflict gets done in love and with the sense that God cares more about the worship and the team than any of you do, then you can proceed with confidence that you don't have to muster up the resources to deal with it all alone. The conflict we had over the video was extremely constructive; it built our team up. We came away with a much better grasp of what it meant to be the multiethnic team we had wanted to demonstrate being. We learned what it cost to love one another.

You can tell you're having good conflict if it energizes you and clarifies the situation. Conflict is useful if you learn from it, if it helps you to a deeper, better understanding of God and people. If you see conflict as a potential benefit, you'll enter into it with hope and some patience. But if you fear and resist conflict—especially if it's already happening, which is almost always the case—you are likely to make the situation worse for yourself and your team. Holding conflict back tempts us not to make peace with a brother or sister before participating in worship (Matthew 5:21-26). It creates tension that can make it

difficult for the whole team to function. Avoiding conflict breaks down relationships and tempts us to sin against one another by not facing up to problems (Matthew 18:15-20). It puts us in peril of *misleading* our congregations.

To work through conflict is to trust that God is at work in us and in our teammates. To "speak the truth in love" requires that we believe that telling the truth will be better for us than not telling it or lying (which are similar), and that we believe our lives are eternal and our neighbors are holy, so that sinning against one another is not just okay. Saying—or hearing—something difficult relies on a foundation of caring for each other's spiritual growth. Good conflict requires that we engage in the disciplines of believing and growing in God and in partnership on a regular basis.

Scriptural Paths for Resolving Conflict

Jesus' words about reconciliation and forgiveness are strong. He clearly values our whole relationships with one another. If the gospel isn't effective in our friendships and partnerships, how can we offer hope that the gospel is good news for a broken *world*? The gospel is very much about a concrete set of relationships. In John's Gospel, Jesus' last words to the disciples and his last prayer to the Father are about the unity and love of believers for one another. His description of his own death is of "[laying] down one's life for one's friends" (John 15:13), and he commands his disciples to love one another in the same way he now loves them (John 15:12). This is serious business, and our relationships with one another are to be held in trust as holy.

The Bible offers some guidelines on conflict that you might want to study in more depth (see Matthew 5 and 18). You can cultivate healthy team relationships by paying attention to Jesus' teaching in this area.

Go to one another right away. Do not allow issues to fester over time by avoiding discussion. And don't continue leading worship and doing ministry when you have not restored your relationships. Jesus said, "Leave your gift there before the altar and go; first be reconciled to your brother or sister, and then come and offer your gift" (Matthew 5:24). Leave your guitar in its stand, and go reconcile. If you are short on time, you may need to pledge reconciliation, which you will work out as soon as possible. (This is what the Urbana team had to do in the example I shared. We led worship with reconciled hearts and talked the matter through later.)

Go to one another and to no one else. It's tempting to talk to Sally about your problem with Bob, but it will not help. In fact, according to Jesus it will make things worse. Go directly and immediately to the person in question, and *do not* involve others until you've made an thorough effort to work it out.

Go in private. Don't use team meetings to air your grievances about one another, and don't use jokes to send barbed messages in public. Talk with your teammate, and raise your concerns. You might be surprised to hear the other person's perspective, and it

will give you a chance to come to understanding in a quiet, reflective setting. Often I find it helpful to have these conversations in a neutral place rather than in the place I've experienced conflict with the person.

If you get stuck, then *invite another person or two to help you work things out.* If you need help, agree if you can on that need and decide on a person you both trust and respect to help you.

Forgive. Forgive again. Forgive as you have been forgiven. Say to one another, "Will you forgive me?" and "I forgive you," rather than "I'm sorry" and "Oh, that's okay." It's not okay if there is sin involved. And it's important to offer and receive forgiveness. To apologize is to make a reason or an excuse for something. When we sin against one another, we don't need excuses; we need confession and forgiveness.

In one sense, forgiven and reconciled relationships are the most significant thing your team has to offer your congregation. Leading worship as a team of people who need help to love one another is the only way to be honest about who we are and who God is. It's the only way to live at the heart of worship, where our need meets God's goodness.

19 Famous Worship-Team Problems

Alison Siewert

As a child, I watched my dad coach a community swim team that eventually produced several champions, including an Olympic recordholder. I remember when my mom and I called him on the phone while he was at the pool, listening to him call out, "Go! . . . Go! . . . Go!" to swimmers practicing timed laps. He was strict.

Latecomers had to perform a push-up for every minute they were late. But he says he rarely had anyone show up late. Team members were motivated by the opportunity to improve their technique and times. Growing into excellence was attractive.

I've never been in a situation to have quite so clear and disciplined a routine with any team as my dad did with his. Coaching swimming and leading worship don't intersect at many points. But the thing I learned and have applied in nearly every leadership context is that a team must have a well-defined sense of purpose and a clear set of expectations. Teams cease to be teams when they devolve into casual gatherings without discipline. I also learned that motivating people to work together and into a common mission is an exciting process but one fraught with surprises and struggles.

Solving the problems that assail teams is hard work. Sometimes discipline is difficult. One person comes late to a couple of rehearsals, and over time everyone shifts to wandering in five to fifteen minutes after the designated starting time. Sometimes relationships get tough. John and Nancy are going out, and when things are good between them, they're great on the team together. But when things get bad—about every second week—they can't focus on leading worship in each other's presence, and the whole rehearsal is tense.

There is no easy formula for good relationships and quick problem solving for worship teams. But some basic biblical principles will help you navigate difficult waters. Let's look at some common struggles for teams and approaches to resolving them.

People Chronically Show up Late

Most of us work hard to jam as much as we can into our schedules. The result is often that things are jammed so tightly that one ten-minute glitch in the morning can develop over the day into a forty-five minute delay by dinner time. It's certainly an understandable problem. But most worship teams could use more, not less, time than they have to practice. So what do you do? Here are some questions to explore.

Are you *on time?* Leaders play a key role in setting expectations and atmosphere for the team. If the leader is there a little early to set up, prepare materials and pray for the rehearsal, the rest of the team will see that this time is important and useful. If the team leader is late, you'll likely see an atmosphere of casual, self-selected starting times. People will think it's not important for them to be prompt because, well, the leader's not there anyway, so what would they do if they arrived on time?

Is your rehearsal time the problem? I once belonged to a college-ministry team that met at 8:00 a.m. every Wednesday. And every week we waited until 8:45 to start because people were late. We finally realized that a bunch of campus staff workers who stay up talking with students until 1:00 a.m. were unlikely ever to do well at early morning punctuality. We changed our meeting time to 9:00 a.m. and started on time nearly every week thereafter. Is your rehearsal time realistic? Can people get there from work or class in reasonably good condition? Check on this before you go any further.

Are team members overcommitted? Trying to do too much is a common reason for chronic tardiness.

Do people understand the importance and value of rehearsal time? It might be helpful to discuss how you want to use rehearsal time to respond to God's call to lead in worship, to prepare well, to lead skillfully and to develop spiritually. Do you work to make rehearsals interesting, energetic and useful? If you're leading the team, make it motivating for people to be there and be on time, for their own growth and benefit as well as the team's and congregation's blessing.

If you have one or two people who cannot or will not come on time, you may need to consider asking them to leave the team. You don't want to be harsh about it, but a team can't function with three starting times and two or three different combinations of people present at various phases of rehearsal. For this reason, these suggestions might be considered for folks who leave early and skip rehearsals, as well.

People Can't Lead Every Week Because of Other Commitments

A consistent team is ideal because it can track a fellowship's progress and be involved in leading together on a regular basis. But at my church, that's impossible. The way I've solved this problem is to create a rotating team schedule. The thirty-two members of the worship team fill out forms each quarter, telling me when they're available. From this information I build a schedule of teams. I try to keep people together if they're usually available at the same times. If George, Rila and Josh seem always to be free the second week of the month, I schedule them together regularly so they get to know each other better and develop musical rapport.

To help us stay together as a team relationally and musically, I have quarterly rehearsal days where everybody on the team meets for a meal and sharing and several hours of rehearsal and music learning. That way we all practice the same versions of the same songs, and the person leading the team each week can be confident when they choose music that all the members of the team have copies and have played it. This time also gives me an opportunity to do ongoing training and reflection so people continue to be challenged.

Our Team Lacks Closeness

For God's people, vision is always connected to his Word. Worship teams need more than rehearsal time. They need time together around Scripture. If you're having difficulty building vision (and even if you're not), make some time for Bible study together. If no one on the team can lead you in it, ask for help from a staff worker or pastor.

Communal worship is meaningful if we have some knowledge of what's going on in the community. How is God at work? How are people experiencing life with Jesus? How do we need to connect with God or re-

ceive from him or be corrected? Give yourselves time as a team to review God's work, to thank him for it, to understand your need for Jesus—and then respond in your own worship!

Worship teams can benefit from doing something together besides worship. During a week of rehearsal and preparation for a major national conference, our team spent several afternoons during our rehearsal week participating in urban ministry. This gave us the opportunity to experience God at work in and through us as a community. Though we didn't all know each other well when we started (members came from all over the country), we ended the week with a deep sense of our connection to each other not only through God's call to lead at the conference but also through how he led us in ministry in the city. We also came to know one another's gifts, needs, fears and strengths as we watched and helped and learned from our teammates.

A Member with a Significant Sin Problem Still Wants to Lead Worship

Would it be okay for a member of the worship team who has a significant sin problem to lead in other ways in the fellowship— teaching Bible studies or leading a prayer ministry? If not, then it's probably not okay for him or her to lead worship either. Since leading worship is leading people, and because leaders make real decisions that affect the lives of others, the state of their faith is important. It's difficult and can work against a person's conscience to continue encouraging others in something that they're personally faithless about. Sin issues drain energy and time and warp judgment— especially if the person fails to repent—in a way that makes leadership a burden and also a danger to those they lead.

When people fall, Scripture makes it clear that we are to restore them through gentle discipline, prayer and counsel. If the person you are working with refuses to repent, even more direct communication and action may be necessary. (See Matthew 18 for Jesus' guidance on this.) A person in the process of repentance needs space for correction and healing. Such a person does not need to be needed. We never need a person on a worship team so desperately that we are willing to jeopardize his or her spiritual life.

Some people run into issues far more complex than just their own sin. Serious problems such as eating disorders and deep depression need to be handled with the help of pastors, counselors and other well-equipped people. Be sure you stay aware of what's going on for people on your team. It's never worth continuing to have people lead if their participation hides, prolongs or exacerbates serious struggles or sin problems. People's spiritual lives always come first.

One Long-time Member Sings Really Out of Tune
Extra help from another singer on the team or lessons from a voice teacher may help someone who needs to hone skills (such as ear training) to lead effectively. But if you've exhausted all routes and resources for remediation and it's obvious a person is using gifts other than his or her own, you may need to redirect the person to a different ministry altogether.

Helping people accurately assess their gifts and directing and redirecting them into places they can experience God at work through them can be difficult, but it's crucial. There is little love in letting a person continue under the illusion that they're contributing to the body when they really aren't. You can help people stop and reassess their involvement in several ways.

Add folks who have new ways of seeing and doing things. They help mix things up a little and expose weaknesses and problems.

This can be hard on both long-term and new people, so it must be done with careful and sensitive leadership.

Open up new avenues to people. Some may have gotten involved in the worship team simply because they never considered anything else or because there wasn't much else going on when they joined the fellowship. With a gentle nudge perhaps they'd be great at some of the other things your group is doing, like leading Bible studies or organizing outreach to homeless people.

Talk to people directly about their gifts. People need to hear from you that you are lovingly encouraging them into something new. It's important to share with them how their strengths have contributed as well as how their weaknesses have been problematic for the ministry. The goal in your discussion is to love people well and to help them get a clearer picture of who they are, who Jesus is and how God has been and will be at work to bless others through them. Be sure to help the person to hope and see that the Lord has a good future of new opportunities before them.

Several Team Members Consistently Resist My Leadership
This can be a significant problem for fairly obvious reasons. A team needs a leader to function effectively. Worship teams are often led in a sort of player-coach format, where the leader coaches others, some of whom may even be equals, and plays on the team too. This creates some complex dynamics for relating well to the team, because you are both leader and member. But you are the leader. And someone must lead.

I once worked with a team that had been through several leaders, in the course of four years. From what I could glean, each leader had struggled to gain the team's re-

> *Servanthood is the core of leadership.*

spect, and each leader had given up in frustration. When I interviewed team members in order to assess what wasn't working, I found out that each leader had introduced a completely different style of working, and the multiple changes of leadership left people confused. In addition, people had their own ideas of how worship should go and felt disappointed when leaders didn't fulfill their expectations. So the leaders stood on one side of the fence, feeling disrespected and frustrated, while the team stood on the other side, feeling directionless and angry. It wasn't pretty.

Servanthood is the core of leadership. To develop respect, you have to gain trust.

And to gain people's trust, you have to cultivate and demonstrate a servant's relationship with them. (An excellent book on this subject is Robert Greenleaf's *Servant Leadership*.) I invited the team to my home for a meal. I studied the Bible with them. I worked hard to listen carefully to people, even when they got whiny, and then to respond to them graciously. I sent notes to individuals. Over time the team came to trust me more and some of the resistance with which we started developed into partnership. It was never perfect—teams never are—but it grew to be much better than the struggle we began with.

20 Practice Makes Better
Rehearsing a Team

••

Phil Bowling-Dyer & Matt Frazier

As worship leaders we function with many deadlines—most notably the upcoming service—so a musical worship team has to use rehearsal time effectively. The rehearsal is the place where the team can hone its musical and leadership skills, a context in which a team can try out new ideas and concepts and an opportunity for a team to bond outside of the stress of being in front of a congregation. Here are some ideas about how to make the most of a rehearsal.

Planning: Objectives
The best way to start preparing for rehearsal is to decide what the objectives of the time will be. The most obvious objectives flow from the ministry task—to have music prepared for the next meeting or service, for example. While this is a good place to

begin, the more clear and measurable the objective, the better. Get specific by asking: Which songs need to be rehearsed? What instruments will play on which songs? Who will lead? Is there one leader for the musical set, or will the leadership be shared? Will we memorize the music? Is there a particular style we're aiming for in each song? How will we begin and end each song?

Other objectives might flow from considering the skills of the team. Does the team play together and in tune? How is the overall sound? Are there distracting habits the team or individual members need to discontinue? Are there communications skills the team can practice?

Within the three or four objectives for each rehearsal, choose at least one objective with a long-term goal in mind. For example, if the team can work on its vocal blend as it prepares for a weekly worship service, it will achieve greater overall vocal health and a lasting improvement. Or if the team works on playing together and following the drummer, its growing skill will affect all your worship times, not just this week's.

Planning: Actions

Once you've identified clear measurable objectives, choose actions (small steps designed to meet each objective) that flow from them. If your objective is learning the special music for this Sunday's service, your actions may be to practice the song in vocal sections for fifteen minutes, then call the vocalists together to take on some shaping from the director. If the objective is to learn a new gospel song, the actions may be first listening to a recording of the song, then having the instrumentalists sight-read the music and, last, putting the instrumentalists together with the soloist and choir. The important thing is to have clear actions planned so you know the objectives can be met.

Planning: Mapping a Rehearsal

Here are some suggestion for rehearsals:

Spend some time praying. Gifted people can lead songs and music, but only those touched by the Holy Spirit can lead effective worship. It is imperative for the worship team to be led *by* the Spirit of God as they lead the congregation *with* the Spirit of God.

Allow at least an hour to rehearse. This is enough time for the team to settle into the task and enjoy one another. If the rehearsal goes for more than two hours, make sure there's a ten-minute break. Your team will retain more if people get a short pause to rest and regroup.

Warm up. A simple vocal exercise followed by an easy and familiar song can warm the group up vocally and instrumentally.

Give people more to work on. Have a few things for team members to practice as they go home.

With clear objectives and actions, you can map out the beginning, middle and end of a rehearsal. You might decide to begin a ninety-minute rehearsal with a ten-minute devotional and prayer time. Following that, you might go on to sing through a familiar song to warm up the team. Then the vocalists could work on four parts for a special piece, while the instrumentalists work out their music. They all come back together, and go through the song. After some time for honing, plan to take a ten-minute break. Following the break and a few anouncements, the worship leader might practice giving clear hand cues to the ensemble (let's say the cues have been confusing for the past few weeks). Following this exercise, the group could hear the recording of a gospel song. The instrumentalists go over some of the more difficult riffs while the vocalists begin to memorize their lines. A soloist then joins them all, and the song comes together. At the end of the rehearsal, the group should review new worship songs and arrangements again and commit to memorizing the gospel song for worship the following week.

As in life, our plans don't always go exactly as we would like when we rehearse. It may take longer to learn a new song than you thought; you'll have to be flexible. Even if you occasionally have to change your expectations, you'll always be better off to have had a clear plan in the first place. You and your team will consistently accomplish more if you work with clear objectives.

Implementing: The Rehearsal

Okay, you've made a rehearsal plan. Now to carry it out.

Explain. Take a few moments early on to explain the objectives for the rehearsal, and what you plan to do. This will help the team members to feel a part of what you are doing together, and to understand the direction of the service. This will also save time in instrument adjustments (percussionists who need different sticks, guitarists who must dig out their capos). You'll function much more like a team if everyone knows the basic goals and plan.

Create. As you begin to rehearse each song, tell the team what kind of arrangement you'll use. You may occasionally want to ask the team members if they have any fresh ideas to approach a song you'll be doing. Great arrangements can come out of such collaborative efforts. Since this takes a lot of time and energy, however, you'll likely want to have an arrangement ready to implement.

Talk. During the rehearsal, get members of the team (especially a small team) to give constructive feedback. Some people feel uncomfortable telling fellow amateur musicians that they are singing out of tune or playing out of tempo, but with enough care, this is possible and even important. It's the task of the worship leader to create an atmosphere where excellence is valued and egos are out of the way.

Being a worship leader includes much more than singing and playing in front of a group. Among other things, serving as a worship leader means taking time and energy to plan and implement good rehearsals.

Part 4
Making Music: The Musicians

21 Practical Skills for All Worship Musicians

••

Matt Frazier

When you're leading worship, you are a worship leader before you are a drummer, a bass player, a singer or whatever. This means that you'll want to focus your primary energies on worshiping God—not on playing your instrument. If you're focused on God, then those you lead will tend to follow you and focus on him too. Since your first role is as a worship leader, you'll want to develop certain skills and habits no matter what instrument you play (including the voice).

Keeping God As the Focus

Consider your visual presentation. Does the congregation get distracted while watching you play? Or do they notice you only as part of a group of people who is helping them to worship God? Ask other team members what they think, as well as members of the congregation. You might even find it helpful to practice in front of a mirror sometimes so you can see for yourself. Keep in mind that the instrument you're playing is only a means to lead others into worship.

Know your equipment. Since your instrument is a means to a greater end, make sure you know your equipment well. The middle of a worship session is not a good time to discover exactly how much your amp is prone to feedback. Make sure your cables are good, your stands are tight and your voice is loose. All this will help to make God, rather than your instrument (and the surprises it may have in store for you and your congregation), the unchallenged focus of worship.

Practice. A critical habit to develop outside of worship times is practicing. Whether you're playing guitar, tambourine or tuba, practice is crucial. One of the best

ways for you to serve your congregation is to feel as comfortable and confident as possible with your instrument. Remember that almost all of us practice at a higher skill level than when others are present. In front of people we get nervous, don't experience as much room to experiment and feel less freedom to make mistakes. So be aware of your abilities and limitations, and don't try to play beyond them when you're leading worship.

A specific practice tool worth mentioning here is a metronome (a mechanical device used to keep perfect time at virtually any tempo). Whether or not you're responsible for keeping the steady tempo on a team (it's generally the drummer's job), having a solid sense of time—being able to play without speeding up or slowing down—is very important. Many musicians who usually play alone are not skilled at this, but timing is important when you're playing as part of a team. Speeding up or slowing down can also be very distracting for those you lead, and it's not very musical. Changing the tempo of a song is not wholly unlike changing the key of a song. Imagine if the piano player on a worship team changed keys by a half-step every verse!

Take lessons. If you find yourself running out of specific skills to practice, consider taking some lessons. A qualified teacher will challenge you to improve your musical skills, learn new styles, explore chords and voicings, use precise rhythms, and more. We all need to learn from others. Check out the teaching faculty at your college or local music store for more information on this. Tell potential teachers what you hope to learn, and ask if they can provide it. (The chapters that follow will also help you get started, but they certainly don't include everything you'll need to know.)

Finally, keep in mind that in many musical situations, *less is more*. Playing simply (or at least sounding that way) is especially appropriate in worship settings. This helps a congregation think about God. If what you're doing is too complex for you to do easily, you may draw the attention to yourself. Do what you can do, and do it well. You'll help yourself and your congregation enjoy worshiping God.

22 Practical Skills for Guitarists

Dan Siewert

The summer before I went to college I worked on the maintenance crew at a Christian camp. I took along my brand new Guild D-25 Sunburst solid-wood, curved-back acoustic guitar, acquired as a graduation gift. As I had anticipated, other guitarists worked there, and we jammed together on everything imaginable. My technical skills improved rapidly, as I had hoped. What I did not anticipate was that I would be asked to go beyond these semiprivate jam sessions and actually—gulp!—lead worship with my guitar. You'd think that strumming "Kum Ba Yah" for a bunch of high schoolers around a campfire would be much less difficult than mastering some Hendrix riff. However, I found out that when you take the average aspiring guitarist and put him or her in a worship setting, it's a whole different thing going on.

Leading Worship

When leading worship, the essential goal is to *lead people into worship*. And the leader's primary role is leading people. The fact that you have a guitar hanging around your neck becomes secondary. The critical struggles for many guitarists leading worship are *not to perform* and *not to focus on the guitar*. Does this mean that the guitar has no part to play? Not at all. But in the hands of an excellent worship leader, the guitar becomes a different kind of tool.

How do you meet these struggles? First, lose the guitar for a while. Good worship leading with the guitar involves a leader who would be effective at leading worship with or without a guitar. If you've never led without your guitar, try leading as a vocalist to get a feel for it. Second, learn to play while focusing on people and on what's being communicated, rather than on your guitar. Changing your focus can be a challenge for the excellent player who is tempted to perform, as well as for the novice who lacks the confidence to concentrate on anything except hitting the next chord. If you struggle with either of these, keep trying; if you have the desire, you'll get it eventually. Finally, build what you do with your guitar around what will help people worship. A simpler yet easier-to-follow strum pattern may be just what you're looking for.

What to Do

Here are some practical tips for good leadership, appropriate focus and effective use of the guitar.

Learn to change chords without looking. This is not easy with some complex chords, but it allows you to stay connected with people.

Memorize. Not having constantly to look at a chord chart keeps you connected and allows you to think more about tempo, cues and what you're singing.

Pay attention to tempo. If you're the one setting the tempo, run a line or two in your head to catch the right tempo before you start. Figure out whether you have a tendency to go too slow or too fast, and work on correcting that. Practicing with a metronome will help assure that you neither rush nor drag.

Play to provide rhythm, not melody. The guitar is usually a rhythm instrument when it's used for leading worship. Whatever you do, provide a clear and steady beat.

Make spare use of improvisational solos. So-los can easily draw people's attention to you and your guitar—not the point of worship.

Learn to play barre (bar) chords. These will give you the ability to play anything, without having to constantly simplify. Learn open chords as well, which create good tone and will improve your overall sound.

Vary strum patterns and volume during songs. This will add richness and variety to the accompaniment. This is not always applicable when you're playing with a large instrumental team but definitely helps when it's just you and your guitar. You may also want to learn finger picking, which will give you additional musical textures to work with.

Learn and practice basic music theory. And apply it—the stronger your basic skills are, the more creative and expressive you can be.

23 Practical Skills for Vocalists

Alison Siewert

I'll never forget the time I was supposed to lead worship for a conference—and couldn't. My voice just disappeared, right before my ears. To this day I'm not sure why it happened. But it was a scary experience I don't want to repeat!

Whether or not you've ever lost your voice, you need to take special care of it when you lead worship. Many pitfalls await vocalists in worship settings: poor equipment that doesn't amplify or monitor you well, halls with funky acoustics that swallow up or reverberate everything you sing, instrumentalists of varying skill—which will include some who play everything as loudly as possible, over which you have to sing. All these can be yours when you lead worship!

Tips from One Vocalist to Another
You can avoid some of these pitfalls if you take a few steps to prevent them.

Stay generally healthy. That's right! Enough sleep, a good diet and adequate exercise all help you sing better.

Warm up before you sing. Learn a few warm-up exercises (if you don't know any, take a couple of lessons or ask a choir director for ideas), and do them consistently. Give yourself ten minutes to warm up before you have to start a worship time or rehearsal.

Take some lessons. Most people need training to learn to sing correctly and effectively. If you're new at it, a group lesson can be cheaper and just as helpful as private sessions. Many community colleges and uni-

Solos
Matt Frazier & Alison Siewert

Many worship teams wonder whether to include solos in worship settings. An instrumental or vocal solo can help a congregation to reflect, pray, focus or otherwise respond if you're sensitive to how it fits into the whole picture of worship. Use them carefully. As you arrange songs, you might include an instrumental verse in the midst of a hymn, or a long introduction to a piece as an opportunity for quiet preparation or meditation on the lyrics just sung or about to be sung. Or you can introduce a new song as a solo first, then invite the congregation to sing it.

Solos are not directly participatory for a congregation, so you need to think through a strategy for their use. Your ultimate goal is to lead people in adoring God. Help people away from the temptation to adore the music and/or the musicians by directing their attention to the purpose of a solo. Interpret what's about to happen. If you want people to reflect on the sermon, invite them to do that as the guitarist plays the melody of a responsive song. Or if you want people to have opportunity to quiet their hearts before the call to worship, tell them that (musically, verbally or visually), and provide a solo piece in the background. You may even want to offer people time to dance to an instrumental verse; invite them to do it, and have some worship-team members encourage them by example. When someone sings a solo before the sermon, show worshipers how the themes connect, so they can listen and reflect on the lyrics. You could also project the lyrics or include them in a handout, so they can follow them well and take them home for further reflection.

Soloists need extra time and energy to be well prepared. They must work at their music until it's easy for them to reach the notes and get the rhythms. The butterflies that for most of us accompany solos are almost impossible to avoid, except with lots of experience—and even then they can still be found a-fluttering! However you proceed, remember that real musical excellence is found in making a contribution to the whole of worship, whether on your own out in front or in the background.

throat and make you unable to perceive pain. If you feel pain, you need to get help to correct either a health or a technique problem. Singing should never hurt.

Use a microphone. Don't attempt to sing over instruments, other leaders or the congregation. Find a sound set-up that amplifies you enough so that you don't have to shout (except, of course, when you shout to the Lord). If you use a microphone, learn to use it properly. Most vocal mics have unidirectional cardioid pickup patterns. They are designed to maximize the vocal sound right in front of the microphone. Holding a microphone or wearing a headset mic, can cue people into a performance. If you have the option, it's usually better to use a mic stand, leaving your hands free. But mic stands are easy to back away from, which may weaken your amplification. Stay right on the mic—one to six inches is standard for vocal mics—at all times. If you feel afraid of singing into a microphone, get some time to practice with it.

Don't sing harmony at the expense of the melody. Someone always needs to sing the melody so that it is clearly audible to the congregation. Don't get all your vocalists singing cool harmonies and expect the group to sing the melody. They'll feel lost! Make sure, especially when you're teaching a new song, that you first feature the melody alone and then the melody above all else in the mix. Otherwise people will learn

versities offer group classes.

Practice. No good track athlete would switch from the four-hundred meter to the marathon without long and gradual preparation. And you should not go from singing only in the shower to leading long worship sessions. Start by singing some each day, and increase your time and effort until you've built endurance.

If it hurts, stop. Get help from someone who knows the voice. Don't keep singing if you feel muscular pain, scratchy pain, swelling or itching. And do not use throat lozenges (even if you have a little cold!) right before you sing, since these numb your some ad-lib or harmony part as the melody!

Lead with your whole self. First of all, the vocalist is a worshiper, and you need to do what's worshipful for you. But you need to do it in a way that also encourages worship in those you are leading. Closing your eyes for long periods of time in the midst of singing, for example, will probably have the effect of making people feel disconnected from you and the worship experience you're having. Ever try having a conversation with someone who's closed their eyes? On the other hand, making overly enthusiastic eye contact with the crowd may leave folks feeling like they've been cheered on at a football game: "Ready, okay!" And looking only over the congregation may convey a kind of ethereal quality that isn't quite what you're looking for either.

The key is to reflect in yourself—your voice, face and body—what you are singing. Think about the words and gently reflect what they mean to you, without performing. If this is hard to imagine, try watching yourself on video or in a mirror as you practice. (This can be painful, but it's helpful.) Do you see the song as you listen carefully to the words? Do you see anything distracting or unnecessary in your gestures or expressions? How does the team look together? Is too much happening, too little or is it a good balance? You don't need to pursue this exercise at length or frequently, but it might be a good reality check if you're having a hard time imagining how to look.

Do your best. You don't need to be _____ (pick your favorite singer) to lead worship effectively. You need to be able to stay in tune, to hit the range of notes, to enunciate clearly and to sing out confidently from up-front. Not everyone has to harmonize, ad-lib and solo.

The Best Advice

The voice box sits right in the middle of many important human functions: breathing, eating, communicating. It involves a great many muscles in a complex, intricate, highly integrated process of producing sound. The voice is the primary equipment God gave us for externalizing what's on the inside. It's a key tool for relating to other people and to God, a way others come to know who we really are. So lead with your real voice. You need not pile on stylistic whines and scoops to make your singing sound ultra artsy. Be yourself, and sing *real*. The better trained and more accomplished you are, the more discipline this will require, since your training probably taught you to embellish, dramatize and attract attention to the voice.

The most important thing a vocalist can do is to let the voice express what God is doing internally. That means you have to invite God to work inside! When you sing out of your experience and conviction that God is good, that he's at work in and through and for you and others, that Jesus is the Life—then you will be leading worship. A leader can only take people where she's willing to go. If you give yourself to worshiping God with all your heart and soul and mind and strength, you will reflect that in your voice.

> *The most important thing a vocalist can do is to let the voice express what God is doing internally.*

$\cdots\cdots\cdots\cdots\cdots\cdots\cdots\cdots\cdots\cdots\cdots\cdots\cdots$

Andy Crouch

As a pianist or keyboardist you have the advantage of playing an incredibly versatile instrument. Melody, chords, rhythm and a wide dynamic range—you can communicate them all, making the piano a great instrument for leading musical worship. If you have a synthesizer, you also have a wide array of sounds to choose from. So what do you do with all that?

Making the Most of Your Instrument
Beyond the basic techniques every pianist needs to master (you are still practicing your scales, aren't you?), here are some key areas to work on for contemporary worship music.

Forget the melody. With a few exceptions, you're better off not playing the melody when you accompany congregational singing. Let the singers and other melody instruments do that. Concentrate instead on providing a solid rhythmic foundation and playing the chords that give the song depth. The melody can actually be heard more clearly if you're not playing it. Really! (The exceptions are when you're introducing a new song or when you're playing a hymn that can be accompanied splendidly by the melody with rich chords beneath.)

Practice your chords and chord changes. To accompany contemporary music confidently, you need to know chords inside and out. As a first step, learn to play chords on sight. When you see an A your hands should move nearly automatically to the basic A position. Get familiar with the basic chord variations that make up Western music (major, minor, minor seventh, major seventh, minor sixth) for

each note in the scale. Can you automatically play a Bm7? If you work at it, you can! The next step is to learn the chords that always go together in a particular key. Most songs in D will feature G and A at some point, and probably B minor, E minor and F# minor too. Get comfortable switching between them.

Work on creating a solid beat. The most important thing you can contribute—even more than getting those minor sevenths right—is a predictable rhythmic foundation. This doesn't have to be elaborate, but it's important that you not be rushing, dragging or both at once since the singers will get confused! To gauge your progress, try playing with a metronome or an indulgent drummer. Many of us who learned piano as kids grew up stopping or slowing down every time we made a mistake. It's much better to keep going.

Listen for countermelodies. Once you have a solid foundation of chords and rhythm, listen for opportunities to introduce melodies that complement the main melody. And if you can study and apply music theory and learn about voice leading, you will also be able to expand your range of ideas and options.

Keep it simple. Listen to recordings of professional keyboardists, and you'll soon realize that while they're really good, much of what they're doing is understated. They don't fill every beat of every measure with sixteenth notes or novel countermelodies; they just do a few things very well. When in doubt, play less. You'll leave more room for the melody to be heard and sung. Don't be afraid to be in the background!

25 Practical Skills for Percussionists & Drummers

Sundee Frazier & Matt Frazier

Musicians refer to the phenomenon that drums and percussion instruments often produce in music as "feel." This is what makes the music *feel* good or makes you *feel* like tapping your feet. It holds everything together by providing rhythmic structure, and it supplies direction for the music. Without this feel, music would lack cohesion and identity. So why even bother with the rest of the band? Well, music also needs a little harmonic structure. Oh yeah, and an occasional melody. But feel is crucial. This is just as true in worship music as in any other type of music because the better the music feels, the more people will be drawn to participating in it.

If you're a drummer or percussionist in a worship setting, you should know that you play a critical part in the sound and effect of the music overall. You help your team play together. Have fun contributing your significant element. If you're just starting out, play what comes easily to you. If playing the tambourine on beats 2 and 4 is what you can do without skipping a beat or changing the tempo of the song, then this is what you should do. You might be surprised how much something this simple can add to a song. Sometimes the best percussion playing in a worship setting is simply leading a congregation in clapping on 2 and 4. (And by the way, unless your culture specifically dictates otherwise, never clap on 1 and 3—it can disrupt the feel.)

We've found that many times a collection of percussion instruments can be more appropriate than a drum set in worship settings. There are several reasons for this: drums are often too loud in small venues; if they are not played well, drums can be distracting; even nondrummers can be trained to play a few simple things on a tambourine or a shaker; it is easier for other musicians who do not have extensive training to play with a percussionist than a drummer; and percussion instruments work better with smaller teams. (If you *are* going to play a drum set with a worship team, make sure there is also a bass player to fill out the bottom end—otherwise the music will sound strangely unsupported.)

Enjoy mastering one percussion instrument at a time. Then figure out how to use them for different musical styles. We've heard percussionists use only a couple of instruments tastefully, adding a lot to the sound of their team. (We've also heard drummers with lots of drums who mostly distract from the worship experience.)

If you want to start playing percussion, here are some instruments to try (probably in this order): tambourine, shaker, afuche/cabasa, bongos and congas or minicongas.

The Tambourine

To practice the tambourine, listen to songs with a heavy back beat and play on 2 and 4 with the music. Then add eighth notes and finally sixteenth notes, keeping the rhythm very steady and continuing to accent on 2 and 4. Be careful not to use too much arm movement, as it will make your feel sound stiff and wear you out physically. On the other hand, too much wrist movement will sound sloppy (it will lack rhythmic definition). Try to find a balance of arm and wrist.

The Shaker

When playing the shaker, steadiness is essential. The shaker is more difficult to control than the tambourine, and you will need to practice for a long time playing just straight eighth notes (don't worry about accenting any beats at first). Make sure you keep your wrist somewhat relaxed—this is where most of the motion should happen. Once you've achieved consistency in the sound of your eighth notes, then try to accent on 2 and 4. When you move your arm to accent particular beats, extend your forearm the same distance from your body each time. This will ensure a more even sound and consistent feel.

The Afuche/Cabasa

The afuche/cabasa is used most effectively for accenting notes, especially beats 2 and 4 (and variations of 2 and 4—for example, 2 and 4 and). You must play with crisp movements and in time (don't rush the feel or drag behind the tempo). This instrument should be used sparingly because it has such a unique sound: it can even be brash if you try to play too many eighth notes in a row.

The Bongos and Congas

With bongos or congas it's best if you can find someone who can teach you proper playing technique. There are also videos available that demonstrate how to play basic Latin rhythms. These fundamental patterns are really all you need to give a worship song a whole new feel.

The Drums

Playing a drum set presents many different challenges and potential benefits to a worship setting. If you are just learning to play drums (or percussion instruments), you should listen to what other drummers and percussionists play. Most people tend to listen to the vocalist in popular music, but you must learn to listen to the drums if you want to play drums—percussive thinking is very different from melodic thinking. Listen carefully to the rhythms, patterns, instru-

mental combinations and feel of good percussionists and drummers in popular music. You should also practice along with professional recordings of other groups with good drummers. This will help you develop your sense of time and feel.

Using a metronome. Even more than for other musicians, you will want to make practicing with a metronome (or some other time keeper like a drum machine) a regular part of your routine. No matter what your skill level, you should always focus on keeping good time and helping other musicians play well together. A metronome will help you to do that. It will also help you if you're called upon to count off the tempi for songs. One helpful way to practice with a metronome is to pick a groove and a tempo and play it for a few minutes, then increase or decrease the tempo slightly, and play the same thing for a few more minutes. Say you try 120 beats per minute (bpm); play it for a while, then increase to 124 bpm or decrease to 116 bpm. Increasing or decreasing the tempo several times in this manner will help you learn and feel the important but subtle differences between tempi.

Volume concerns. Drums add a lot of excitement to music, but in worship settings they sometimes add too much sound with that excitement. Occasionally you can get away with simply exercising more musical and physical control and play at a lower volume. Since drums are an acoustic instrument, however, they tend to resonate and sound as they should only if played with a certain amount of force. In other words, a drum played too softly doesn't sound much like a drum.

Some drummers cut the amount of sound their instruments produce by adding all sorts of muffling devices to them: tape, rags, pillows. However, their instruments no longer sound like drums really should. Others have invested in sound-cutting shells that surround their set. The original purpose of these shells is to keep the drums from bleeding into the vocal mics in a tight acoustic situation (like a television studio). They are only meant to be used where an extensive sound system will reinforce the drums. Otherwise, many important sound frequencies get cut along with the volume, and then the true drum sound is gone.

Another common solution to the volume issue is electronic drums. This approach gives you drums that sound "just like the record" at a volume you can control. Though this may be the least painful of the sacrifices drummers make in worship settings, this solution is a significant financial investment and doesn't feel much like you're actually playing drums.

So is there really an answer? There's not an easy one. The main thing we recommend is being aware of what is happening acoustically beyond your drum set. How large and loud is the congregation? How much sound will the rest of the music team create? You'll want to match it. What about the acoustics in the room? Choose your instruments and playing technique according to your situation. For example, I (Matt) would rarely ever use a metal snare drum (or a piccolo of any construction) in most church sanctuaries—these kinds of rooms are too live because they're built for vocal music. A 5-inch or a 5 ½-inch wood snare would likely work best. I also would not expect to have an opportunity to thrash myaggressions away behind my set in most worship contexts. But our own *musical* ex-

perience is not as important as the *worship* experience of those we lead.

As you learn how to play these various instruments, at some point you'll need to start experimenting with what you think sounds good and adds to the feel of an arrangement. This is where faith comes in! Just try things while you're practicing, even if you're not sure it's going to sound good. Until you try it, you can't hear it. Experimenting in practice will give you the confidence—not to mention a lack of self-consciousness—to jump in at the right time and to keep a whole worship team at a consistent tempo.

Playing percussion can also feel risky because people in a congregation will easily take more notice of you and your instruments: they sound *and* look unique (and can even be flashy), produce high volumes and are often introduced part way through a song or are used sparingly throughout. Being a percussionist has helped me (Sundee) not to worry about what others think about me and instead to concentrate on worshiping God and serving the people who are being led in worship.

Drums and percussion help worshipers feel the music they are singing and therefore relate to it (and hopefully the whole worship experience) more. If you become a thoughtful player with appropriate skill, these instruments will help you lead and participate in worship in a whole new way.

26 Practical Skills for Bass Players

• •

Jun Ohnuki

Although the bass usually occupies a supporting role in music, you're still an important player in leading worship. The challenge is to contribute to the focus of worship and to remove as many distractions as possible. As a bass player you'll meet that challenge by taking charge of several issues regarding your equipment, playing and presentation.

Your Equipment

Equipment should keep a low profile. Approach your equipment knowing it's there to serve, not to distract, and use common sense to this end. For example, amps shouldn't obstruct movement, and they need to be securely plugged in— preferably in a grounded outlet for safety and hum reduction—where they won't get tripped over. Unless your amp hisses or hums, avoid unplugging patch cables and switching off amps during worship meetings. Whenever you're not playing, turn the master volume off; just mark or remember your level. This will eliminate unpredictable noises. Many an intense prayer has been interrupted by a bass player who accidentally whacks the strings en route to scratching his or her nose!

Always check your strap connection. I've noticed many straps can twist a half-turn while the bass is being donned, leaving a tenuous connection which either pops off right away or, more insidiously, at some indeterminate point later on. Having your bass unexpectedly fall off is, um, really bad. If you know you'll forget, get strap locks that require a button push to release.

Use a guitar stand or find a solid place to set your bass when you put it down. And keep patch cables untangled, so you and your teammates don't trip on them.

Equalize the tone of your amp to the acoustics of the room. While the specifics of tone are mostly a matter of taste, there are general guidelines to follow. Try to achieve a full tone, but not one that's so bass heavy that notes are difficult to distinguish. Your EQ will change from room to room. In a

The challenge is to contribute to the focus of worship and to remove as many distractions as possible.

mid-sized room with carpet and acoustic tile, much of the sound will be absorbed and your tone can be pretty full, with the low and mid-range frequencies at moderate to high levels. However, if you play in a big gym with no acoustic damping, then you should turn down your low frequencies, as these will echo all over the place. Learning to EQ takes practice. Get someone with experience or at least a good ear to help you out.

Balance your volume. Amp placement and volume balance are also essential, and can be trickier than they sound. Your volume should be balanced with others'. But if you, like me, like to hear yourself at higher volumes, tilt your amp back so it points at your head and only blasts you. Better yet, use a direct box, which allows your sound person to adjust your levels independent of you. Then you can place your amp beside or in front of you as a monitor.

Playing the Music

The bass has several functions in worship. First, it fills out the sound merely by its presence in the lower register. Be aware, though, that you share low notes with the keyboard player; coordinate so you don't play conflicting lines or make a muddy, bass-heavy mess. Try not to spend too much time in the upper registers, either, since this can conflict with vocalists. Be aware of how you enter a song. For slow, contemplative songs, it's often nice to "ease in" with a descending riff, before you assert your presence with a low note. With louder songs, it's nice to slam right in with a big, open E or whatever.

Another function of your playing is to help the team direct the dynamic of a song, swelling from quiet and reflective to full and powerful. This is controlled by the relative complexity and volume of your playing. It's good to start out with simple lines and establish the feel, playing mostly roots, fifths and thirds. Especially on slow songs I may not play at all for the first verse, perhaps sneaking in (often along with the drummer) during the first chorus and holding the root with whole notes. On a second verse I might start playing a defined line. As a song builds momentum you can begin to em-bellish your lines, adding syncopation and fills, and increasing a bit in volume. You can also alter your lines substantially, going into double time, etc. Try to keep the same basic idea moving through the whole song, providing a consistent sonic foundation. Even in songs where dynamic range is not wide, it's still helpful to develop subtly; most songs need to "go somewhere."

Using an Equalizer   Andy Crouch

The equalizer is probably the most commonly neglected component of sound in amateur settings, but few pros would go anywhere without one. Learn something from professionals, and include an equalizer in your sound system.

Sound that seems muddy, harsh or even unpleasantly loud is the result of "coloring" by the room and speakers. The ideal room and speakers would allow all frequencies to be heard equally, but in fact every room and every set of speakers tend to reproduce and amplify some frequencies while muting others. In addition, speakers on stage (such as monitor speakers) tend to feed back into microphones at certain frequencies. An equalizer allows you to compensate for these effects, bringing all the frequencies back into equality. (Get it?) Using a row of sliders that adjust the volume of narrow bands of sound, from the lowest to the highest frequencies, you can cut frequencies that the room or your equipment tend to boost, and boost those that tend to get lost. In other words, an equalizer is like volume controls for specific frequencies, allowing you to "flatten" the sound so no single sound sticks out, and all the different frequencies are present.

For most applications, a one-third-octave equalizer is appropriate. *One-third-octave* means that the equalizer allows you to adjust the levels of thirty different bands of frequencies one-third of an octave wide. (Compare that to the treble and bass controls on your car stereo—a kind of two-band equalizer.) Once you've set up the equalizer (usually inserting it between the outputs of the mixer and the inputs of the amplifier—if you're running a stereo setup you'll need a stereo equalizer) and set all its sliders to the flat position (neither cutting nor boosting any frequency), you are ready to "tune it" to the room. While there are many sophisticated ways to do this, one simple way involves setting up a single microphone (preferably omnidirectional) in the middle of the room and gradually turning up the volume until feedback (the ringing you hear when a frequency is overamplified) just begins to set in. Figure out which frequency band is ringing and lower that band's slider slightly until the feedback goes away. (In a square room the first band to ring will very often be 250 Hz.) Turn up the overall volume and repeat the process until you start to hear ringing in several frequencies at once. Now when you turn the volume down to a normal level, the sound will seem much more natural and will have less of the boominess or harshness that comes with poorly equalized sound.

Another role for the bass player is to add rhythm and movement. What you play can either reinforce what others are playing or provide counterpoint. Other times, your line can create the "groove" which drives the song. The specifics of what to do and when are the substance of bass playing; to go much further would be beyond the scope of this chapter. But if you're just starting out, here are a couple of basic tips:

Coordinate with your team. Look to rhythm players and play the same rhythms they're playing. If there's a drummer, play with the kick drum.

Start with the roots of the chords. Add fifths, thirds, passing notes and inversions as you get comfortable with them. Eventually, build a consistent bass line for each song. Watch for chord chart annotations that place the bass note under the chord: E/B, for example.

Presentation

How you present yourself in the act of worship

is significant. You are a worship leader before you are a bass player. This means your technical proficiency and aesthetic sensibilities should serve the purpose of worship, not vice versa. Play at whatever level of complexity you feel comfortable so you can devote most of your energy to focusing on God and encouraging the congregation to do the same. If you're intensely focused on your bass—head down, hunched over, trying to play some tough lick—then you're able to focus on God that much less, and others will focus on where you've led them: your bass.

This is not to say you have free license to be a bad musician; certainly you must take responsibility for your musicianship. Just don't get distracted from the primary task of facilitating worship. If you practice that tough lick enough that it becomes easy, then you can throw it in wherever you want, because you don't have to think about it, and you're free to look up and out and engage the congregation. In worship you are neither the main attraction nor an unaccountable mercenary. You are a key member of the worship team.

Since the bass is less common than some other instruments in worship, it can lend itself to showiness. Steer clear of rock star affectations—splayed legs, excessive jumping around, head bopping (burning instruments is usually unhelpful as well)—and be aware of how you present your music. It's fine to express worship with your body if it draws others into worship with you.

If all these details seem overwhelming, don't worry. With practice and experience, many of them will become automatic. More importantly, the ultimate responsibility for leading worship lies in God's hands. If he wants to touch people's hearts, even your biggest flub won't stop him. You have tremendous freedom to worship God as you lead others. The trick is to balance this freedom with a relaxed but alert cognizance of equipment, music and presentation issues. Finding the balance is the challenge of leading worship, whatever your role. Have fun!

27 Sound Systems

••

Andy Crouch

To know what kind of sound system you need for worship music, you need to know *why* you need a sound system at all. People worshiped God just fine without sound systems for thousands of years—why start now? If you don't have a good answer for that question, your resources are probably spent better elsewhere. And as much as your bass player may protest, to pump out a five hundred-watt wall of heart-rate-altering sound is not quite good enough.

Why Do You Need One?
While there may be many reasons why musicians want a sound system—from saving their voices to altering your heart rate—there's really only one good reason for investing in one: communication. More specifically, *a sound system is a tool for intimacy.* Let me explain.

The hallmark of contemporary music, and consequently contemporary worship, is that it is intimate. That is, we like music that comes close to us. We want performers to be real people; we want to see them up close; we want to hear the nuances of their voices. The lyrics of contemporary music are also quite intimate, about personal experience and (more often than not) love. Intimacy, in the sense of being close enough to someone to know the details about them, is a value in our culture.

The problem with valuing intimacy in this way is that it's impossible to have in a large group. Take vocal music, for example. There is a kind of vocal music that's designed to be sung without amplification for hundreds or even thousands of people—it's called opera. But the kind of vocal technique needed for good opera singing is not very intimate—for one thing, it's quite loud! At the end of an opera you may be impressed by the quality of the singers' performances, but you don't feel like you've been close to them. Or consider the way one has to speak to get a message across to a large group—say, five hundred—without any amplification. It's possible, but you have to speak in a way that isn't much like everyday speech.

With a microphone, on the other hand, someone can speak in a natural, conversational tone of voice and still be heard clearly by a large group. Similarly, we can sing songs that are intimate and yet accessible to everyone in the room, rather than the much smaller group we could sing to without amplification.

Sound systems by themselves don't create intimacy, but they can be a tool that lets us communicate clearly and personally with many people at once.

So the primary purpose of a sound sys-

Microphones   Andy Crouch

Good microphones are essential to sound reinforcement because sound systems operate on the familiar principle of "garbage in, garbage out." If your microphones are inadequate, no amount of expensive (or loud) equipment can make the sound clear.

When you shop around, you'll find several general kinds of microphones. *Unidirectional* (also called *cardioid*) mics pick up sound only from the front of the mic. They work well for vocals, since vocal sound comes from only one direction, and they do a good job of avoiding feedback from monitors and other sound sources like amps and drums. *Omnidirectional* mics reproduce sound evenly from any point around the microphone. They are used very little in live sound but occasionally come in handy. *Dynamic* mics are most commonly unidirectional and less expensive; they are also the most rugged, a treasured quality in mics used by singers in live situations. *Condenser* mics are more responsive than dynamics but often require external power (through a battery or a so-called phantom power provided by the mixer) and are somewhat more fragile. They are best used in situations where they will not be extensively handled.

A good reference point for vocals is the Shure SM-58, a dynamic unidirectional mic. It's deservedly popular: solidly built, offering a boost for "thin" vocals when it's used up-close, and widely available for a reasonable price. There's really no good reason to buy anything cheaper than an SM-58—in the long run you won't be satisfied. There are many mics available that sound professionals like, including Audix's OM line (the OM-3 is comparable in price to the SM-58) and Shure's own Beta 58. If you can find a way to afford them, you won't regret it. If your budget won't allow the expense, consider buying a smaller number of higher-quality mics and borrow or scrounge until you can purchase a full complement of good ones over time.

For acoustic instruments avoid the low-frequency boost that vocalists love so much in SM-58s and similar dynamic unidirectional mics, and look for an instrument mic. The SM-58's cousin, the SM-57, is a good starting point. There are lots of options and lots of opinions about the options. The best way to sort through them is to find someone with professional sound reinforcement experience, preferably in the kind of venue and style you're pursuing, and learn from them.

tem is intimate communication, the kind that is one-to-one and personal. Some groups can communicate quite well without any artificial help. If your group is under fifty persons, strongly resist the urge to buy a sound system. With that size, microphones and amplification are likely to create as much distance as intimacy. It's like having someone in the same room talk to you over the telephone! Between fifty and one hundred people, you may or may not need any amplification, depending on the strength of your worship leaders' voices and the instrumentation you are using. For over one hundred people, a sound system becomes important if you do mostly contemporary music.

What Kind of Sound System?

The highest priority in a sound system is *clear reproduction of sound.* If the sound system gets in the way of the musicians, singers and speakers by coloring or altering their sounds, it's not doing its job. The most basic factor in clear reproduction is quality equipment, so buy the best components you can afford—especially microphones (see the sidebar) and speakers, which are the two ends of the sound chain that make the most difference in the sound. Also, strongly consider including an *equalizer* in your system. Equalizers make the difference between muddy and transparent sound, and they can make up for a lot of deficiencies in the equipment or the room. (See the sidebar for more on equalizers.)

God made us to be near to him and to one another.

The reason to buy *powerful amplifiers* is not, as most people think, so your music can be loud. Different groups have different tastes, but in worship you're rarely going to want to blow people out of the room. That doesn't help them focus on God's presence, which is powerful enough without amplification. Rather, more power lets your system reproduce sound more clearly, even at relatively low volumes. Take my word for it, or ask an engineer; more power means clearer (not just louder) sound. Just don't turn it up to eleven!

If you're not installing the system perma-

nently, *portability* will be something to consider very carefully. There's nothing that can sap the morale of a worship team more than lugging heavy equipment back and forth every week. There are many options on the market today that are lightweight yet produce high-quality sound. Be careful, though, not to get something that is light because it's cheap—you'll be disappointed.

Getting the Most Out of It

Once you've purchased your system, here are two principles for maximizing its use:

Find a "sound person" to join your team. It doesn't help the worship leaders' concentration to be preoccupied trying to get the sound right. You need a person whose only job is to mix the instruments and make sure the overall sound helps the congregation worship. This person should not only be technically skilled but also have a worshipful heart —use all the same selection criteria that you would for any team member. Ego problems don't exist just *on* stage—the off-stage kind can be just as bad or worse! Make sure this person has a servant heart, and include him or her fully in the team's prayer and preparation.

Try not to become dependent on your sound system. Only a tiny minority of Christians in the world can afford sound systems to accompany their musical worship. We can easily become dependent on the products of our affluent culture, but God really doesn't care at all what kind of music we play—he cares about our hearts. A sound system is a helpful tool, but it's just a tool. Have unplugged, even nonmusical, worship times frequently to remind everyone that it's not music we worship, it's God, and he can be known and worshiped in many different ways.

Intimacy with God is our birthright as Christians, and a sound system used with excellence and with prayer can serve a small but important role in drawing us to him.

Part 5
Making Music: The Music

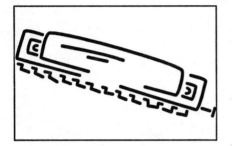

● ●

Alison Siewert

Of all the questions I'm asked about worship, the most frequent is, "Where do you find music?" Recent expansion in worship music marketing by Christian companies has produced a plethora of material. With the resulting library of music books, sheets and recordings, it's a daunting task to locate a song you know, let alone search out good new pieces for your group. It can be very helpful to join forces with other worship leaders to do the research necessary to build a good, useful worship repertoire. There's really no way to do it short of putting in some time and effort to review lots of material and choose good songs to sing with your congregation.

Where to Start Looking

Commercial publications and recordings. Most Christian book and music outlets provide listening stations so you can check out recordings before you buy. Take a member or two from your worship team along with you, and spend some time listening to new worship releases. Jot down the names of the songs and the authors of the selections you like and might want to use. Many recordings are marketed simultaneously with music books. Check to see if what you want is in the book. If not, you can try contacting the music company; sometimes lead sheets are available for hard-to-find songs. If a recording contains several pieces you like, you might want to purchase it so your whole team can listen to them.

Hymnals. I'm happy to say it has become more popular to use hymns in both traditional and rearranged forms. Hymnals are chock full of both great music and deep theology. They are fuller statements of faith

than most contemporary worship songs, so including a number of them in your repertoire can help make your worship times more substantive. You can use the metrical index to change tunes around (see chapter 29) and do some creative arranging of your own. Try setting the melody to a new rhythmic feel. One team did this by taking "O the Deep, Deep Love of Jesus," which was written in a rolling 6/8 and minor key (sounding mournful to the modern ear), and shifting it, in the same key, into a reggae 4/4. The result made the hymn sound much more upbeat and helped a new generation worship.

Other worship leaders and churches. I have a friend with whom I exchange song lists once a year. He sends me all their titles and publishing information, plus copies of new original pieces he's using with his team, and I do the same for him. I respect my friend's theological acumen and share his musical taste, and our worship teams are at about the same level of ability. So I've been able to use a great number of suggestions from him. Many student fellowships find their best music by sharing. Trading ideas is faster than doing all the searching by yourself, and you have the added help of hearing from someone who has already tried the song with a congregation. If you don't know other worship leaders, call fellowships and churches in your area, and ask to talk to the person in charge of their worship. Also check Christian music, leadership and worship sites on the Web.

Missions trips, international visitors and crosscultural resources. When you or others from your fellowship go on summer projects, be sure to send along a small tape recorder so you can gather songs from your host culture. That's the best way to share worship with people from all over the world—and that way you'll have intimate, authentic knowledge of the origins and uses of particular songs and traditions.

Testing a New Song

What do the lyrics mean? The first thing to look at or listen for in a song is the lyrics, because no matter how catchy or cool a tune is, a crucial focus of our musical worship is the words we sing. Do they reflect an accurate picture of the God of Scripture and of the Christian life? Are the lyrics appropriately carried by the music? I once heard a song whose tune caused the lyrics, predicting God's vengeance, to come off sounding downright *chirpy*! Are the words concrete and clear—or highly abstract and religious? A pile of theological words like *sanctify* and *glorify,* or talk of "the beauty of God's holy and righteous situation on Mount Zion" may sound really spiritual but leave your congregation singing about stuff no one quite gets. It's impossible to have real agreement and community in worship if we can't sing together with understanding. Do lyrics encourage us forward in real faith by convicting or inspiring us? Do they offer a fresh or different perspective on the gospel? Are the words poetic and well put? Look carefully at the lyrics.

How relevant are the lyrics? Make sure the words are relevant for your congregation. For example, you may want to avoid archaic formal language (thees and thous) and look for language that includes both genders. Especially in hymns, be on the lookout for obsolete terms and phrases such as "I will suffer nought to hide Thee" (in "Jesus, Priceless Treasure") and obscure ideas like "this terrestrial ball" ("All Hail the Power of Jesus' Name"). Figure out

ways to interpret them effectively or reword the song. If you're looking at something in a foreign language, be sure that you know precisely what the words mean and that you offer a meaningful translation to your congregation. You can interpret or translate when you first introduce the song, but remember to review occasionally so newcomers and forgetful people aren't left wondering why you all keep asking Jesus to let you fly to his bosom ("Jesus, Lover of My Soul"). For songs in anything other than your community's first language, try putting the translation under or next to the lyrics in a different, smaller type. This allows people to follow the meaning line by line as they sing.

What's the song's theme and purpose? Will it add anything to your repertoire or do something better than a song your group already knows? Look for new pieces that expand the subject matter available for worship times rather than adding more of the same to your list.

Testing a New Song's Music

Is the music singable? Review the tune, singing it several times through. Check for the following:

1. Range. Between low A and the E2 (in the top space on treble clef) is preferable for congregational singing. Remember to check the range again if you transpose the song. Pay attention to where the majority of the notes fall (the *tessitura*). If the song hangs out in either the upper or the lower register for long periods, it may be too difficult for people to sing.

2. Hook. Can you remember the tune an hour later? The next day? This is a good sign that it will be easy to catch on to.

3. Simplicity. Does the tune move easily so that people will feel confident hitting the notes? Is the rhythm clear enough for people to get without feeling frustrated? It's okay to do music that challenges people as long as it's attainable with reasonable practice. Make sure it's of good enough quality to be worth the effort.

4. Fit with the lyrics. Do the tune and lyrics match each other in tone, style and feel? Can you sing the lyrics in rhythm without getting tongue-tied or running out of breath?

Is the song musically accessible? Can your team play this piece? If the original arrangement includes sophisticated wind parts, can you simplify it for your two guitars and tambourine? If a song can be pared down and still sound good, it's probably a solid piece musically.

Does the song add something new, fresh or otherwise needed to your musical choices? Does it fill a particular role, such as giving you an upbeat alternative for confession? Does it expand your musical culture or range of styles in a useful direction? No single song has to do everything, but look at each new piece in the context of what you already have.

I run new pieces through this sort of a check as I evaluate and choose. But then I try them in a live worship setting. Before the team creates an all-out arrangement, I want to hear a group sing the song. Every so often I find that something I thought was perfect is much harder or less compelling than I imagined it would be. I solicit feedback after we introduce a new song. I've been surprised when a piece I was only lukewarm about turns out to be a great encouragement or connection point for people in the congregation. In the end, it's not what I like but rather what helps people to worship God that I want on my song list.

29 Hymns—For You, Not Just Your Grandparents

•••

Andy Crouch

Why sing hymns when there's so much exciting contemporary worship music? Many churches and fellowships have decided that songs written before 1980 (or 1990!) have lost their value for contemporary Christians. The words can seem unfamiliar or obscure. "Here I raise mine Ebenezer . . ." Huh? The music can be hard to sing or just dull. Most of all, perhaps, hymns from earlier centuries don't play to a lot of our late twentieth-century North American preferences. Often they take their time getting to the point. Their texts require mental effort; their tunes require physical effort.

So Why Bother?

Well, why bother decorating your dorm room with posters or your home with artwork? Those plain walls had a certain appeal, didn't they? In many areas of our lives we're willing to go out of our way to make life more beautiful, more complex and more rich with personal meaning. Hymns can be one of the best ways to take your worship deeper. Once you've tried them you won't want to go back to worship without them.

Hymns exercise our mind and heart at the same time. You can dig into a theology textbook—lots of truth, but deadly dull. Or you can watch an AT&T commercial—long on emotion but short on anything beyond warm fuzzies. Or you can sing a hymn. A good hymn sets strong statements and images of the truth about God to music that draws our heart into the truth. When our hearts and minds work together, we are much closer to a personal relationship with the One who is truth.

Hymns connect us with our past. We're not the first generation to know the love of God in Christ. In fact, we would never have heard about him without hundreds of previous generations passing on their knowledge and experience of God. Isn't it likely that they have something to teach us? From a former slave trader to a blind woman to an Oxford-educated overachiever who gave up the perks of status to serve the poor, the writers of historic Christian hymns ("Amazing Grace," "Blessed Assurance" and "O for a Thousand Tongues to Sing") have been radical followers of Jesus.

Hymns have stood the test of time. A lot of things around us are built to wear out within a few years, worship songs included. If you grew up in a church, I bet you can think of more than one song that you sang over and over again in high school that you'd just as soon never hear again. The best hymns, though, have been sung for decades or centuries without becoming trite or tiresome. Even great hymn writers like Isaac Watts or Fanny Crosby wrote a lot of stuff that wore out within a generation. But "When I Survey the Wondrous Cross" and "Blessed Assurance" will continue to be sung as long as people contemplate the mystery of the cross and the wonder of God's love. A few of today's songs and choruses will last too, but only a few.

Ironing Out the Wrinkles of Age

One of the high priorities of the team writing this book has been to make hymns a central feature of worship without losing a contemporary sound. Several tricks we've learned along the way may help you do the same.

If you like a hymn text, don't be afraid to change the tune. Tunes can sound dated long before words do. Most hymn texts are written in a regular *meter*, which means that each line has a fixed number of syllables. So "Amazing Grace" has eight syllables in the first line, six in the second, eight in the third and six in the fourth of each verse—a pattern that's written 8.6.8.6 for short. Many tunes have this same pattern (which happens also to be called Common Meter or CM because it's so, well, common). If you don't like the tune a given hymn text is printed with, look in the *metrical index* in the back of most hymnbooks for other suggested tunes with the same meter. Or think of contemporary tunes that have the same pattern. Dozens of songs are written in 8.6.8.6 meter, including the "Gilligan's Island" theme song. Consider your options! (Judiciously.)

Teach hymns carefully. Because the words and music are less familiar sounding, your group may need help to feel at home with hymns. Spend time explaining the words and what they can mean to us. Especially take care to explain any strange expressions. (And explain them more than once so new people don't wonder what you've already told everyone else!) Sing the hymn line by line until the group is comfortable with the tune. Then use it often. You're much less likely to get tired of hymns than most contemporary choruses, so don't be afraid to sing them several weeks in a row.

Mix hymns with newer music to form a well-rounded set. Make a hymn like "All Hail the Power of Jesus' Name" or "Jesus, Lover of My Soul" the centerpiece of a time of worship, surrounding it with other, more contemporary choruses that focus attention on the same theme.

Try reading hymns aloud as a group before you sing them. Similarly, give the group time to read the whole hymn to themselves

> *Hymns can be one of the best ways to take your worship deeper.*

while the worship team plays the tune several times through.

As with all worship music, be discerning. Hymns from earlier eras can be just as overly sentimental as today's lush pop choruses. Hymn writers in earlier generations were just as susceptible to triumphalism (imagining that there is no more need for suffering or struggle in the Christian life) as song writers can be today. Especially be on the lookout for phrases that, whatever they meant to their original hearers, now exclude people. Few contemporary African-Americans want to sing about Christ's blood "wash[ing] the Ethiop white" (Charles Wesley's words in one of the original verses of "O for a Thousand Tongues"). And many women find constant references to "man" (when humanity is meant) distancing and off-putting. Find ways to rework these kinds of expressions, or find another hymn.

If you—and the group you lead—are willing to put in the extra effort to sing hymns well, you'll find all of your worship life becoming richer. You'll be stepping into the midst of a great cloud of witnesses who cheer you on in the Christian race from their vantage points in the tenth, eighteenth or twentieth centuries. You'll discover, in fact, that the great songs of faith, whenever they were written, are always and everywhere contemporary.

30 Arranging Music

Matt Frazier & Andy Crouch

Whether you're leading worship with one instrument or with a team, you will be making decisions about musical arrangements for each song: the tempo, rhythm, chord structure, instrumentation and overall feel of the piece. Rather than just strumming (or jamming) away, take some time to think about the arrangement to make it more effective. This will ensure that your musical choices will be intentional and thoughtful rather than accidental or arbitrary.

Good arrangements for worship are interesting and evocative—they encourage the congregation to participate in the music. On the other hand, they are not so fascinating or peculiar as to distract people from focusing on God's presence. Good arrangements also musically represent the mood and sentiment of the lyrics. A celebrative text like "O for a Thousand Tongues to Sing," for example, can be sung to many different tunes and in many different ways, but it probably should never be arranged mournfully! Your musical arrangement should fit your text. The best arrangements help a congregation understand and relate to a lyric, make them want to sing it and lead them into worship more deeply as they sing it.

Tips for Making Good Arrangements
Use styles that are relevant and attractive to the congregation. Then they'll want to be part of the music. Listen to the music that those whom you lead listen to. If it's not your favorite music, that's all right—try listening anyway. You don't necessarily have to imitate it (often you will not be able to), but you can incorporate aspects of what you hear.

Listen to and incorporate music from around the world. The styles and rhythms of other cultures not only add texture and variety to our sometimes overused Western forms, they also give us a taste of the variety of God's family and, consequently, the many-splendored character of God himself.

Always use arrangements that your musicians can play confidently. Practically speaking, your arranging will be influenced by the musical background and skills of your worship team. You may well have ideas for arrangements that are challenging for your team (and maybe for you) in terms of tempo, key, chords, feel and so forth, but resist the temptation to stretch too far. You will only create distraction for them and your congregation!

Of course, this doesn't mean that we shouldn't grow in our musical abilities. Practice at home, though, not in front of a congregation. If a guitar player in your team is just getting started on the instrument and can only play songs with D, G and A in them, then use arrangements that have a lot of D, G and A! Encourage the guitarist to learn a broader spectrum of chords—maybe have them sit out on songs that other musicians can carry—but for now D, G and A will probably have to dominate.

Shape your arrangements around your team's strengths. What does your team do particularly well? Use these strengths strategically. If you hear one of the members of the team playing something that sounds interesting during a break from rehearsal, for example, think about whether there might be a song that could be shaped by what you heard. Maybe you won't use it that night or even that month, but remember it for later. Someday it may be useful. Even if your team members are not exceptional musicians, you will often find that they have one or two creative techniques that you can apply.

In a local church where I (Matt) led, I worked with a guitarist who played folk music when he was younger and was particularly skilled in finger-picking. When he played in worship with me, I always used finger-picked guitar prominently in one or two songs. I'd have him play the first verse alone and have the rest of the team join in on the chorus. Or I'd have him play the last verse of a song alone and transition straight into the next song with him still playing alone.

Try arranging music as a team. The Urbana 96 worship team did this with a song based on the text of Micah 6:8: "He has shown you, O people, what is good and what the Lord requires of you: but to do justice, and to love mercy and to walk humbly with your God." Most of us had led the song at a previous conference using an arrangement that was so unique that in three years it was stylistically out of date. (Popular musical tastes change quickly!) We liked the text a lot but weren't sure what to do with it. One day I (Matt) was thinking about the song (listening to it in my head) when I discovered a drum groove that I thought might work well. I wrote it down and set it aside. Some months later I shared it with a few of my teammates in a living room with my hands playing on my knees and my feet stomping on the floor. In spite of the acoustical limitations, the others seemed interested, and when the whole team gathered to rehearse (with real live drums this time), I played it for everybody.

At that rehearsal one person remarked that it sounded a little like a train. With the bass line added (which the bass player heard implicit in what the drums were doing), it sounded like an urban train. Because of our backgrounds, many of us think of the city when we think of the justice and mercy Micah describes. So we started working with it further. Picture an urban train, and you might think of a city like Chicago. Musically speaking, some blues guitar licks

> *Variety makes music and worship come alive.*

fit this picture, so our guitarist tried that. The pianist started experimenting with different chord voicings and extensions (the chord structure of the tune is quite simple), and the keyboardist tried some different organ lines. It did not come together quickly. In fact, we left that rehearsal not sure if it would work at all. A few of us continued to think about it, however, and listened to some music to get more ideas, and shared them with one another. Eventually, it turned into a good arrangement that the congregation related to well. Creative arrangement attempts don't always work out with happy endings, but when they do, it's worth the work.

Variety makes music and worship come alive. Try different styles—even *within* songs once in a while. But don't hesitate to do a few songs "just like they're always done." You'll never have the time or the creative energy to arrange every song like a masterpiece. Remember, God, not our music, is the center of worship.

31 Writing Music for Worship

Matt Frazier

Accomplished songwriters and compos-ers have been producing wonderful worship music for many generations. Your church pew and your local Christian bookstore are abounding with musical options for your worship times. Your own bookshelf might be equally well-endowed. So why would you ever want to consider adding to such a huge collection of material? I hope to suggest a sufficient answer to this question as well as some ideas for how to go about writing meaningful worship music yourself.

Have you ever witnessed God moving in your church or fellowship and wanted to help people respond to the specific thing you saw God doing, but couldn't find just the right song or hymn to do it for you? If you haven't yet, you probably will. Recently in my own fellowship, many of us have been discovering that God uncovers buried anger and helps us to deal with it. As a leader, however, I realized that there aren't many worship songs out there about dealing with anger. So I thought it could be use-ful to write one, and I started to work on it. When God is moving in a new way among a particular group of people, it can be more meaningful to create an original song or two to celebrate Jesus' work.

Another reason to consider writing worship music yourself is because you may want to have a larger variety of worship songs that appeal to the theological values (and after all, all values are theological) and musical tastes of your fellowship. It seems that lots of contemporary worship music gets written about similar themes and in similar musical styles. There may be worship themes that you would simply like to see more songs for. I've noticed a lack of songs related to evangelism, the Word and racial reconciliation. You may have noticed other issues that are scarce in the array of worship music available commercially.

So if you want to mark the movement of God's Spirit in your congregation, or if you've more generally noticed a gap to be filled in the needs of your worshiping body, you may want to try writing a piece of worship music yourself. If you have some understanding of how the fundamentals of mu-

Five Steps to Help You Write a Worship Song   Matt Frazier

The creative process is different for everyone, but here are a few suggestions that might help you. You may want to take them in a different order or even come back to some of the steps multiple times while writing a song.

1. *Pick a theme or Scripture on which to base your song.* What has God been saying to you or your community of faith recently? Have you discovered particular ways you need to grow in your worship of God? What is it about God that you and your friends have been excited about recently? Are there particular kinds of sin that God has convicted you of through individual or corporate Bible study? Answer one or more of these questions, hone your ideas and start to write some words.

2. *After some time to revise your lyrics, decide on the structure, emotional mood and musical feel the song should have.* Is it about celebration, repentance, God's greatness or his righteousness? Is a folk-music feel fitting, or should you try for something with a monster groove?

3. *Informed by #2, choose an approximate tempo and feel (they can change later), and write a melody.* Keep it in a good range for group singing, and remember to make it simple enough to learn after having heard it a few times. You'll also want it to be interesting enough to remember.

4. *Set your melody to a chord progression.* If you don't know much about the structure of harmony, you may want to get help from a friend who does. Or take a class so you at least know what rules you're breaking if you chose to do so (like, direct and parallel fifths and octaves), as well as which rules you'll definitely want to keep (chord progressions that actually do progress).

5. *Revise, get input from others, pray and reflect about final decisions—like choosing between words, notes and chords—and try the song out in a real worship setting.* Perhaps you'll start with your own worship times or maybe with a worship time with a friend or two. If no one else ever hears the song, you still have something special to share with God anytime you want (and if you want to know just how special it is, check out how parents get excited about the crafts their kids make in Sunday school sometime).

sic work (melody, harmony, rhythm), you may be ready to start. If not, you can take a few basic music theory classes, or even team up with someone who has this musical training. If you've not written much in popular verse, you can do some studying or even pair up with someone else who has more expertise in this area.

General Guidelines for Song Writers

Begin with the Bible. Lyrically, Scripture is always a great place to start for material. We know it's always true and reliable, and it was originally written for everyone to relate to. We may have great ideas about God, but nothing is as sure as God's own words. As you write songs based on Scripture, you might also try writing songs that provide a response to it or an application to it for a particular group of people.

Find a balance between the general and the specific. Keep in mind that a good song does not necessarily make a good worship song. A song whose poetry and music are great but whose lyrical themes are so specific that only two or three people in the world can really relate to them will not make for a good group worship experience. On the other hand, the market is glutted with overly general worship songs. (You know the ones: "Lord, I praise you. I really praise you. Lord, I really really praise you. Gosh, Lord, I'm so serious about praising you that I can't stop repeating myself.") So we can happily avoid that direction as well.

Try to write something a whole group of people can sing. Good songs lend themselves to being sung by a group in worship. It is possible to write something that is interesting and yet lacks complexity of operatic proportion. Songs should be memorable and relatively easy to learn. In terms of range I try not to write a melody line above a d^2 or e^2 since most people simply can't sing any higher. I also try to stay above an a or b—the altos and basses will do okay below that, but the rest of us will strain and jump up an octave so we can keep singing.

Take time to evaluate the song, and get others' to critique it too. Along the creative process path, you'll want to take time to let your ideas settle on paper. Then come back to them a while later. This kind of space will help your self-evaluation. You should also consider getting others' comments. I have a friend who often looks over worship songs I've written and gives me his thoughts (he's a very good song writer and a committed worshiper). He tells me how the words affect him and critiques them poetically. He sometimes suggests a few different melodic or harmonic options that I had not considered for an area of the song. He's also good at telling me when he thinks something just doesn't work. I don't always agree with his advice, but even when I don't, I still come out of the discussion more sure about what I want in a given song both musically and lyrically. I also come out with a better song.

How One Song Developed

I'll give you an example of how it all worked with one of the first worship songs I wrote. Several years ago the fellowship I was a part of was studying John's Gospel. We had been studying the book for several months, and God taught us many new things. Among them was the reality that he alone is able to satisfy our many deep, true needs. When we studied John 4, we identified with the woman who had been in many marital relationships but was still as empty as ever. She needed Jesus to fill her thirst, and he was offering to do just that. While on a personal prayer retreat, I spent some time reflecting on this passage that

my friends and I had been studying. In my car on the way home, I became more and more excited at the promise of what Jesus offers us. As my joy swelled, a song began to come out of my mouth. At first it was just a few lines: "I want to thirst no more, I want to hunger no more." But it was the beginning of a song that I completed later called "Thirst No More." It was rooted in my own very specific experience with God, but the song has proven fruitful in many worship times for many people over the last several years.

Of course, the song didn't finish itself. I considered the lyrical and musical content for a long time. I heard others' thoughts about it, and I revised it a lot based on my own and their observations. I even tried it with a group of ten or fifteen friends and got their reaction—without telling them I wrote it at first. If you've heard the song, it's very different now than those first days, in part because of the suggestions I got and flaws I worked on after trying it out.

Sharing music we've written with others can be a little risky. Since your songs came from inside of you, they feel like they're a part of you. When others respond, it's easy to think they're responding to you. I heard some joking about "Thirst No More," for example, when I first tried it in group worship. Eventually, it caught on and proved useful. The truth of the matter, however, is that even the best songwriters have "duds," so don't expect every song you write (especially early on) to be fantastic or easy for others to connect with spiritually. Writing bad songs, or good songs, doesn't change who you are before God.

Writing worship music can be a great way to meet a specific need in your own fellowship and enjoy to God in a new way. The music you write may be meant only for your local congregation, but God's care for you and those with whom you worship is sufficient to motivate your efforts in writing.

Using Music with Integrity

Alison Siewert

As we planned music for Urbana 93, my teammates and I discussed using a song called "Let Us Adore." Many of us knew it and thought it would be a great addition to our worship. But as we discussed our ideas for the piece it became clear that the "Let Us Adore" I knew was different from the one Phil knew, which was different from the one Andy knew . . . and so on. If you've been leading worship for more than six months, you've probably had a similar experience!

Songs and parts of songs get passed around from fellowship to fellowship and leader to leader, often making their way into repertoire without any reference to the original written piece. In many cultures this sort of oral tradition is the norm. However, the people of these cultures are generally quite skilled at passing on information with great accuracy. In most places in the United States we neither operate this way nor possess the skills to do it effectively.

Viewing Music as Art

I went searching for "Let Us Adore" in written form so that we could confirm one or another version before disseminating it at Urbana. Sharing a song with twenty thousand people at once pressed us to take careful responsibility for what and how we shared. Over the course of an afternoon I located the original music for "Let Us Adore" —and was surprised by its origins. This song had come from a Jewish Shabbat service written by a composer named Julius Chajes. I purchased a copy of the original so I could take a closer look.

I was humbled to find that neither my version nor my partners' were correct. We were all quite wrong! It was thrilling to find that the original song was even lovelier and more interesting than what we had heard or could have imagined. Locating the piece in its original context also helped me understand its full meaning and how it fit together with the whole picture the composer wanted to share.

I have just illustrated for you one good reason to seek out the original versions and origins of songs you use in your gatherings. You will usually gain better perspective on a song when you find its roots and see the author's original intent. To transmit songs in sloppy or inaccurate forms is unfair to the artists, and can deprive your group of the beauty of the original. Of course in some worship cultures, music gets altered to fit a particular feel, to work with a type of band or to make it accessible. I'm not talking about specific, decisive arrangement choices. Many of us can, do and even *must* adjust certain things. I'm talking about taking the time and effort to care and to take art seriously.

Seeking Permission and Accuracy

Let's say your friend wrote a poem about God and shared it at a large group worship time. You want to quote the same poem a month later for your worship service. Do you guess at what the words were and ap-

> *Remember that a song is a work of art, an expression created for the worship of God.*

proximate the poem? Probably not. Suppose your poet-friend plans to accompany you to the church service. In that case, definitely not! Of course you would call your friend and ask for both an accurate quote and permission to use the work. To quote it with permission and accuracy is no imposition on its ability to speak worshipfully or to be meaningful to you. Indeed, this is why you are quoting it in the first place!

One summer, a friend left a folder at my office. When I opened it to see what and whose it might be, I found a raft of chord charts that had been assembled for use at a camp by its song leaders. To my dismay, I discovered that it included "Thirst No More"—a song written by my friend and Urbana teammate Matt Frazier—written with mostly wrong chords. Since I know that Matt gladly and freely shares the music for this song whenever he is asked, I approached my friend and asked where that version came from. She didn't know. When I told her the chords were inaccurate, she argued that they had been simplified for the sake of the guitarists. My husband, a guitarist, pointed out that the incorrect chords were actually quite a bit more difficult than the

original and that the chords did not fit the melody. To this, our friend said, "Well it

Copyrights   Alison Siewert

It's so tempting: You hear this cool song at a conference, and your friend on the worship team could maybe . . . make a photocopy for you? Nay, O nay!

Why are copyrights such a pain? It seems like such a bother when it's just one copy, and it's just music.

The reason copyrights exist is to protect the people who write music. If you wrote a great song, it'd be kind of a drag to have someone else get hold of it and claim *they* wrote it. They'd be stealing your work. You'd hope this sort of thing would never happen in a Christian context, but it's not unfathomable.

In addition to identifying the rightful creators and owners of music, copyrights protect writers' and publishers' profits from the music they write and publish. I have a good friend who has written several popular worship songs. He doesn't make much money from them, but with the little he does make he was able to save up and buy a keyboard. (He'd been going to college practice rooms and churches to use pianos.) I want him to have his new keyboard because I know that, in addition to making his life easier and more fun, it will be a tool for writing more songs. I like my friend's songs. I want more.

So when you actually pay for your worship music, you help support people who are actively writing more music. In addition to buying musical equipment, they can also use their profits to purchase food and clothing. This seems like a pretty good deal. They eat, we sing.

I know what you're thinking, and I'm thinking it too: A lot of profit goes to giant companies who handle publishing and licensing. Yeah, that's true. But not everyone involved in Christian music publishing is rich. Trust me, I've met some of the poor ones.

You can get a copyright license from an agency such as Christian Copyright Licensing (CCLI), which covers most of the worship music on the commercial market. It's a pretty good deal financially, covering your basic uses (overheads, church bulletins, service recording), and it gives you access to CCLI's research capabilities (which are serious), in case you only know the middle two lines to the song but want to find the title and publishing info. They also provide kind and clear explanations of what you can and can't do. Find them on the Web at www.ccli.com.

You can't copy commercially published music unless you have written permission from the publisher. You can print words on overheads and bulletins for use in worship with a license (as described above). You can't copy the music from the book. You can, with certain limitations, create "custom arrangements" (CCLI can give you details) for use with your team.

But you can't photocopy the music from the book or from your friend. Stay legal out there.

doesn't matter. A song is just between you and God."

Well, yes, you do sing to God from your heart. However, you sing in the context of Christian community. If everyone knows and sings music differently from each other, it becomes very difficult to experience community around musical worship. At the very least, we need agreement about notes, chords and words to have singing that sounds like a song, rather than a cacopho- nous train station! Of course songs acquire extra and occasionally undesirable notes, riffs and harmonies—sometimes by arrangement and sometimes purely by accident—when large numbers of people share them. But as worship leaders we bear a responsibility to do the best job we can of transmitting creative information as fully and with as much integrity to the original art as we can.

33 Teaching New Music

....

Andy Crouch

You can't have congregational worship unless your congregation learns to sing. As churches have become more sophisticated in contemporary music, many have begun employing very talented worship leaders. You may well be one of them! While these musicians have wonderful gifts, it's easy for everyone involved to sit back and let them do the singing. It is a very short step to sitting back and letting them do the *worship*.

Worship leaders can't allow this. The real joy in worship is when a whole community of people come together to declare dependence on God. Think about how unusual this is in our culture. There are endless opportunities to watch professionals sing, or for that matter worship. Just turn on the radio or the television. But how often, outside of Christian churches, do ordinary people sing together? Almost never!

As a worship leader you have a key role in leading your group toward the remarkable experience of singing and worshiping together. You need to be more than just a singer or musician—you need to be a teacher.

Guidelines for Music Teachers
Pick singable music. All the teaching in the world won't help if the music is beyond your group's ability. What is singable depends a great deal on who you are leading and will vary considerably among cultures, between generations and even within your own congregation. In general, though, look for melodies with stepwise motion (small intervals between the notes rather than sudden jumps), a singable range and some repetition in the song structure. Songs with a verse-chorus structure are often easy to teach because the chorus—both words and music—repeats frequently. (For more on this see chapter 28.)

Help the congregation learn to learn. While it's important not to stretch people too far too fast, don't underestimate how well a group can learn to sing together over time. At the time of the Reformation, preachers could assume that their congregation knew the entire book of Psalms by heart. Just a few years ago, I visited a charismatic church whose congregation had a repertoire of over 150 original songs, most with multiple verses and elaborate melodies, entirely memorized. No overhead projections required! (They kept songbooks in the back for newcomers.) As you make learning songs a part of your life together, people will be able to learn more in quantity and quality.

Be encouraging as you teach. Most people feel very insecure about singing. They need lots of positive feedback. When they get a song right, tell them! Don't worry about fueling their pride by focusing on how well a congregation sings; trust me, insecurity is a far greater distraction.

Take time to get it right. Learning a song is a great opportunity to work together and to build your relationship with the congregation. Even people with very little musical training can sense when something's not going right—don't be afraid to acknowledge it and help them fix it. Don't be afraid to use gentle humor to encourage people: "Okaay, let's try that again!"

When possible, "line it out." Early Americans would often sing songs one line at a time, with the congregation following a song leader (often the one person in the church who could read the words and music). This is a beautiful way to sing in its own right, and it's invaluable for teaching. Sing one line, then let the congregation sing it back to you. If they don't get it, sing it again. You may want to use simple hand motions to visually indicate the "shape" of the musical line.

Turn the teaching time into worship time. Try praying through a song line by line. Don't step out of the presence of God to teach. As long as you remain prayerful, chances are your congregation will too. At the same time, be sensitive. There are some times when a new song is not helpful. For example, sermons introduce plenty of new material (we hope), so with rare exceptions, songs that serve as a response to preaching should be familiar so people can continue meditating on the Word.

Minimize musical distractions. Use very simple instrumentation, and avoid vocal harmonies (unless you're teaching them to the congregation). Save the full arrangements for a time when you're quite sure the congregation is comfortable singing their part.

Revisit new songs early and often. This can be as soon as thirty minutes later in the same meeting. Repetition is a key to learning. There's nothing wrong with doing a song more than once. You are picking songs that have musical and theological depth, aren't you? Even if you don't use the song again in the same worship service, be sure to come back to it within a week or two, or you will need to teach it all over again. Remember, repetition is key to learning.

Behold—unlike Jesus—worship leaders should not make all things new. One or two new songs per session is about all most groups can comfortably learn. Make full use of the songs your congregation already knows, carefully adding songs that will serve well over time. There is new meaning to be found in even the most familiar songs—and you don't have to teach them!

> *When a whole congregation participates with joy and delight, worship is a unique sign of the power and presence of God.*

Part 6
Show & Tell

Alison Siewert

In the story of Ezra and Nehemiah's rebuilding of Jerusalem's wall and calling God's people to return from exile to worship, Ezra brought out the law and read it to the whole assembly of Israel. The Scripture says, "He read from it facing the square before the Water Gate from early morning until midday, in the presence of the men and the women and those who could understand; and the ears of all the people were attentive to the book of the law" (Nehemiah 8:3).

What an amazing picture! Can you imagine your fellowship paying attention to the reading of Scripture all day long? But Ezra had two things going for him as he communicated. First, he lived in a culture with a powerful oral tradition— people were accustomed to listening intently to discourse, law and stories. Second, he read to people who had been in exile for so long they had forgotten what the Scripture said and desperately wanted to regain their grasp of God and his Word.

We live in a visual culture. Cultural virtues and laws are seldom transmitted by long readings to gathered communities. And stories are told not around campfires in words but around TV screens in pictures, music and dialogue. Since our worship gatherings include the communication of God's Word to God's people, we must consider how we communicate the gospel story effectively in a visual age.

For most of us, worship gatherings typically include some singing, a welcome, announcements, prayer and confession, perhaps special music, and a sermon. The sermon has traditionally been the focal point in American Protestantism. Scripture has a huge story to tell: We miss a great deal when it's communicated in words alone.

Adding Drama with Sketches
One of the best tools we have to bring Scripture to life is the Word enacted: Sketches. With a sketch you can bring the humor, pathos and relationships of Scripture to life for your congregation to see as well as hear. With drama, the Bible moves from being a dry, monotone reading that seems so ancient and distant we can't relate, to being a real-life situation that real people dealt with then and that we can relate to now.

Scripture has a huge story to tell: We miss a great deal when it's communicated in words alone.

Make sketches humorous. Humor is one of the most important bases of effective communication. Those of us who grew up in a TV-and-marketing world tend toward cynicism when it comes to things performed for us. Much of our experience of culture is tainted by market values, people attempting to figure out how to get us to buy. If sketches bring out humor, even poke fun at our consumer culture, they cease to feel like slick performances. We appreciate authenticity. If we focus in a sketch on the authentic comedy or tragedy of a story, we're more willing to receive the story itself as valid.

Keep them within your range. Likewise, sketches communicate well if they are appropriate to the context and resources available. If you try to do something as slick as television but you don't really have the skills or people to pull it off, you lose ground on both believability and authenticity. If you have the people, time and talent for a reading, do a reading. Simple is okay, and in fact, it's better if it's what you can do well. Remember, most Americans take in a huge volume of sophisticated, high-tech sight and sound. People know what's good and what's cheesy.

Leave some questions unanswered. Don't try to make sketches tie everything up into neat theological packages. Drama is rooted in the experience of human conflict. No conflict, no drama. (Have you ever noticed that Dante's *Inferno* is more *interesting* than his *Paradiso?*) Sometimes you need to have the tension get resolved; other times you can merely raise tension and let the sermon

or some other element of worship work at the resolution.

Find people with a knack for sketch writing. You need to have "an ear" for writing believable, manageable dialogue and interesting, nondidactic plots. So value the folks who do; draw them into the creative worship team, and help them cultivate their unique gifts for building worship.

Comedic and dramatic sketches will help you build a worship experience that communicates in accessible ways. For people to have real, life-changing encounters with God in worship, they need to understand what God is like and to hear what he's saying. Well-executed sketches can clarify and enliven the picture of God your congregation sees.

35 Writing Sketches for Worship

●●

Alison Siewert

I began writing sketches for worship out of necessity. When I started working as a worship designer, resources for drama were limp and limited. Today there are many books and even some subscription services devoted to sketches. Willow Creek Community Church publishes script books accompanied by videotapes of excellent material.

But I still write almost all the sketches we use in our services. I don't have the resources of a megachurch: no drama team, no sophisticated lighting, not even a real stage. At this point in the development of our service, when we want a sketch, the musical worship team has to perform it! This gives us limited time and energy, as well as a pool of untrained actors to work with. I've found it more effective to write material for the people I have than to find material that

makes me wish for a set-up I don't have.

I find that when I write the sketch, I can work much more closely with the sermon and other parts of worship to develop a piece that highlights more exactly what we want to bring out. One of the things that makes Willow Creek's theatrical ministry so successful is that they do just this: work closely together with everyone involved in the service to create an integrated hour of communication.

I also write our own material because I can make it reflect the local culture and current issues in a fresh, authentic way that's hard to get even from the best book. By working together with my team we can create sketches that feel germane, and therefore accessible, to the congregation.

My hunch is that my church situation is

similar to that of many other fellowships and churches. Most of us don't have—at least not yet—the capability to pull off well-crafted, intricate dramatic works. Good drama ministry grows through experience: You have to do it to improve it. So where do you start?

The Making of a Sketch

Begin with a Scripture passage. One of the easiest and, I think, most enjoyable kinds of sketches to write is based on the text of Scripture itself. People often circumscribe the Bible as historical and almost legend-like. I mean, can we really imagine what it must have been like for Moses to lead God's people through the sea? It probably didn't look like Charleton Heston on a sound stage. Or what about when Jesus multiplied fish and bread? Can you fathom what the disciples must have been thinking as they looked over the crowd, passing around the food? (Anyone got ketchup?) Biblical stories are vibrant, engaging, humorous, poignant and real—yet they get bound up in gilt-edged books and flattened out on fuzzy felt boards. Acting them out can do amazing things to revive texts.

Study the text—with others, if you can. I want to find out what the author was trying to communicate to the original audience. What's the main point? Look for how the point is communicated. Is there humor? A confrontation? Poetry or rhetoric? What visual images are set up? Stories always have dramatic tension, some conflict or problem to be resolved. That's what makes them stories rather than mere descriptions of action, and that's what makes for a good sketch. We have to identify the dramatic tension in the story and illustrate it.

Find the theme. For one service the preacher wanted to talk about Genesis 11's story of the tower at Babel. Rather than have the passage read in dry form, I illustrated it with a sketch. Since I had studied and taught Genesis 11 many times, I returned to my notes and looked for themes and how they were communicated. I remembered that the narrative plays humorously upon the building techniques and the Babylonians' desire for conquest, and decided we'd go for comedy.

A main point for the story was that humans consistently work to exalt themselves and to control the world through their own achievements, but in the end only God has the power, authority and wisdom to control things. The Babylonians worked to dominate their world by "making a name for themselves" through tower building. The sermon examined how we build towers in our own hearts and how God in judgment and mercy brings them down so that we can know him as Lord and receive the blessing only he can offer.

Review your resources. That week I had a musical team of four men and two women. I knew then I had six people to work with and that I needed parts that would work for more men. I also noticed that of these six, only two were very proficient at dramatic skills, and we only had about an hour to rehearse. I knew then too that I had to come up with a piece that required few and short lines for each person and allowed for some bloopers.

Look for modern parallels with the story. With these parameters in mind, I began to visualize how we might illustrate what happened at Babel. I tried to come up with some context our congregation would recognize. Our church recently completed a

> *Biblical stories are vibrant, engaging, humorous, poignant and real—yet they get bound up in gilt-edged books and flattened out on fuzzy felt boards.*

building program, so it wasn't too long before I imagined a building committee meeting—they had seen plenty of those! In my area of the country, many roofs are made of slate because, though expensive, it's very durable and attractive; our church's committee had set samples of different slate roofing materials outside our office so they could all see and decide on how to cover our new building. This paralleled the discussion in the Babel story about what building materials to use.

Then I thought, wouldn't it be funny—and probably frightening—to be sitting in a meeting, working on a building, and go from a fine conversation to sudden and complete incomprehensibility? Your friend Bob is telling you about the doors he ordered and next thing he's speaking Estonian! I realized both the comedic potential and the creative options for an illustration of this.

Writing a Sketch

Set the scene and tone. It needed to be clear that this was a meeting—a kind of meeting we've seen and can relate to. I thought about how funny "meeting culture" can be in itself, how people get caught up in their agendas and their ways of doing things. I wrote to poke gentle fun at a culture we all know so that Babel was in our backyard, right where the composers of Genesis wanted it to be.

Picture the characters. The men at the meeting, Ray, Moe, Hank and Jobab (we needed some Bible-name flair) begin with blustery discussion of roofing choices. The dialogue here needed to sound like real people sound in real meetings. I tried it out in my head as I wrote it, mimicking things I've said and heard said. Dialogue has to jump out of the Scripture and sound natural.

"Come, let us make bricks and burn them thoroughly," became:

MOE: But slate's pretty pricey, Ray. How you gonna pay for that?

HANK: Yeah, it's pricey, and hard to get anywhere in Babylon. How 'bout

we go for brick? We can get everyone together on a Saturday and have a work party to make 'em by hand.

No one I know would say, "Come, let us" do *anything,* let alone burn bricks. Sketches can do a great deal to vivify the text simply by rewording things in modern language. The language can be local too. If I were writing this sketch in my homeland of southern California, I might have written, "Dude. Let's like, get some gnarly bricks and rack up some serious towerage!"

Be careful with language. If you write in dialect or accent, make sure you have a good working knowledge of its sounds and meanings so that you can be consistent. Beware of imitating things in ways that might be or sound racist or otherwise stereotypical in overly negative ways. If you're not sure, ask someone for help or choose a different direction. You don't want to lose the point of the sketch in inappropriateness or controversy, and you do want to honor the people and cultures joined in Christ's body.

I had the Babylonian Building Committee continue to meet, covering all the topics Genesis 11 says the Babylonians discussed. I especially wanted to convey the motive behind their building: to gain the advantage, be the best, dominate the world, "to make a name for themselves" (11:4). Since the Olympic Games were in progress at the time, many new commercials appeared, touting the marvels of human culture—especially communication. I used quotes from these commercials in the committee's dialogue because they were so perfectly relevant to the passage and to us.

Increase the tension. The text makes it clear God *descended* to Babel, creating a situation the Genesis writer treats with a little humor. The picture of the Lord going down to earth to see the little human tower is funny, especially in light of their purpose: to build a tower "with its top in the heavens." (I guess they didn't quite make it!) When God makes it from heaven all the way down to their building, he "frets" that they will be able to do anything, now that they've built their great tower. I wrote a reaction for an offstage God voice (that person didn't have to memorize lines) that gets at this edgy humor.

Then came the really fun part! I wrote dialogue in "Babel," where every character speaks in mostly English words that are put in totally nonsensical order. (Hey, it was easier than teaching people Cebuano!) One character stayed in comprehensible English, serving as a narrative device. One of the best things about this sketch was that all the actors—except the guy speaking regular English—could drop words or mix things up without affecting the sketch too much. And humor came not only through what the actors were saying, but also in how they said it. I built the section so that they get increasingly frustrated and finally blow up:

MOE: *[becoming more frantic as he tries to get others to understand]*: Earnest looby? Ray, earnest looby? *[yelling]* Earnest looby? Earnest looby! Earnest looby!

RAY: *[attempting to calm* MOE *down]* Uh . . . looby, Moe . . . injinx equestrian antependia. . . . Norse something to the eponymous Abu Dhabi.

MOE: AN-TI-HIS-TA-MINE!!!

I had Moe yell this, stressing every syllable. It needed to be a word that the congregation knew so that pulled out of its normal context and placed in the nonsensical—we all know what an antihistamine is, but we would not likely yell it in utter frustration—it would evoke humor. It did.

Show just enough. Sketches for worship usually need to be short, so I wrote just enough dialogue to get the point across and make it funny and enjoyable. Had this piece been any shorter, people would have had difficulty tracking what happened when the builders started speaking incomprehensibly. It took folks a minute to figure out that it wasn't their hearing aid or the actors mixing things up by accident. It's not every day someone tells you, "It'll become clearer when ironing boards defoliate."

Don't answer all the questions. Plenty of religious dramas end with everything lined up neatly, contained in a box you could take home. But since people do better when they're engaged with a question rather than presented with an answer, I left the resolution incomplete, which (we hope) provoked their interest in the sermon. When you use drama in concert with the Word preached, sung and prayed, you don't have to wrap it all up in your five-minute segment. Sketches are at their prime when they humorously or poignantly raise a question, set a tone or enliven a picture of Scripture that will be further explored in the community of worship.

Note: A complete script and other script samples follow in chapter 36.

....

Excuse Me, What Did You Say?
A Sketch on the Tower of Babel
by Alison Siewert

Cast of Characters
Ray, Moe, Hank, Jobab
(the first Babylonian building committee)
God (offstage)

[The building committee sits in a meeting discussing how to build their new tower. They speak as "experts" with a clear sense of how it should be done and done right.]

HANK: Welcome to our regular Babylonian Building Committee meeting. I'd like to start by . . . *[interrupted by Ray]*

RAY *[interrupting]*:   I say we go with slate! You can't do better than slate. It'll last a thousand years!

MOE: But slate's pretty pricey, Ray. How you gonna pay for that?

HANK: Yeah, it's pricey and hard to get anywhere in Babylon. How about we go for brick? We can get everyone together on a Saturday and have a work party to make 'em by hand.

MOE: Yeah, and then we can superfire 'em so they'll last as long as slate.

RAY: Well, okay. I still like slate, but I guess brick, with some sticky stuff, that oughta be durable enough.

JOBAB: *Durable* is what we need in a tower! Just look at these blueprints! We're gonna have the highest tower known to humankind. It's a beaut, alright. Just think how other nations are gonna envy us when they see our advanced technology! With this tower we'll be able to broadcast, forecast, telecast, stratocast, cast for fish. We'll dominate!

MOE: We'll dominate every world market! We'll control oil prices and troop movements, cultural trends and fashion. It's all ours for the taking. It's our manifest destiny, gentlemen. We were meant to have it all.

JOBAB: My friends, we are about to become the Transcendent Society. When people *communicate,* anything is possible. We can do this! We'll be gods in our own time! We'll make a name for ourselves. We'll be the Great Babylonian Building Committee—known for our splendiferous tower!

GOD *[offstage]:* Oh, my! If they become gods in their own time, then what will I be? Help! Help! *[pause]* No, not really! How can we remind them that they're just creatures . . . made by *me?!* Aahh . . . I've got it!

HANK: So, Jobab, what do you think of the capybara tiddleywinks go tifftuff kersnoozes?

JOBAB: Excuse me, what did you say?

MOE: I think Hank was trying to say that scissors butterscotch coronation make tortilla echinacea.

JOBAB: Moe, I didn't understand a word you said.

RAY: That's okay, Jobab. It'll become clearer when ironing boards defoliate otorhinolaryngology out mountainous obfuscation within under over under over under over *je ne sais quois.*

HANK: Vituperous schooner argy-bargy about the pen pencil in the williwaw truck floribunda?

MOE *[becoming more frantic as he tries to get others to understand]:* Earnest looby? Ray, earnest looby? *[yelling]* Earnest looby? Earnest looby!! Earnest looby!!

RAY *[attempting to calm* MOE *down]:* Uh, looby, Moe . . . injinx equestrian antependia. . . . Norse something to the eponymous Abu Dhabi.

MOE: AN-TI-HIS-TA-MINE!!!

JOBAB *[looking around, completely befuddled]:* Whoa . . . I have a new name for ourselves: Call us *confused!*

[Each wanders off in a different direction looking for someone who understands. Their voices trail off, ending with JOBAB'S.]

HANK: Schooner argy-bargy in the simultaneous truck! Schooner argy-bargy in the simultaneous truck!

MOE: Earnest looby? Sagacity! When tulips north transubstantiation? Sagacity? Sagacity!

RAY: Oh, well. Norwegian something to the eponymous Abu Dhabi. Sawubona!

JOBAB: Uh . . . I guess the meeting's pretty much adjourned. Right, guys? See ya next week? Everyone? Guys? *[He fades out, walking off]*

Whadoyahaveta Do?
A Sketch of Mark 10:17-22
by Alison Siewert

This sketch is more of a montage than a story, but it incorporates the stories of the rich young man from Mark's Gospel with our own stories, and poses the question, How are we related to this man? And what do Jesus' words to him have to do with us?

Cast of Characters
Voice 1, Voice 2, Voice 3, Rich Young Man, Jesus,
Businessman, Woman, Daughter or Son

VENUE 1
Voices 1, 2, 3 all in rhythm and each line beginning within the preceding line

VOICE 1: Whadoyahaveta

VOICE 2:   Whadoyahaveta

VOICE 3:   Whadoyahaveta—*do?*

RICH YOUNG MAN *[nearly vaudevillian in rhythm and movement]:* Hey! What do I have to do? Good Teacher, Good Teacher! WhadoIhavetado? WhadoIhavetado now to make it, to get there? Good Teacher, Good Teacher! WhadoIhavetado?

VOICE 1: Whadoyahaveta do? What is it?

VOICE 2:   Whadoyahaveta do? What is it?

VOICE 3:   Whadoyahaveta do? Whadoes *he* haveta do?

RICH YOUNG MAN: WhadoIhavetado? WhadoIhavetado to *get a life??!!* *[pausing, catching breath, breaking rhythm, kneeling]* Good Teacher, What do I have to do to inherit eternal life?

JESUS *[calmly]:* Why are you calling me good? God is the only one good.

VENUE 2

BUSINESSMAN *[on the phone]:*   Look, what do I have to do to convince you to set this thing up? I mean, we're both looking for the same thing, right? A good deal is a good deal!

WOMAN *[on the phone to fiancé]:*   You know, Brian, I'm just not sure I want to move to South Dakota. I love you! But I have a lot of reservations about . . . well, you know, my family's here and everything. And it's cold in South Dakota. I mean, who goes to South Dakota? I love you, but I guess what I'm saying is I'm not *that* sure about this relationship. You know what I mean?

DAUGHTER OR SON *[on the phone to parent]:*   Look! What do I have to do to please you? All I've ever wanted is to make you happy, and it never works. I'm sick of it, and I can tell you I don't care if you take me out of your will. Go ahead.

BUSINESSMAN *[still on the phone]:*   Well that's a great idea! Let's see if I can do something for you, and you can do something for me. You're a good human being, Don. Now, what do I have to do to get you to sign on the dotted line?

JESUS: You know the commandments . . . [Businessman, *on phone, mimes along and chimes in demonstrating he knows it all]* Don't murder; you shall not commit adultery; don't steal; don't bear false witness; don't defraud; honor your parents.

BUSINESSMAN: Of course, of course, Don. We all know the code of conduct.

JESUS *[to audience, matter-of-factly]:*   There's one thing you lack: Go, sell what you own, and give the money to the poor. And you will have treasure in heaven.

The Perfect Relationship
by Scott Brill

This sketch will require some memorization and rehearsal time as well as some acting and comic timing, but it might be a very humorous complement to a talk on romantic relationships or an evangelistic sermon on Jesus as the perfect relationship.

Cast of Characters
John, Pete

JOHN *enters the room as* PETE *sits at a table, looking intently at a piece of paper.*

JOHN: Oh, my . . . *[walking around him]* Oh, my, oh, my . . . . Look at this! The King of the Recliner is . . . what? Actually studying?

PETE: Well, not exactly.

JOHN: Whew! What a relief! The world's not coming to an end, then. So . . . if you're not studying, exactly what are you doing?

PETE: I've decided it's time for me to get into a romantic relationship again. I'm ready to fall in love.

JOHN: Egads! This is even worse than studying! Peter Williams? In a relationship?! The same Peter Williams who, his freshman year, broke up with a perfectly nice woman simply because she thought *Southpark* was a new soap opera? Wow. Well, I'm stunned.

PETE: Well, I'm over it. Besides, this time it's going to be different. I've been burned before, so I'm going to make sure it's the perfect relationship.

JOHN: The perfect relationship? The perfect relationship would not have you in it.

PETE: Ha! Very funny. Come on, man. You've got to help me. *[handing* JOHN *the paper and a pen]* Here. Give me some ideas of categories for compatibility, and write down what I say. Then I'll have kind of a profile of the perfect woman for me.

JOHN: All right. Something tells me I shouldn't go for this, but I am your roommate

. . . and servant. . . . Let me think. Okay, let's start with leisure time. What are your nonnegotiables for relaxing?

PETE: Saturday morning cartoons. *Monday Night Football.* ESPN2.

JOHN: Don't forget *WWF All-Action Pro Wrestling!*

PETE: Right. *[thinking more] Walker, Texas Ranger. Homicide. NYPD Blue.* . . . I guess those are the nonnegotiables.

JOHN: What about hobbies or interests? Culture? Out-on-the-town?
[he waits through very long pause as PETE *tries to think of something]* Never mind. I'll just write, "See leisure time." Next topic. What about personal appearance?

PETE: It's important. I'd say, decent-looking, but not the kind of knock-you-out looks. Hygiene is key also—occasional showers and brushing teeth. *[looks around the room]* But she absolutely can't be a neat freak. She has to be able to put up with a certain amount of, uh . . .

JOHN: Chaos?

PETE: Lack of order.

JOHN: Got it. Let's move on to personal tastes. Music is probably the most important. What do you think?

PETE: Sensitive ballads of the late seventies and early eighties. Air Supply. Dan Fogelberg. Christopher Cross.

JOHN: What?!

PETE: Hey! It's a highly personal thing.

JOHN: All right. Air Supply. Whatever. What about food?

PETE: Let's see. McDonald's, Burger King, Pizza Hut. Donuts.

JOHN: No. Not places to eat—what kind of food?

PETE: McDonald's. Burger King. Pizza Hut.

JOHN: Right. Got it. How about family background?

PETE: As long as she doesn't have any sociopaths as close relatives, it really doesn't matter.

JOHN: Demeanor?

PETE: No, of course I don't want to demean her! I don't want to degrade her either. Who do you think I am, asking that?

JOHN: No! Not *demean* her—*Demeanor,* you know, like how she presents herself. How she interacts. Demeanor.

PETE: It would be nice if she could do that.

JOHN: Never mind. Here's a big one. Personal goals.

PETE: A desire to make as much money as possible with the least amount of effort.

JOHN: So deep. Any others?

PETE: Nope.

JOHN: Study habits?

PETE: The best grades possible with the least amount of effort.

JOHN: Religion?

PETE: Some kind of religion would be nice. But nothing too weird. I'd like to avoid extremes. You know, no yoga meditation in red pajamas, but no door-pounding, Bible-thumping either.

JOHN: Okay. That's about all the categories I can think of. Let's see what we've got here: You want a woman who has virtually no life outside watching copious amounts of TV, is somewhat good-looking, has a handle on basic personal grooming, has bizarre musical taste, is addicted to junk food, no skeletons in her closet, no recognizable direction in her life, hasn't flunked out of school yet and is religiously nondescript?

PETE: Yeah. That's it.

JOHN: You know, Pete, this sounds frighteningly like you.

PETE: Yes! Yes!! Of course! Why didn't I figure it out earlier? The perfect relationship would be with someone exactly like me! I want to fall in love with me! If I can just find myself in a woman's body, I'm set. *[He starts to leave]* Thanks, man. You're awesome—you've been a total help. I'm so excited. I'm going out right now to look for her/me. *[Leaving]* Don't wait up for me.

Luge Chute
A Sketch Introducing Luke 5:17-19
by Alison Siewert

This sketch illustrates a story from Scripture in a modern setting. It requires only three guys and a bag of chips.

Cast of Characters
Mikey, Joey, Scotty

Three friends sit around a living room, eating chips and discussing the Olympics.

MIKEY: Hey, you guys! Did you watch the Olympics last night?

JOEY: Yeah. Whoa, that was amazing. What was up with that luge thing?

MIKEY: Wait! Was it luge or bobsled? I can never tell the difference.

JOEY: Uh . . . I'm pretty sure it was luge.

MIKEY: Yeah, luge.

SCOTTY: Anyway, what happened? I was at the laundromat. Some guy had pro wrestling on the TV there, and I couldn't get him to change it, even for a buck.

JOEY: Oh! You didn't see it? Well, there was this one guy . . .

MIKEY: The luge dude.

JOEY: Yeah, the luge dude, and he and his teammate—of course they were the Americans—because everyone knows Americans are bad at luge. I mean, do you ever see luges by the road here in America? No. It's a non-American sport. Anyway, they were going down the chute thing that they luge down, you know that thing?

SCOTTY: Yeah, the luge chute.

JOEY: Okay. So they're going down the luge chute, and they get stuck. I mean, they were supposed to slide down the thing, right?

MIKEY: The luge chute.

JOEY: Yeah. So then, they like, flipped and landed sideways, and they couldn't move. They were totally entrenched. You know?

MIKEY: In the luge chute. They were totally stuck.

JOEY: So then, the one guy in the front got up off the luge thing and just slid the rest of the way down the chute on his rear.

MIKEY: Right down the luge chute.

JOEY: Right down the luge chute. But then the other guy, the guy in the back or whatever, he was like caught by his latex suit under the luge in the chute.

MIKEY: Caught by the suit under the luge in the chute.

JOEY: And then he couldn't breathe right. But they couldn't get his suit unstuck, so they needed a doctor.

MIKEY: Is there a doctor in the luge?

JOEY: But there are, like, twenty thousand people lining the sides of the course, you know?

MIKEY: People lining the luge chute.

JOEY: So they had to like, bring this doctor in by helicopter, but the doctor is in regular clothes, not one of those special luge suits. So he can't negotiate all the ice and the turns and stuff. So a bunch of guys from the Swiss team and the Namibian team, they all basically carry the doctor from the top of the luge chute all the way down to where the guy was stuck.

MIKEY: From the top of the luge chute to the bottom of the luge chute.

JOEY: And then, it got even more amazing. 'Cause to get the luge dude unstuck, they had to take pickaxes and shovels and stuff and, like, demolish the luge. There was no other way to get the dude unstuck. They just like, dismantled the thing. And like, the Olympic guys are freaking out because the luge competition wasn't over yet, and where are they gonna luge? But the Swiss guys and the Namibian guys are, like, who cares about luging? We gotta get this guy out! Get some priorities! So they pretty much just dug apart the luge chute and unstuck the dude.

SCOTTY: Wow. Sounds pretty amazing. So what happened to the guy?

JOEY: Oh. Hey, Mikey. What happened to the guy? You know?

MIKEY: The guy stuck in the luge chute?

JOEY: Yeah, the luge chute guy.

MIKEY: Oh. The doctor got his breathing working right again, and they had to cut him out of his luge suit to free him from the luge chute. But he's gonna be alright.

JOEY: But the luge competition just had to be called off totally, because there's no more luge chute.

SCOTTY: Oh, well. It's not like they were showing any of the luging anyway.

MIKEY: Yeah, that's true. But dude, you shoulda seen this luge chute. Demolished!

JOEY: Destroyed!

MIKEY: Destructo!

SCOTTY: Sounds a lot better than pro wrestling.

[They exit, still talking and eating chips]

Help, Help! We Need Help!
A Collage of Psalm 121
by Alison Siewert

This sketch employs multiple media and can be used to introduce Psalm 121, raise an evangelistic question or open a time of confession in worship. When using City of Hope, you will have to fast forward to the very end—past some, uh, unchurched language—to find the scene described for Scene D. Note: You may need a license to use the movie clip (available from Motion Picture Licensing Corporation at www.mplc.com).

Cast of Characters
Johnny, Nicky, Joey, Questioner, Marcia, Kim,
Reader,
Video Operator (offstage)

Scenes take place on stage and around congregation. Two video monitors are positioned at front corners, facing audience at diagonal. Live scenes play individually, then repeat sporadically (except Scene C, which is continuous), simultaneously, to the start of READER.

SCENE A

JOHNNY *[setting up ladder]:* Yo, Nicky! Can you help me wid'is ladder over here?

NICKY Yo, I'm busy. Ask Joey.

JOHNNY: Hey, Joey, can you help me wid'is ladder over here?

JOEY: No way! The Steelers is startin'. Ya wanna come over and watch?

SCENE B

QUESTIONER: Is there a God? And if there is a God, why can't I find him?

SCENE C

KIM: Uh, Marcia, can you help me get this coat unzipped? I'm stuck.

[Marcia and Kim work at getting zipper unstuck for duration of sketch, with appropriate ad-lib verbalization]

[After Scene C has been completed one time, begin repeating all scenes through film clip, until READER *begins]*

SCENE D

[Final scene from John Sayles' City of Hope (David Straithairn as the town fool crying, "Help! We need help! In the building! Over here! In the building!" etc.) plays on video monitors. Scenes A and B repeat; Scene C continues to end. At end of video segment, before credits come up, all players stop and quietly focus on READER.]

READER *[as* City of Hope *ends, stepping to mic]:*   I look up to the hills—Where will my help come from? My help comes from the Lord, who made heaven and earth. God will not let you down; our God who keeps you will not fall asleep on you. The Lord is your keeper; he's shade when it's too hot out. The sun will not beat down on you during the day, and the moon will not overwhelm you at night. The Lord will keep you from everything that's evil; he will hang onto your life. Our God will keep your going out and your coming in from now on and forever.

[Lights fade and players exit]

Electronic Breakup
by Scott Brill

Here's a sketch that requires only one actor, who can have the script taped to the computer on which e-mail is being written.

Cast of Characters
Voice, Jill

JILL *sits facing the audience and her computer screen.* VOICE *announces the sketch.*

VOICE: Sitting at her computer, Jill contemplates an e-mail message from her boyfriend. We get to listen in to her thoughts.

JILL: I can't believe it! There is no way. I cannot believe that he would be this heartless. He broke up with me by e-mail? What a weasel! And he sent it to me at 7:20, when he knew I'd be out running. *[staring at the computer]* Three stupid lines:

"Dear Jill, I'm really sorry we didn't get to talk more about this, but I think it would be better is we didn't go out anymore. It's not anything with you—I just don't think I can make this kind of commitment right now. I hope we can still be friends. Love, Steve."

This really rots. What am I supposed to do? I can't even talk with him about it. I guess I could try to write back. But what am I supposed to say? *[thinking for a moment]* I could try begging. *[Begins to type]* Steve. Please, please, please don't do this to me. Let's talk first. I know we could work it out. Maybe if I gave you a little more room in the relationship. I'll call less. I think that . . . *[stops typing]*

Oh, man. This is humiliating. I can't do this. It's not worth crawling on the ground. I've got to save some shred of dignity from this. *[thinks again]*

Okay. He says he still wants to be friends. That has possibilities. Let's see . . . *[begins typing]* Dear Steve, I got your e-mail, and I'm trying hard to understand why you don't want to go out anymore. I appreciate the fact that you still want to be friends with me. And I want you to know that I would still like to have some kind of friendship/relationship with you. I've always tried to hold onto our relationship with open hands and not have a lot of expectations . . . *[stops typing for a moment to think]*

Is that really true? Can I actually write that? *[pause]* Yeah, I guess . . . *[types again]* I believe in that statement—"If you love something, let it go. If it comes back to you, then it was really yours. If it doesn't . . ." *[anger rising]* " . . . hunt it down and kill it!" Maybe that's it. Maybe I should just express my true feelings. Maybe I should just tell him how mad I am . . .

Dear Mr. Davidson. You little, pencil-necked geek. You have once again given another piece of evidence toward the fact that all men are pond scum. Could you be a little less sensitive to me? You say you still want to be friends? Fat chance! I'd rather die than look you in both of your faces... *[stops typing]*

This isn't working either. I just can't express to him what I'm feeling. I can't even figure out for myself what I'm feeling. I'm mad. I'm disappointed. I feel rejected. I feel used. This stinks!

But you know what stinks even more? He doesn't feel any of this. And he probably doesn't want to know what I feel. Why else would he tell me this by e-mail? Nine months going out, and . . . this? So I'm left to pick up the pieces of my dreams for our relationship while he hides in his geeky computer closet—just hoping I'll what, get over it? *[stares at keyboard]*

Forget this. I'm going running again. *[turns off computer and walks off]*

37 Directing Sketches

Alison Siewert

So you've found or written a sketch you want to use next week. Now, how do you put it together?

Even a small amount of well-used rehearsal time can make a sketch better than a reading. Your goals for rehearsing a sketch need to be clear. You need to know what the sketch is doing for the movement of worship. Is it designed to raise a question? Identify a key issue? Review an episode in Scripture? Shed new light on something people figure they already know? Be clear before you begin, so you can use your time and energy well. Sketches typically require several players to do many things, so any rehearsal time must be organized lest it become chaotic and ineffective.

A Basic Rehearsal Plan

Read through the script. Have the players sit together and simply read the entire script. This will help you get an idea of the shape and character of the sketch in a way that was more difficult when you were just imagining it in your head. It will also tell you what talent you're working with, whether people are able to do the accent you hoped for, whether they understand their characters, whether they'll need help speaking loudly enough. I often have a group read a script twice—the first time to get a feel and the second to work on parts and ideas.

Block the sketch. Blocking refers to the process of arranging actors' movements and gestures. You don't need to create complex motion for every line (especially if you and your actors are new at this), but you should be ready to give people some direction. For instance, if the sketch includes three disci-

ples in a boat and Jesus on the shore—but you are not using an actual boat and have no shore scenery, except what you pantomime—you need to define where the boat is. Otherwise, you'll likely end up with some disciples in the boat and others walking unintentionally on water! Likewise, decide where the shore stops and the boat starts so Jesus doesn't fall into the boat! When you block, *be sure you keep actors turned toward the audience,* especially for their lines. Inexperienced players often speak their lines to one another at the expense of the audience's hearing and sight. Teach people to speak outwardly and loudly—unless you have lavaliere microphones for every actor—more loudly than will seem comfortable to them.

Rehearse the sketch. Have people go through the sketch, from top to bottom, at least twice and up to five or six times if you have time. It's fine to use a run-through to stop for corrections, but most of the time it's helpful to wait to the end (sketches are usually short anyway) and give people notes about their performances, answer questions and adjust lines and blocking. Then run through it again. However many times you rehearse a sketch, you need to give players a break between rehearsal and the start of worship.

Some Tricks, Devices and Handy Tips

1. If people need their scripts, try to find creative ways to hold them. Because of the constraints of our overall schedule, I often rehearse sketches from 4:45 to 5:20 p.m. for a 6:00 p.m. worship service. I have no drama team, so the musical worship team also gets to perform sketches. (They don't mind too much!) This stretches people's memory capacity to just about maximum, so I generally don't expect that folks will memorize lines, even if they get scripts a week ahead. I often have characters (a secretary, a doctor, a reporter) hold clipboards on which they can carry their scripts. Magazines, newspapers, tables, Bibles and scrolls can also be props and script holders. (Hey, most filmed actors get teleprompters, so don't feel too bad.) If you write your own sketches, you can plan this. One person wrote a monologue for a character reflecting out loud at her computer. (The script for "Electronic Breakup" is included in this section.) I sometimes write just one or two on-stage parts and some offstage roles. For a worship theme on Jesus the Light of the World, I wrote a dialogue for three voices in the dark (they read from off stage, using flashlights); another time, I had one actor responding to messages on his answering machine, with all the "phone voices" offstage on microphones (with scripts in hand).

2. If people need their scripts, teach them not to bury their faces in the paper. Coach players to look up as much as they can. Use highlighters to mark each actor's script so they don't get lost or create dead space while looking for their next line. Get actors to memorize and pay attention to what comes just before them, and to secure the last few words of each speech, since that's what other actors will be listening for as a cue.

3. Use few props. Props can be great, but too many of them in a short sketch can be overwhelming. Add to that the fact that most of us have little or no technical stage help (and certainly no prop master!), few hiding places for props and little rehearsal time for complicated work with props, and you'll see that the simpler, the better.

4. Check your sight lines. Most worship spaces were not built for theatrical drama, so they aren't arranged like theaters, with the audience on a slope looking at the stage from an angle. Most congregations sit on a flat plane, which can make it difficult to see what's happening up front. You can elevate a staging area for worship, but that's a limited solution—you don't want the worship team towering too far above the congregation. You can also keep things simple, so people don't have to follow a complicated chain of movements they may or may not be able to see. If you do have sight-line problems, don't have players to sit or lie down. You'll have to suggest those positions using stools, poses and props, such as a person "sleeping" by standing with a pillow on their arm under their head.

5. Go easy on special effects. Effects (or FX) can be really helpful used sparingly and really distracting when loaded on. Say you have a cool ringing telephone sound on your keyboard and want to use it when the Bob character answers the phone. The keyboard player is playing Bob, so the violinist offers to play the telephone sound. But during the worship service the keyboard player forgets to set the keyboard for the phone sound before he transforms into Bob the character, and the violinist doesn't know how to reset it. So you get to that ringing telephone part, and the violinist is still frantically trying to figure out the keyboard. There's a moment of silence, so the keyboard player playing Bob makes his own ringing sound and picks up the phone and starts his line, but just then the violinist figures it out, and it rings and . . . well, you get the picture.

Do what you can do well, even if it's simple. And challenge people to new skills and risks in a way that allows them to continue their focus on leading worship rather than their sketch anxiety.

38 Planning for the Eyes

For many people the eyes are the primary channel in and out of the heart and mind. Just as an out-of-tune note or inappropriate language distracts from worship, poor visual planning can diminish the worship experience. As a leader, part of your job is to think visually about a number of obvious worship aspects.

What Do You See?
With your worship area in mind, take a look at the following list. Can you improve on any of these aspects of worship?

Dress and posture. Worship leaders can enhance or distract from worship based on how they appear and act. (See "Your Fashion Statement" in chapter 13 for specific suggestions.)

Background. A dull one can easily bore and a busy one overstimulate; our aim is to help people focus.

Lighting. Can people see you? The words? Each other? The aisle to the restroom?

Slides. These need to be legible and neat, not thrown together with crayon.

Screen size. A general rule is that the diagonal dimension ideally should be one-eighth the depth of the room.

Handouts. These can express the theme of worship.

Be aware too that the more abstract visual elements like contrast, color and shape can either lead people into worship or make it more difficult for them to concentrate.

Artists, cinematographers and designers know many rules for visual communication. You may want to find an artist to add to your worship team just to help think about things which improve and detract from communica-

tion. Visual design is complex, but worth exploring in regard to worship.

Three Basic Principles
1. The eye is attracted to light. Most people's eyes will be drawn toward the brightest thing at the front of a room. If that is a window, bright light or a white board, and not the leader's face, it will produce a subtle tension for many and make it harder for them to concentrate on worship. God created us with a little bit of white in our eyes: That is where we connect when speaking directly to another person. It is very important to place speakers and leaders in a spot where light will fall on their faces.

2. Horizontal lines feel more stable and calming, while vertical lines tend to create more tension. Film makers often use strong vertical shadows or lines in the background of scenes filled with tension or suspense. Panoramic scenes with long, strong horizontal lines tend to be more peaceful. Applying this theory in a worship setting may be difficult, but it is worth noticing what is behind the leaders. You may be able to neaten some things and make it easier for a group to worship.

3. Warm colors (reds and yellows) tend to reach out toward the eye; cool colors (blues and greens) tend to recede away from the eye. Color has a profound effect on our feelings. We even use color to describe our moods. "Are you feeling blue today?" The color of light, clothing and background can add or detract from themes in worship. Have you ever noticed how often in advertisements the most important idea is presented in red or yellow type? Artists know those colors tend to come off the page toward the audience. That does not mean everything should be printed in red, but you may want to consider when just a little color will help people enter into worship more deeply.

In addition to working with these principles, you should do some visual planning in the musical worship team's space and your fellowship's entryway.

How can your worship team arrange instruments and vocal mics so they can see each other, the congregation can see the leaders and lyrics, and the whole scene looks relatively well-organized and tidy? You don't want a jungle of cords and amplifiers cluttering the front of the room. Think about using the careful placement of equipment as well as plants, backdrops and other screens to focus and clean up the overall look of the room. Also spend some time trying out various arrangements until you figure out what kind of space you need and how to use it well. Ask some visually oriented people to visit and give you feedback.

The entryway, reception area, narthex or foyer—whatever you call it—is the first contact people have when they enter the worship experience. Using the basic principles listed above, examine your entry. What does it communicate? How might you arrange, color and light it in ways that would improve its welcome?

You may find planning for the eyes a stretch beyond the planning for the ears you're used to, but in an increasingly visual culture we must design for eyes if we want to communicate to hearts.

39 Using Media in Worship

Scott Wilson

In order to use any commercial videos—beyond fair use—you need a license. You can apply for a license with the Motion Picture Licensing Corportation at www.mplc.com. They'll negotiate a reasonable fee.

We live in what is sometimes called the media age. The media have become a powerful shaping force in our culture and often try to seduce us into worshiping the wrong things. As Christians we can be so leery of them it is hard even to imagine using media in worship. Actually, this is not a new problem: the ancient Israelites were strongly warned against using their technology to make anything which would lead them to worship God's creatures rather than the Creator himself. Likewise, any time we use media in worship, God is to be our focus, not the fabulous technology or techniques, or the wonderful producers or actors. Used in this light, media can greatly enhance worship.

The right medium can take what is old or familiar and infuse it with new meaning. When we sing about the deep, deep love of Jesus rolling like a mighty ocean, and we see ocean waves, it can intensify our understanding of God's love and bring an old hymn to life. When we talk about a thousand tongues singing God's praise and we see pictures of other faces, a wide variety of other ethnicities, the breadth of our perception of God's family can be increased. When we pray for a people group in another part of the world and see their faces, their villages, their lives, we pray with more understanding and often with more passion. The old adage about a picture being worth a thousand words is true. Using media can eliminate long verbal explanations, often saying things better than words ever could.

Creating a Visual Context for Worship

Media, like music, can speak languages of the heart. Pictures can set moods and encourage feelings in a way that helps people into worship. Media can also offer concrete information about God's world and his people. Here are some ideas to get you thinking about using media in worship. (See the note on copyrights on page 127.)

Use a clip from a movie at the beginning of a meeting to set a context for worship. The clip doesn't need to express accurate Christian theology to be useful. You may try showing a short film clip in which characters express their fears as a prelude to a time focusing on the God who meets our needs. The clip could remind us that we are all human and often afraid.

Find a short news clip or some newspapers which discuss a situation in the world for which your group wants to pray. Use the news to introduce the prayer time and increase the congregation's comprehension of what they are praying about.

Pick an image or images to project behind or around your song lyrics. Choose something that will help participants meditate on the words in a fresh way. With all the computer and projection technology available today you can usually find someone in a group to help make this happen. It may be a significant way of allowing some people with different talents to contribute their gifts in worship.

Use a music video in your singing worship. You can find many videos to choose from among the growing number being produced, or you can produce your own. (Again, find some talented folks and invite them to contribute.) You can show a video much as you would a movie clip, or if it would work for your group, invite the congregation to sing along. If you have click-track technology available (a click track is a metronome beat heard through earphones by the drummer or pianist, which makes it possible for the musical team to stay in sync with the visual), you can even have your worship team (if they have ample rehearsal time and are ready for this) play the music rather than using the prerecorded track on the video.

Find a clip that allows people an opportunity to reflect in their own hearts and minds on a strong message or moment in worship. It might even be a short documentary piece showing how someone else has responded to the Scripture text or to challenges similar to what the congregation has just heard preached.

40 Visual Arts in Worship

••

Alison Siewert

From the carvings of the Celtic Christians to Bernini's columns for St. Paul's Cathedral, from the icons of the Orthodox Church to Kent Twitchell's Los Angeles freeway murals, visual arts have been used to adore God and declare his benefits to people. Visual arts in the church have dissipated since the Reformation questioned the excesses of opulent decor in light of the gospel's call to simplicity. But it is possible to live simply and also spend wisely on visual art. You don't need a huge budget to find and cultivate talented people in your congregation to contribute beauty to worship.

Opening Worship to Artistic Expression

In preparation for a Pentecost celebration at one church, some artists drew a growing flame in pencil on one side of a large white fabric sheet. Right before the service they dampened the sheet with water and displayed it on posts at the front of the church. It still looked white to the congregation. But when the service host introduced the theme for worship and began reading the Pentecost passage, the artists, standing unseen behind the sheet, squeezed liquid dye along the lines of their pencil drawing. The dye spread into the wet sheet, creating a beautiful, vibrant illustration of the spreading flame of the Pentecost experience. The flame-covered banner stood in place during the service and afterward as a reminder of the Spirit's movement through the congregation and through history.

Another congregation created fabric letters to make the words of the gifts of the Spirit for a sermon series. They made each word a different solid color and sewed it to a larger piece of netting the same color. The words-on-net were then suspended from the ceiling by fishing line, which made them appear to be floating down—as if from God.

Included here is Scott Wilson's backdrop design for an InterVarsity national conference that covered creation, the Fall and redemption. The art on the backdrop progressed over the course of the week to illustrate what God was showing the conferees about themselves and the world. The effect built a visual reminder of what had come before and helped people focus on the subject at hand. The whole of the developing backdrop gave people a sense of God's work

as they learned about it in Scripture and celebrated what he was doing in them throughout the conference.

On one campus, a fellowship met in a large, old, drab classroom. To make the space more celebrative and to help overcome the fact that most of the students had sat through way too many lectures in that room, a group of art majors worked to transform the chalkboard that traversed the entire staging area, about twenty-five feet in length. When the focus was missions, they covered the area with maps. Occasionally they covered the entire board with very well-executed chalk art. And they designed and made a banner that covered the entire chalkboard. It bore three horizontal sections: at the center was an intertwined vine and crown-of-thorns that flowed evenly across the banner, showing the interconnection between Jesus' death and the new life ("I am the Vine") he offers us; the lower section was scarlet, signifying Jesus' blood shed for us;

and the top section was purple, celebrating Jesus' royalty, and through him, ours.

When producing a musical in my college's chapel, I found that the center dome (about fifty feet up, over a dais of black marble) created a sound vacuum for anything spoken or sung under it. This was a problem, since we had a whole production moving in and out of this space. After consulting a sound engineer, we tried filling the dome with helium-inflated weather balloons. It turned out not to solve the sound problem all that much (we found other remedies), but it gave me an idea for the future! We'd always had trouble decorating the sanctuary because there was no backdrop and nowhere to hang anything. I realized that using this "technology" we could hang streamers of various materials from balloons released into the dome. We did this several times, using fabric, ribbon and paper streamers of all sorts to achieve different effects for different celebrations.

Many churches use bulletin covers bought from large publishers, but I try to get artists from our congregation to create bulletin covers that reflect the theme of each service. My home church took this idea a step beyond bulletins and invited ten artists to create ten paintings to reflect each sermon in a series. The result was a tremendous variety of excellent art. The artists, who ranged from an exceptionally talented high-school student to a professional painter, made beautiful, meaningful contributions to worship as each of them explained their work (displayed at the front of the sanctuary) on the Sunday of its use. Then all the paintings were hung together in the fellowship hall for people to review and enjoy for several more months.

Visual Symbols in Worship

Scott Wilson

The ancient Israelites surrounded themselves with visual symbols which reminded them of their relationship with God. The shapes and space divisions in the temple, the fringe on the corners of their clothes and the lines carved into the armposts of King David's throne were all visual reminders to them of aspects of God's character. The prophets often used strong visual illustrations like broken pots and even underwear to make their points. Jesus often told stories about the kingdom in settings where people could actually see the characters he described. Visual symbols are a powerful addition to worship.

Lots of things make good visual elements in worship. My church recently used a pile of broken sports equipment and appliances at the front of the sanctuary to remind people of our brokenness before God.

Beautifully wrapped presents might symbolize God's gifts to us. Many Bible passages have built-in symbols, like 2 Corinthians 4:7: "We have this treasure in clay jars." Through the years Christians have used some symbols so frequently that they have become widely known and accepted. Doves, flames, crowns, crosses, fish, bread, a lamb, a lion—these carry meaning for many Christians, and this makes them accessible and easy to use in banners and other worship art.

Three Questions to Ask When You Plan Symbols for Worship

1. What symbol will make the theme stick in people's minds?
2. What symbol can bring a fresh understanding to an idea in worship?
3. Will people get it? People should eventually understand.

Guidelines for Using Symbols in Worship

1. *Tie in symbols by referring to or explaining them in your meetings.* Not everyone thinks the same way. Even the best symbols will be obscure for some people.
2. *Don't offend people just to get their attention.* Choose appropriate symbols; this usually means those without a double meaning.
3. *Find a few strong symbols.* These have more impact than throwing a bunch together in hopes that one will make sense. Work to use a few symbols in complementary ways.
4. *Evaluate how the use of a symbol affected the worship experience.* What did people gain from using it? Check back days and then weeks later. How has it helped people to remember the symbol and the ideas or challenges it represented?

Getting Creative with Other Media

Multimedia expressions offer another realm in which to create and show visual art. I used the forty-foot, stark-white concrete walls of a very modern church building as screens to project slides illustrating a song. As a group sang a cappella, the slides, which were set on a lap dissolve (making them fade in and out, rather than flashing from one to the next like Aunt Erma's vacation pictures), created a wonderful visual effect, in part because they filled the walls and in part because they were apt illustrations of the song.

InterVarsity's Twentyonehundred Productions creates video expressions of worship songs. They make a sort of "moving stained glass" that illustrates songs and builds worshipers' connection with the lyrics. It was especially helpful to use videos with hymns such as "O for a Thousand Tongues to Sing" and "For All the Saints," where there are many lyrical images and some unusual expressions elucidated through pictures. Using videos with worship music is a little tricky since you have to incorporate use of a click track, but if you have the technology to do it, it's worth the work.

Find the visual artists in your fellowship, and invite them to join you in leading worship through their gifts. Encourage them; set aside a special offering or some budget for them to purchase materials; and pray for them as they create expressions of God's Word and work for the whole body to enjoy. You'll only have more to celebrate as you worship.

Part 7
Speaking the Word

The Preacher Is on the Worship Team!

Alison Siewert

The first time I brought up the idea of generational differences at my church staff meeting, I handed out a sheet of several quotes marked, "Some words from GenX." *"Genks? Is this a typo?"* one pastor asked. Another didn't understand the phrase "God rocks." "When you say, 'God rocks,' " she asked, "is *rocks* a noun? Like, the rocks of God? Or is it a verb? And what would that mean?"

Hmm. Sometimes the people with the same goals and from the same church and even on the same staff team can have remarkably different vocabularies. And that's a big issue when you're building new forms of worship. The worship team plans and leads the service, but the preacher usually gets to say more. And it's not at all unusual for a preaching pastor and an artistic worship team to come from different generations. The way we talk about the gospel is directly influenced by background and training, generation, cultural influences, even gender. So it's also not rare to find a pastor whose frame of reference is quite different from the others on the worship team. The people planning the service together may have very different ideas of how to communicate the same things.

Many pastors have had extensive training in homiletics—the art of preaching—in seminary and practice. I have noticed among my church staff colleagues, whose training came primarily from two large and very different seminaries, that preaching can be strongly influenced by the nuances of a seminary. Worshiping a new way may require preachers to approach the task of speaking the Word differently from the way they have always done it.

Reaching the Next Generation

Share your own experiences in connection to the text. Younger congregations—"Generation X," for instance—often appreciate stories from a pastor's own life. Appropriate self-disclosure gives you an authentic kind of authority. You aren't laying out some dispassionate explanation of the Bible's meaning but drawing people into what it means to grapple with the reality of living out the Word. I know several pastors for whom including their own stories feels awkward and even risky. However, as they've taken the steps to talk about how they've struggled and prayed with the Scripture and how God has come through for them, people have responded by valuing their teaching all the more. They can see the preacher dealing with the text, not just talking about it. The preacher's identification with the process the congregation must go through makes the Word accessible and gives people hope.

Watch your language. I lead a service which aims to be a gathering place for people who want to worship God in an intimate, informal setting. Many of the folks who worship with us are not members of our church. A majority are between twenty and thirty-five and are part of a generation who ignores delineations such as denominations and organizational structures. Talking about how Reformed we are or how the church budget is organized does not help to create the kind of warm and authentic environment we're aiming for. In fact, it can create suspicion in people who don't want to be drawn into large institutions. Our preaching team has to work hard to adjust language like,

"We Presbycostalians . . ." and "as we always do here at First Church."

Include application ideas that go outside the boundaries of institutional programs and structures. If the only calls to respond we ever make are to do organized activities like teaching Sunday school, inviting more people to the Easter pageant or getting involved in a small group, we lose the ground of trust we need with people who feel alienated from church structures.

Be a part of the planning process for worship. This is helpful in several ways. First, preachers can help shape the service from the inside out if they share which part of a text they'll focus on, what stories they'll tell and what they think God wants the congregation to hear and respond to from the Word. If you want to have integrated, meaningful worship, you need time to listen to God and to one another. Ezra and Nehemiah saw the need for Israel to reconnect with God's law, and with God himself, after a long period of exile. When they planned the service, everyone focused on this one need and how God was meeting it. The result was that Israel understood and acted on what they heard and saw. They repented and celebrated what God was doing, and their lives were never the same.

Second, it's much more effective to build worship experiences together with all who will direct and lead the congregation than only to get a Scripture verse and sermon title two days ahead of time. Most pastors are extremely busy, and few have time allotted in their schedules for being part of a worship building team. But if artistic worship leaders and pastors can come to some agreement about the potential and importance of working together, and if they can allow themselves enough time to think creatively and thoroughly about worship, they'll find it so re-

warding and useful that they'll soon seek to extend their time allowance for team processes. In one church I know, the worship team, including preachers, spends a day each month with sheets of newsprint posted around the room. They pray and talk through each of the next month's texts and brainstorm ideas not only for the sermons, but for music, responses, dance, drama—you name it. Together they select some of their best ideas, and the team members responsible for various areas take responsibility to develop those ideas and execute them. Of course, not every idea ends up coming to fruition, but because they've invested the time to think and pray together, they have more to start with if they have to change plans or re-create on short notice.

The elements of a service should work together to make a single, clear call to God's people.

Finally, working together to plan helps to sharpen all the leaders involved. Pastors can play an important role in encouraging and developing the gifts of worship leaders, who are sometimes drawn on for their gifts but not given much feedback and help. Leading worship is a very public sort of activity that exposes its practitioners to adulation but also to critique and complaint. Worship leaders need pastoral care, and pastors can help them by giving it. Preachers, who also need pastoral care which may be drawn from colleagues such as worship leaders, are just as much in the public eye. They need response and encouragement in order to grow in ministry. Preachers can benefit from a team experience by receiving constructive criticism and reflective affirmation from other worship leaders. Worship teams are often very close to the congregation and can help preachers grasp what is and isn't working: what language needs to be adjusted, where to expand storytelling. We can work on the preaching task together, even though not everyone actually gets homiletical!

Sundee Frazier & Alison Siewert

In our turn-of-the-century culture, people experience *truth* as relational rather than propositional. In other words, I know Dad loves me because he shows and tells me, not because it's been stated somewhere that fathers always love their children. This perspective changes things: A three-point sermon about why the resurrection is a basis for faith may no longer win people over. The resurrection is still a basis for faith, of course, but we have to explain and exemplify it differently. Rather than an abstract rationale for belief, our culture challenges us to present a relational God and to help people interact with the person of Jesus.

What Do People Want?

People long for meaningful relationships. They hope to find them in worshiping congregations. This part is not new. The call of the gospel includes offering ourselves in relationships where people can experience the love and truth of who God is. But if people are focusing on relationship over and against propositional truth, they may value charisma over content in a teacher. Speakers might be judged on entertainment value rather than the substantive reflection they offer in a message. In fact, the idea of "doctrine" is unknown to a very large percentage of young worshipers. Of course, what people believe makes all the difference in how they live, so we must help others develop comprehension of the Christian faith, worked out in theology, rooted in Scripture and offered by a relational God.

People want to know what works—not what's true. What will make my life worth living? What will give me hope? What could fix the seemingly irreversible problems in my life, not to mention this crumbling world? People want to know what works but also how to proceed. Listeners need to know how to apply what they hear. What am I supposed to *do* with what you're telling me? This is good for the gospel! Jesus emphasized that we must both hear and respond if we want to have more (see Mark 4:1-20).

Listeners challenge us to present a faith that's relevant to their lives. In fact, most people are concerned that teachers themselves find their own teaching relevant; they can pick up hypocrisy a mile away. We have the opportunity to tell about a living God who is active and involved in our world, and who can and does respond to all the problems we see; *and* we have the opportunity to be held accountable to live what we teach.

People want quick results. We are used to acquiring, moving and making things *fast.* As we preach with a pragmatic perspective, people may be tempted to seek immediate results. Instead, we need to help them develop a pragmatic *long-term* faith that is the hallmark of mature believers (described in Hebrews 11).

People want to take action. Accepting grace from God has been a universal human struggle. However, since modern people are increasingly aware of huge global problems and put great stock in human ingenuity to solve crises, grace seems even more unattainable—in part because they're trying to reach it rather than receive it. In response, we need to help others focus on *being,* rather than *doing.*

People desire personal experiences. Today people are more highly experiential and more visually oriented. They measure truth by experience. This is becoming the spirit of the age and not just a characteristic of younger generations. If something feels right or makes me feel good, then it must be true. "I think, therefore I am" has been replaced by "I feel, therefore I am." All of the senses, not just vision, are more highly valued than ever. Look at advertisements, which are a great barometer of culture. Ads appeal to our senses, not our logic. They often make no linear sense, but they sure stimulate visually and viscerally.

The good news is that people want to experience loving God with all their hearts, minds, souls and strength.

The good news is that people want to experience loving God with all their hearts, minds, souls and strength. Once turned to Jesus, people have a capacity to feel and speak passionately about him. The desire to experience God with all the senses makes music and other creative forms powerful vehicles for knowing God. This cultural curve, in fact, makes music and other art forms a means of discovering and developing faith. Expanding the role of the arts beyond expressing what is already known and believed makes them primary communicators of doctrine, major evangelistic tools and indispensable basics for any ministry. Worship, which has always been sensate and experiential, has moved from being only for committed believers to being a venue in which belief is demonstrated and experienced by believers *and* newcomers to Jesus.

We need to talk to God and each other about how he works to connect with people in their desire for relationship, their need for practical help, their focus on action and their commitment to personal experience. Each context is different, but we have lots to learn from one another as we minister to a changing world. Let the real needs and hopes of this world and your congregation affect how you teach, preach and lead. We can teach the whole truth but teach it in different ways if we are willing to experiment, take some risks, be uncomfortable. We must strive to present our fellowships mature in Christ (Colossians 1:28-29).

Some Practical Things to Try

Get out from behind the podium or pulpit. People want to see you up-close and personal! Leave your robe on the hanger and dress casually if that's allowable.

Keep it lively. In some cases you may need to *keep it short;* in other situations, even if time isn't an issue, you may need fewer points and more stories.

Go noteless. At the very least, don't *read* your message. Put notes on cards, and only refer to them for transitions in your outline.

43 Interactive Teaching

Sundee Frazier

The singing is over, the congregation sits and the speaker comes to the front of the room to teach. In most places the message is where everything has been leading. But have you noticed how often it's when the speaker starts speaking that the room falls flat? People who were worshiping with life in their voices just three minutes earlier have suddenly gone comatose, a glazed look coming over their faces and into their eyes? If you've spoken to groups much, you know what I'm talking about.

I often feel like I'm looking into the eyes of a crowd of television viewers: people with "TV face." It's almost like I'm not a real person. I'm a prerecorded talking head, and the people I'm addressing are the TV audience who've come to ingest another half-hour of information. Unfortunately, much of what I say is added to a mostly unused store of thousands of other bits and pieces of information. (And, by the way, I've been in the congregation enough to know that it's not just *my* speaking. The same thing happens to others too!)

The Teacher's Challenge

At this point in history, we who speak, preach and teach are facing audiences of people who are saturated with information—too much information. It is not humanly possible for us to respond to the overwhelming amount at our disposal every day. This is the greatest challenge facing teachers today, because Jesus said that our hearers' response is everything.

The good soil in the parable of the sower (Mark 4:20) represents those who hear his words and accept them. Jesus says we need to be good soil. We must accept his words.

Accepting a person's words includes integrating them into our life and acting on them. I haven't accepted my husband's request to meet him for lunch if I stand him up and go to the gym instead. We accept Jesus' words when we integrate them into our lives, use them and act on them.

Our goal as teachers is to help people integrate Jesus' teachings into their lives so they can respond to them. Without integration there is no real response. Interaction is one thing that facilitates integration. If we want our message to be absorbed into peoples' daily lives, then we need to *help them interact with that message*. And we need to *develop interaction between them*—times where people can work together to talk and think about what they're hearing. Ultimately, we need to offer opportunities for interaction between our hearers and *Jesus*.

Some bemoan the influence of the TV, computer and Internet—major sources of our information glut. One positive point of their influence is that they've increased people's hunger for engaging stories and interaction. Jesus was the master storyteller and interactive teacher. His teaching was engaging because it was full of the drama, stories and tensions of life—like a good TV series. He used visual aids often, like the World Wide Web. And he prompted response from and interaction with his audience, like CD-ROM programs do. He knew how to engage the whole person with his words, and he wants us to learn how to do the same. We must, or we will lose generations of people who, from here on out, are going to retain only that information which seems most immediately useful in their busy, overcrowded lives. It's a good time for us to return to the interactive methods of teaching that Jesus used.

Encouraging Interaction Between People

God's truth is relational. Relationships are becoming more important and desirable to people, even though many of us are increasingly unable to build and sustain deep ones. Give your congregation a chance to interact with what they've heard in a sermon in the context of relationships by having them get in small groups right after you speak. Allow them to discuss what stood out to them personally from the talk, or give them a specific question to answer or an assignment to carry out. After a message about how Jesus came to serve and not be served, I might ask people to break up into groups of four, share one specific need they have and then pray together in trust that Jesus wants to serve them by meeting those needs.

If your context allows for this, you can also have people get into groups to create and then perform simple skits that illustrate what you've been teaching. In our fellowship at Lehigh University, after a semester's worth of teachings from the Beatitudes, the students got into small groups, and I gave each group a Beatitude and asked them to create a skit illustrating its meaning. To get their creativity flowing, I told them that every skit had to have the same three components: a watch, an old man and two dollars. The result was a lot of laughter, some good teamwork and relationship building, and a positive experience. The interaction got people to think about what they had been learning and what it really meant. Of course, preparing and performing the skits took up the whole meeting, and left no teaching time. But it was a good use of time because it reminded people of the truth they had heard in previous weeks. Through interacting with each other, they interacted with the Word and had fun in the process.

Encouraging Interaction with God

Give others a chance to relate to God corporately and individually in the context of learning from him through the teaching. Interaction with God is our ultimate goal for worshipers.

I'll never forget when we had a speaker teach on the parable of the friend at midnight (Luke 11:5-13). Most Christians (and many nonbelievers) have heard Jesus' command to "ask, seek and knock." But how many of us are really bold enough to do as Jesus commands through this parable? After the speaker had finished teaching on how we can be bold because we have a heavenly Father who loves us and wants to give us good gifts, she asked us to pray as a large group right there and then. She exhorted us to pray out loud and boldly for whatever we needed, one at a time. It took quite a while for someone to begin (proving that we don't really believe Jesus' invitation to ask, seek and knock, or maybe that we're too afraid of what others think of our prayers.) As I sat there trying to think of the exact phrasing with which to make my request, I realized that I too, as a full-time Christian worker, was holding back. It was a powerful lesson for me, and since then I've tried not to hold back with my heavenly Father or worry about how I sound, whether I'm praying in a group or alone.

You can also give listeners the chance to interact with God one-on-one. Quiet reflection times (with or without questions to prompt thinking) will help them begin to assimilate what they've heard and to apply it to themselves. Quiet worship music playing in the background helps some people. At times I've also used music as the focal point of reflection after a sermon. I choose a song with lyrics that reinforce the point of the message and then have people listen to it, giving them a chance to experience hearing from God through another medium.

Giving Multiple Options for Response

One feature that makes the World Wide Web so appealing is the number of options for response it gives its users. Give people multiple options for how they can apply what they're hearing. One person's acceptance of Jesus' teaching might look very different from another's! Consider your worshipers. No matter how homogeneous your group, people are at different stages—spiritually, emotionally and experientially. How might you break down application of your message to relate to, say, three different groups represented by your listeners?

When I spoke on being persecuted because of Jesus (Matthew 5:11), I ended by saying, "You are probably in one of three places right now." And then I went on to describe those three places. The first application was for those who didn't really believe Jesus is the only hope for every person in the world. I encouraged these people to study more, reading and investigating Jesus and what he says about himself. I told them to ask God to show them how Jesus is a person's only hope. I said they ought not give up until they were convinced one way or the other. The second application was for those who already believed this but who hadn't considered that there are people in their lives God is calling to know him. I encouraged them to start praying for these people, that they would come to have a relationship with Jesus. The third group were those who already pray for people's salvation but who have never tried telling anyone about Jesus. I pointed out that anyone who they consider a friend should know about their relationship with Jesus and how important he is to them. Finally, I invited everyone to share with the person next to them which of the three applications fit them and what next steps they were going to take in response to Jesus' teaching.

Later, a student wrote to me (via the Internet, of course!) that she was in the second group of people I mentioned. She had a classmate she had criticized in her heart because he was loud and obnoxious. The next time she went to class after she heard me speak, he came to class drunk. She realized there was a lot of pain behind his rudeness and that he was someone God was putting in her life for her to pray for. Having multiple options for response helped her see there was a step of faith she could take to apply Scripture. She wasn't ready yet to share the gospel with her classmate, but she could pray for him regularly. This step represented a big change in her heart because she had only been critical of him before.

Give people multiple options for response, and they will more likely realize it is possible for them to act on what they're hearing. All-or-nothing applications are appropriate at times, but often they intimidate people into choosing nothing rather than going for the next step. But Jesus' hope and ours is that they will step out in faith.

Tips for the Interactive Teacher

I hope that contemplating the challenges that face us as teachers has only bred excitement (and not dread) in you. God is giving us the opportunity to work alongside Jesus by helping others engage with and respond to the Word. He also offers us the opportunity to develop our own creativity, to become more like Jesus in our teaching styles and to have fun along the way!

Imagine how you might encourage interaction with God, his Word and others in your congregation. Recruit a couple of creative partners, throw off your limitations and let yourselves dream up the craziest schemes imaginable. After you've ventured to the edges, then and only then go back and modify your plan based on reality (time, money, people resources). Ultimately, you don't have to have a lot of money, or even use that much more time or energy, to incorporate interactive components in your teaching. God provided everything Jesus needed to help people integrate and respond to the gospel.

If you haven't already, explore the World Wide Web. Try an interactive computer program (CD-ROM *Monopoly* is fun!). See what interactive media is like for yourself, because more and more people (not just kids) are using these resources on a regular basis at work and at home. This is becoming one of our culture's key sources of information and diversion. It can be a great asset to us if we are familiar with it and understand why it is so compelling to those thoroughly engaged by it. Ultimately, Jesus, his words and his people are much more compelling. But we need to cooperate with him for others to see that this is so.

Finally, don't give in to the mentality that you must entertain. You don't have to keep people laughing just so they'll stay with you and maybe get the deeper point you're trying to make. But humor is a component of what makes someone an effective teacher. (Jesus certainly had a great sense of humor, and his keen wit shows up in many of his teachings.) Our goal is to open up channels through which people can hear from God; we need not work for their approval. Interactive teaching does not require compromising on content. Interaction can take the content of God's Word deeper, implanting his truth, not replacing it.

44 Using Visual Aids

●●

Sundee Frazier

The fact that Jesus used visual and tactile aids in his teaching tells me there is something universal about our need to learn with the help of concrete objects, pictures and examples. It's not just a modern thing—it's a human thing. Having something visual and concrete allows us to interact with it on more than just a conceptual level. We need to learn from Jesus how to use the commonplace and material to teach about spiritual realities.

Jesus: The Ultimate Visual Aid Expert

When Jesus wants to teach his disciples the true definition of greatness, he tells them the greatest people are servants of everyone. To make his point clear, he puts a child in the midst of them. When none of them embraces the child, Jesus does, and says, "Whoever welcomes one such child in my name welcomes me, and whoever welcomes me welcomes not me but the one who sent me" (Mark 9:37).

With poignant visual clarity, Jesus says without words, "The greatest are those who take in and show compassion to the weak, such as this child here."

When Jesus wants to teach his disciples how great the value of a single life is, he lets a herd of two thousand swine—most likely an entire town's livelihood—be destroyed so that one man can have his life back. Talk about a lesson that won't be forgotten! When he wants to teach them about the provision and generosity of God, Jesus feeds more than five thousand people with five loaves of bread and two fish and makes sure that each disciple gets a basketful of leftovers to carry back. Jesus puts a tactile aid into their hands to teach them what they had recited for years and years in synagogue school: that God is good, and his steadfast love endures forever.

Can't you just see Jesus holding a sparrow as he says, "You are of more value than many of these"? Or pointing to the birds in the trees as he says, "Consider the ravens: they neither sow nor reap . . . and yet God feeds them. Of how much more value are you than the birds!"? (Luke 12:24). With a mere coin he challenges the Pharisees and Herodians to give themselves to the One to whom they belong, the Creator in whose image they are made. And he uses a dead tree (one that he had cursed and caused to wither) as an illustration of the end of the temple and its corrupt administrators.

> *This picture helped the congregation grasp the emotional weight of the words they were hearing and not just their theological implications.*

Teaching with visual aids helps people learn about God. This was Jesus' method, and it can be ours too. Maybe we won't ever cast demons into swine, but we can bring a child up to the podium to make a point.

Five Ways to Use Visual Aids

1. *Take a cue from the Bible.* All of Scripture (not just Jesus' teachings) is full of images from the natural world. It's ripe with ideas for "show and tell" in our teaching. "For as the heavens are higher than the earth, so are my ways higher than your ways and my thoughts than your thoughts" (Isaiah 55:9). That's a powerful statement. It's also a visual statement. What if you have your congregation sit outside on the day you speak from this passage so they can look up and be reminded of just how high God's thoughts are above ours? That would be a memorable sermon. Maybe you can't take your whole congregation outdoors because the group is too large or because you're preaching from this text in the dead of winter, but perhaps you can have everyone look out a sanctuary window. Work with what you have, but by all means do what you can! Don't give up because something doesn't seem feasible.

2. *Be creative.* When you teach with visual and tactile aids, the sky is literally the limit! One church had a potter come and cast the face of Jesus on her pottery wheel while the speaker taught on the crucifixion. When the speaker began to describe the scourging of Jesus, the potter, sitting on the stage next to the speaker, struck the clay face she had made, leaving gashes and making the face look beaten. This picture helped the congregation grasp the emotional weight of the words they were hearing and not just their theological implications.

3. *Use technology.* My husband once used a picture downloaded from the World Wide Web—a sailboat, *The Stars and Stripes,* in dry dock. The photo, projected on a large screen behind him as he spoke, illustrated a point about making sure we have a "large keel" (depth of character) underneath the water (behind our façades) to ensure that we won't tip over in the race of life. The visual image added memorable visual strength to a powerful metaphor.

4. *Give people a reminder to take home.* I once handed out a rock to each person in the congregation after a talk on John 8 (the woman caught in adultery). I wanted it to be a tangible reminder that God wants to forgive all our sins and calls us to forgive others who we might be tempted to "stone." Many months later, a student told me she remembered the talk vividly because of the rock. She still had it. After a talk on God the promise-keeper, I passed out promises from Scripture that I had typed on slips of paper. I asked people to pray in pairs that God would help them believe the promise they held in their hands and give them an opportunity to see how he was keeping that promise to them sometime that week.

5. Tell a visual story. Jesus taught with stories, which are visual too. If you don't have a concrete visual aid, you can still tell stories and create word-pictures, offering mental images for listeners to grasp.

Note: If you do use visual aids and you have blind members in your congregation, make sure someone sits with them to describe the visuals when they are shown. This will help to include those brothers or sisters in the experience.

45 Testimonies

Matt Frazier

Testimonies can be a powerful way of communicating God's nature to a worshiping congregation. Sometimes, they're remembered better by a congregation than a sermon because they are real-life examples of the struggles, joys and faith of real people. Strictly speaking, giving a testimony simply means saying what you've seen. It's about telling others what you've seen God do. It doesn't have to be about the day you converted to Christianity. It can be about how you saw God work last year, last week or even yesterday!

Effective testimonies are brief (they often last five to eight minutes) and focus on one central conflict that is resolved by God. It's tempting to tell every detail of a story about God working in your life until you end up with a forty-minute soliloquy of monumental theological complexity. Be careful not to preach a whole sermon (testimonies shouldn't be preachy or didactic), and be cautious not to tell your entire life story.

A Sample Outline
Define the tension. I was a self-righteous Christian, and I was secretly taking drugs.

Identify how the tension got addressed. I was in a Bible study, and God spoke to me.

Describe what you did to respond faithfully. I made a hard choice to cut off a sinful lifestyle and to confess my duplicity to others.

Show how God has changed and blessed you since. My friends and family can't believe how different I am, and I enjoy God and Christian community instead of being self-righteous and secretive.

Each of these points should have specific details filled in and should be told in a way that others can relate to. It's important to tell people about yourself, but your testimony is ultimately about what God has done for, in or through you.

Practice a testimony with a friend before you share it with a group. This will help you feel more comfortable with the material you're going to share. You can also check your time by going through it just like you'll do it. If you realize you have too many themes in your story, cut something. It will be better for others to listen well to the few things you say than to be overwhelmed or unable to take in information that simply distracts from your point.

If you're a worship leader, use testimonies to celebrate God's work among the people you lead. Ask someone who has been experiencing growth in their relationship with Jesus to share a testimony with your congregation. Use this chapter and your own experience to coach and help them prepare. Call on people to testify, to encourage your whole community. Testimonies offer hope that as God has worked in the lives of people telling their stories, so he'll work in the lives of those who hear them.

46 Reading Scripture

• •

Alison Siewert

I've heard some really bad Scripture reading. One church I attended had a very formal, almost pompous style of reading. The pastor set the tone with a sort of James Earl Jones-in-a-tux feel. It wasn't exactly bad. Here you were, going along in worship, singing some choruses and a few hymns, greeting each other, and then it was . . . Shakespeare time! When the pastor read, it was, well, kind of odd. Unfortunately, when other readers tried to do the pastor's style, *then* it was, well, kind of bad.

I'm pretty sure that when David wrote, "Bless the LORD, O my soul, and all that is within me, bless his holy name" (Psalm 103:1), he was neither overdramatic nor boring, flat and dry. The psalms, like other parts of Scripture, were written by real people who were really experiencing what they wrote. And I doubt that Mark, on finishing his Gospel, put down the pen and thought, "Well, it's a little drab, but it gets the information straight." If God is who we say he is, our voices should sound convinced. And if the Scriptures are true, then our reading should reflect it. The Bible wasn't written in monotones, and it shouldn't be read that way, either. As Dorothy L. Sayers said, "If this is dull, then what, in Heaven's name, is worthy to be called exciting?"*

Read it like you wrote it.

There are plenty of places where reading is not a universal skill. Literacy is not available to every Christian in the world. Throughout Christian history the telling out loud of the gospel story has been a foundation of worship as well as evangelism and discipleship. To speak the words of the Scripture is one of the most radical, lifegiving things we can do, because it allows ordinary people to hear the thoughts and history and promises of God, to learn the story of Yahweh and his people. Since not everyone can or will read the Bible, and because the sophistication of electronic media has raised standards for things seen and heard, it's critical that we get the story out in a compelling and caring way.

Study the passage, in a group if you can. To read Scripture well requires understanding it to some extent. If you have a choice of readers, choose people who are in some kind of regular Bible study together. You might even encourage your fellowship to offer opportunities to study the week's text together. My home church has fifty people meeting every Wednesday at lunch to study the same text (usually a series from

---

*Dorothy Sayers, "The Greatest Drama Ever Staged," in *Creed or Chaos* (Norwich, England: Jarrold & Sons, 1954), p. 3.

one book) that will be preached the following Sunday. So at least fifty people have some idea of what it's about. That's a pretty good start for a pool of readers.

Teach your readers. If you're not good at reading, find someone who is and who can teach other people. Perhaps you have an actor, a teacher, a radio person or a translator in your group. Many professions and hobbies cultivate good reading and speaking skills. If you only have one or two skilled people available, get them to develop skills

end the reading. Some forethought about transitions in and out of readings will help you avoid distractions and keep the parts of the service more connected.

Train all your readers evenly. My husband, an expressive and confident reader and worship leader, got up to lead the responsive Scripture reading at the start of a service. Most of the time the people who read these are nearly bored. Dan got up and read, "Praise the Lord! I will give thanks to the Lord with all my heart," as though he really meant it. He read it like he had written it. He identified with the psalmist in his joy and said it from his and the psalmist's shared point of view. The congregation was shocked. They were so accustomed to boredom that they were perplexed by excitement. They read the response, "In the company of the upright and in the assembly, I will praise the Lord," with a kind of stunned amazement.

My hope is that we won't respond with surprise to good reading because we'll help people learn to read Scripture with all the passion, force, clarity, thrill, depth, drama and confidence it evokes. Real people wrote

Reading the Whole Story   Alison Siewert

Have you ever considered spending an entire worship time reading Scripture? Five members of the worship team at my home church performed the Gospel of Mark—the whole thing—at one of our services. We divided the gospel into segments by stories and events, and retold them simply but vividly as a performance. There were no costumes or props, no intricate moves, no dialogues—just basic lighting, stands for our reading texts and stools for us to sit on. We wore plain jeans and T-shirts, and created a simple, abstract backdrop.

We spent several weeks reading, studying and rehearsing on our own and together. Most of us had done extensive study in Mark's Gospel, so we knew the material well from a Bible-study perspective. But the challenge was to tell it as a story, engaging people and making characters and events as lively as they were to Mark and the others who were there to see them. We wanted people to get a taste (Hey, we wanted to get a taste of it too!) of what it was like for first-century people to hear these stories told and retold—before they took on the gilt-edged packaging of our modern Bibles. We tried to almost memorize our texts so that we could focus on meaning and expression.

The results were worshipful, to be sure. People loved hearing the whole of the story told at one time, and told in a way that moved them, encouraged them and gave them a clear picture of Jesus. It was cool for us to see our congregation respond not to the usual songs and sermons but just to the Word itself and the portrait of God in Mark.

in others. Invite people to learn to read—Scripture, that is—and create a short training course. You should explore how to study the text for meaning, how to express that meaning as you read and how to use microphones or to speak loudly enough without them. And though this may seem very basic, you should work on how to get up and down and how to introduce and

about their real experiences with God, and it is left for us to understand them well enough to reconnect our hearts and the congregations' ears with the author's original intent and God's overwhelming work. Read it like *you* wrote it. And may God continue to write new words on our hearts in worship.

Part 8
Putting It Together

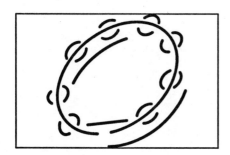

47 The Movements of Worship

Alison Siewert

When two of my friends recently married, they held a reception that gave me a great picture of worship. First the couple entered the room, and the emcee introduced them as "Mr. and Mrs."—helping us remember (not that we had forgotten) and celebrate that they had just been married. Then the couple led the whole reception in feasting on all the elegant, delicious food that had been laid out for us—enjoying the abundance of life together ahead of them. There was a time of toasting in a Canadian tradition (the groom's background) where a dozen close friends and family members stood in a prescribed order and blessed the couple and their future—creating expectation for the fulfillment of promise in their lives. Finally, the groom eloquently toasted the bride—an exquisite act of adoration that moved everyone in the room and made us ready to dance for joy at what God was doing in their relationship. (Of course, the wedding reception lacked a time of confession and repentance: I don't think any of us would want silent confession in the midst of cake cutting!)

I've been in worship services that do a great deal to be hip and contextual, lively and theologically correct. But even the most sophisticated and technically masterful worship service isn't necessarily worshipful. The critical transaction in a worship time is *worship*—it's people adoring God, seeing God for who he really is, celebrating a God who is worthy of all our celebration. The byproduct of worship is that we also come to see ourselves for who we really are, which, of course, leads us directly into more worship. It's a little like an onion, happening in layers without end.

Planning worship is fundamentally a pastoral task, a work of guiding God's people, and it helps to think of it that way. The journey we make is toward God, to enjoy him and be enjoyed by him. This is a reflection of comprehending who God is in light of who we are. But we can break that journey down into some movements of worship that may give us an idea of how to plan and work with the substance of worship, what each part of worship means.

> *The journey we make is toward God, to enjoy him and be enjoyed by him.*

I'll list some movements of worship for you here. They might not always be described in the same way, and they don't always have to go in this order. But you can use this list to help you think about your worship experiences and the worship you see in Scripture.

Ask for Help

In "O for a Thousand Tongues to Sing" Charles Wesley made a request for help in worship and witness: "My gracious Master, and my God, assist me to proclaim, to spread through all the earth abroad the honors of your Name!" We need God's help to worship him. We cannot, even with our most forceful effort, produce hearts of worship on our own. Our hearts, mucked up in sin and pride and distrust of God, must be in God's hands if we want to worship him. Like Saul (Acts 9:8, 18), we need the scales removed from our eyes in order to see Jesus clearly and to welcome a relationship with him. On our own we can't worship God (let alone lead others to worship him). So we need to pray, to ask God for help even as we

What Time Is It?   Alison Siewert

Start decisively and on time. Have your guitars tuned, your music in place, your hair combed, your technical teams at their stations *before* you get up to lead. And start on time. You create an expectation for confident, prepared leadership or for sloppy and uncertain guidance from the minute you begin. Even if you're nervous, pray, smile and go for a good start!

And end on time. Every worship context carries its own set of expectations. If you live or worship in an event-oriented context, it may be fine to let worship continue until it's "done" and you feel God has released you to end the service. Many traditions encourage services to go on for the sake of hearing more of God, seeing people receive healing and prayer, and encouraging ongoing praise. If you're in that sort of situation, enjoy the open-ended time it can provide.

If you worship in a linear context that tends to be very time-conscious, create clear expectations for service length, and stick with them as much as possible. Be prepared to adjust your musical sets and announcements if you need to. When I know a preacher tends to go long or additional elements are included in the service (such as a commissioning or baptism), I prepare the worship team in advance by identifying which songs we won't do if we need to trim the service.

Of course, we should never override a clear prompting from the Spirit just because it isn't convenient to our schedules. But going longer than planned may require interpretation and even giving people an opportunity to leave if they need to. You may need to offer, "It seems as though God is calling many to prayer. But I know that the child-care workers require parents to pick up their children in the next five minutes, and some of you may have other commitments. If you need to go, please feel free to do so; if you're able to stay and pray for others, or if you'd like to be prayed for, you are invited to remain. The worship team will lead us in singing so we can continue as God moves us." If you start on time and think sensitively about God's leading and your group's needs, you'll bless people by helping them focus on worshiping every minute you're together.

start on the journey of worship. Find some ways to do this as you prepare and then begin leading a worship service.

Remember

It's important to remember what God has done. The people of Israel got lost when they forgot who God was and what he was like. And forgetting God's work through ancient, global and immediate, personal histories puts our hearts in danger of ungratefulness, distrust and stubbornness based on the way things feel or seem at the moment. It's important for the gathered people of God to review God's work among them and rejoice in a Lord who has proven himself good and trustworthy over time. Remembering helps us to override heart conditions that defy worship. Worship is not about how we feel emotionally; it's about who God actually is. So taking some time to get clear on that point can help our hearts line up on days we just can't locate the impulse to leap into the sanctuary shouting, "Praise the Lord!"

Adore

Upon remembering God's goodness and at many other points in a worship time, people need opportunities to respond in praise and thanksgiving to God. To adore God is to enjoy him thoroughly from many angles: as redeemer, provider, healer, creator, judge, adoptive parent, dancer, way, truth, life—there are so many! When we adore God, we acknowledge our right place in the relationship as children, creatures, dependents. To attribute worth to God is to speak and hear and celebrate what's really true of him.

That is what was so moving about my friends' wedding reception. It was one of those marriages that everyone could see was brought about by God's hand, so it was a pleasure to speak truly about how lovely a thing this was, how blessed, how beautiful. All you had to do was look at the couple and know the story to see what a great thing was happening and to appreciate it. When the groom toasted the bride, his words were some of the most apt praise I've ever heard. He clearly knew who he was marrying and saw her for the amazing person she is. His words of adoration, publicly expressed, confirmed and filled out what all of us had witnessed for ourselves.

Confess

When we see God rightly and see ourselves rightly, how can we do anything but confess how we have not attributed him worth? We need opportunity in worship to be honest about our sin, to admit how we have attempted to usurp God by playing gods in our own lives and others', how we have thrown contempt on Jesus by calling him untrustworthy. And we need opportunity to receive from him forgiveness and restoration, to be healed from the wounds made by our own sin and the sins of others against us. We can be motivated to confession by God's promise to heal and restore us.

Receive

"If we confess our sins, he who is faithful and just will forgive us our sins and cleanse us from all unrighteousness" (1 John 1:9). Worship can be an extraordinarily free place to re-

ceive forgiveness and cleansing from God.

A few years ago several members of my team fell into serious sin. We had lived and worked closely together but found ourselves painfully pulled apart. We had heard confession and suspended our normal planning processes to spend months praying and rebuilding broken relationships. Nine months later, we met for a retreat to listen to God. In our opening time we heard from the several staff who had been rescued from sin. They shared what they were learning, how God had healed them and what it meant for them still to be a part of our team and following Jesus. Then we prayed in thanksgiving for their lives and hearts and our restored team. At the end of the prayer time someone asked if we could sing "Amazing Grace." I never knew that song was so true as I did in that moment. We shared an extraordinary time of God's blessing: his mercy, his healing and his restoration of our team.

Go Out

We come to worship knowing we cannot remain in its assembly long. But worship can and must remain within us, assembled in our hearts as we leave its sanctuary. To practice true worship is to live it out. As we attribute God worth, as we receive his blessing and healing, we become more like him. We grow up to look more and more like our Father. To go out from worship is to enter the world reveling in God's parenthood.

48 Coffee, Guitars, Jesus
Planning Worship for Informal Settings

Alison Siewert

One of the most important tasks a worship leader performs is putting worship together. No matter how well your team plays or how great your songs are, good organization and clear communication are basic to any service. Worship is a process of communication between the congregation and God, and God and his people, but it's also between the worship leaders and congregation. In liturgical traditions, much of the planning is done by the liturgy itself. Worship moves through a series of responses that have been refined and burnished by decades, even centuries, of worshipers and leaders. But in nontraditional settings planning can seem more of a mystery.

Most often I've found that nontraditional worship actually does have a liturgy. Churches and fellowships who've never opened a hymnal or prayer book tend to follow a pattern that could be described as liturgy, or a system of worship. That's not to suggest you must follow a pattern, only that most of us do. It's helpful to consider what kind of pattern you actually want, rather than doing three songs, a sermon, the announcements and a song just because that's how the service has always been. One of the advantages of a nontraditional setting is that you have many options available. However you go about it, you should develop a general sense of what elements you want, where you want them and how they fit together to build a worship experience. You might want to build a service from a basic outline and change it as needed for particular services. This is easier than creating a service from scratch every time—how exhausting!

Many informal worship meetings take place outside regular church sanctuaries, at unusual times, and are geared to welcome specific people groups. It's important for you to have some vision for where you're headed in the overall picture. For example, you may want to offer food or drink: I've often wondered why the churches avoid eating and drinking in services, when the first Christians, it seems, combined food and worship on a regular basis. In one church I've worked with, they offer coffee and doughnuts to people as they enter the room for worship. It's very cool to help people wake up so they can really enjoy God, and the church has become very attractive to people in their twenties who are adjusting to the early hours of the working world and never feel excited about *weekend* mornings. The food and drink smooth the way for them. My InterVarsity chapter had a dinner—appropriately titled "Dinner Together"—after our worship meetings. It gave us an opportunity to talk about how God met us in worship and what we learned from the Scripture, and to become friends. There are as many options for worship settings as there are fellowships. Discover yours through prayer, discussion, study and listening.

When you've developed a vision for the service, you can get down to the planning process for regular meetings. Think in terms of the congregation's experience. Your group will need information and direction about what is happening and why.

Show the Group What to Do
Your group will need basic directions from the leader in order to act as a group, to ex-

perience community and to work together with you and each other to worship God. With enough information, people are freed up to focus only on the worship at hand; with too little information they become distracted by anxiety over what is happening next. Have you ever been in a worship time where the worship leader didn't give clear direction? It can be very difficult to find your way through the ambiguities—particularly if you're a newcomer! Your attention can shift very quickly to worrying about what you're supposed to do next and what might happen if you do the wrong thing out-of-turn. So if you're going to kneel, tell everyone clearly that this is what you're going to do. If there's openness to raising or not raising hands, and you want people to feel free to do either, let them know.

The worship leader is like a tour guide, pointing out things that might be missed and connections that aren't obvious in order to make the experience more meaningful.

Tell Them Why They're Doing It

Several times I've been asked (usually by more tradition-oriented people), "Why do you keep repeating the chorus? Why not sing it once and get on with it?" This may seem obvious to those of us accustomed to new worship—we repeat things in order to move from information to meditation—but it's *not* obvious to everyone! People are helped into worship by the guidance of a worship leader. Like a tour guide, your job is to help others focus on the things that are most significant and to understand how God is connecting with the congregation in worship.

It's okay to talk as you lead worship. Many worship teams like to use a musical segue between every song to "keep the worship flowing," but often, brief introductions can help people to move into worship even more fully.

Think of yourself as a guide to the throne of God, and look for ways to point people toward the meaning of their experience.

To do a good job of communicating about the service, you have to take time to plan it! It's popular in some circles to resist advance planning in favor of "letting the Spirit lead." But to limit the Holy Spirit only to spontaneity is as limiting as limiting him to your plans! In the Scripture we see clearly that God's Spirit works in both ways: well ahead *and* in-the-moment. (And really, what may seem spontaneous to us is deliberate on God's part.) An effective worship leader is sensitive to the whole of the spectrum. If you plan ahead, you'll have the opportunity to include the whole worship team (pastors and other leaders too) and you'll have more time to be creative. You can always adjust your plans to God's.

How to Build a Worship Design

Pray. Ask God for insight, creativity and wisdom about how to lead your congregation into life-changing worship. Aaron was to carry the names of all the families of Israel over his heart every time he went before God (Exodus 28:29). We also must carry our congregations in prayer and on our hearts from the very beginning of our leading. If you are leading the team, you need some time prior to your team meetings to pray on your own. You might also invite some supportive friends to pray for and with you and your team on a regular basis.

Gather a team. The synergy created by a group of people thinking and talking about a service is much greater than even the best energies of an individual. And if some of your partners can be people on the worship team, all the better. When they stand up front, these people will lead with a deeper understanding of why you're doing various things as a part of worship. Try to delegate authority and responsibility for various areas of the worship experience. You can't, and shouldn't, do everything. Find someone who's really gifted to build hospitality into the meeting; invite a talented writer to create sketches. Take the opportunity to function as an interrelated, interdependent body.

Organize. At least twice a year, clean out the "worship closet," and you'll benefit enormously from your effort. Make a list of your group's repertoire and equipment, gather your lyrics and put them in alphabetical order. Create a schedule for your musical and other arts teams and your technicians. Keep old worship plans in a file so you can keep track of what you've done and when. Gather a roster of people with special talents you can call on. Use these lists to stimulate ideas for your weekly plans.

Clarify the themes for worship. If your meeting includes a talk or sermon, get the preacher involved in planning. Talk together about the themes of the message, important points and any significant illustrations. You can synthesize much better—and your speaker can connect with the music and other worship elements much better—if you have some images and ideas in mind. (See chapter 41).

Make a song list. The way I get a plan rolling is to list all the songs in our repertoire that apply or relate to the current theme, as well as any songs I sense God leading me to employ. If our topic is Jesus the Living Water, I might list "Thirst No More," "Living Water," "As We Gather at the River" and "Come, Thou Fount of Ev'ry Blessing," for starters. This exercise helps me explore the theme and its subtexts and opens me to more than the obvious.

Know your resources. Take a look at your worship team. Who is available for what? There are some weeks I have a violinist participating in our music. I need to know as I

plan that I can include music that draws on his gifts. One man on our team is a professional actor. When he's helping to lead, I know I can write a sketch with at least one challenging part, because I have someone who can handle it easily. On the other hand, I might have a week when all our percussionists are on retreat, and I won't plan heavy percussion into the music because I've accounted for this ahead of time. Figure out who and what gifts you have to work with.

Work out a plan. Making a plan is making decisions. You decide what is most important and most effective for leading your group into worship. Has God given you any specific direction for this worship time? Pay attention to the Spirit's prompting. God will never steer you wrong about worship! Ask yourself some questions: What will help people celebrate? Understand? Confess? Receive forgiveness and freedom? How will you encourage worshipers to live differently as a result of their time in worship? I reflect on these issues as I begin to choose songs and work them into sets.

As you plan, envision the worship. Get a sense for how the worship will flow, and double-check your plan. Some worship leaders even sing through a few bars of each song to test the feel and flow of the worship. Pay attention to the following:

1. Tempos. Do we have upbeat songs in the right places? And more meditative songs where needed?

2. Lyrics. Do the words complement each other from song to song and from song to reading? Do they work together to invite people more and more deeply into God's presence? How do translations of foreign-language songs fit in? New songs?

3. Transitions. Where are the transitions (for example, from a quiet, reflective mood to a time of thanksgiving)? Do they make sense? Where do we want breaks in the action, and where do we want to go immediately into the next thing?

Of course, you can't anticipate everything that will happen in worship, but I've witnessed many awkward, non sequitur and low-energy moments in worship that could have been avoided by doing this step.

Make sure you have everything you need. Call folks ahead to let them know if you have something special for them to do. Make a logistics checklist covering everything you need to take care of. This may include items as basic as "meet custodian to have room unlocked and turn on air conditioning" or as complex as "call technician to adjust lighting for scene 2 of sketch." Whatever it is, make sure it's on the list. If others are working with you, give everyone a list, make responsibilities clear and plan time to follow up if necessary. As much as you're able, plan not to be the person responsible for things like adjusting lights and having rooms unlocked. You need to focus on letting God prepare your heart and how he's leading his people. An important step in planning is to *plan yourself out of some tasks!*

Rehearse. The main goal of your rehearsal time should be to prepare your team to lead. This is different from working out groovy riffs or making the sketch funny. A good worship team leads people into worship by doing things easily and well and by avoiding distraction, so that both team and congregation can focus on God who is the object of adoration. A wrong chord or missed cue can divert people's attention from God to the worship team. Now, God is able to overcome our weakness—we need not be nervous about our inadequacies overwhelming him!—but we bear responsibility to love our congregations by doing our homework. During rehearsal you may find that some ideas didn't work as well as you thought they would, or that your team isn't ready to do a particular song. Give yourself time to adjust things.

Worship. Toward the end of rehearsal I like to go back through some of what we've already been over, but with the focus on worshiping. This helps us hear the songs and words and silence we'll be using to lead others as a worshipful experience for ourselves first.

Once you've done these things, you've *planned* worship. Lead your team into the worship gathering with confidence, and be ready for the God you praise to work in your life and in the lives of those he's gathered with you.

49 Fitting into a Traditional Worship Service

· ·

Andy Crouch

While many churches and fellowships have whole worship services of the sort we've been describing in this book—using contemporary music and very little formal liturgy—you may want to incorporate some of the elements of what we're describing into more traditionally liturgical settings. Here are some ideas for bringing the two together.

Including More Music
One of the great gifts of the contemporary worship movement is the extended time that's given to music, allowing a theme to develop and people's hearts to focus in a way that they cannot when music happens in one-song segments. Try looking for points in the service where extended musi-

cal worship makes sense. Early in the service is a great time for a medley of songs. If your liturgy includes communion, you may have a built-in time when congregational music can add immensely. You may also want to include some extra music after the sermon as a way of leading the congregation in response to the Word.

Don't be afraid to use music in unexpected places—you may be surprised how much freedom is actually present (even encouraged) in even the most formal liturgical traditions. I've found some wonderful places for music that aren't usually used. Appropriate music can follow the confession and declaration of pardon or absolution; it can follow (or if your church allows this, stand in place of) the affirmation of faith; and it can provide a way for a large congregation to express their prayers together. One of the most beautiful opportunities for musical worship is during the offertory or the setting of the communion table.

Transitions Between Music and Liturgy

As you plan and lead, it is very important to understand that in liturgi-

Everyone Loves a Good Announcement

Alison Siewert

Part of living in Christian community is sharing information and doing things together, so announcements are often a feature of worship gatherings. Here are a few tips to make your announcements effective and focused.

1. *Keep 'em short.* If you have several things that need to be communicated, write them down and hand them out in a bulletin or announcement sheet. You could do the restaurant-daily-special thing and write them on a board for people to read as they enter. You can even go movie theater and project them on a screen as people first sit down.

2. *Don't announce anything unless absolutely necessary.* If it can be written, write it. If it involves just a segment of the group, use the phone chain or e-mail or skywrite it. You might even be able to avoid announcements altogether: Newsletter? Postcard? When you can, do anything but announce.

3. *Organize those puppies.* Put the announcements in some kind of logical order so you don't go from the memorial garden to the bake sale to the new Bible study in Obadiah and back to the memorial garden.

4. *Get them on paper.* Rather than having people stand up and give random announcements, ask for written announcements at least an hour before the service or meeting.

5. *Announce only the most essential details.* People won't remember long lists of minutiae, so skip them. Include essentials (date, time, place and one-sentence purpose) but omit fascinating details such as which letters of the alphabet bring a hot dish and which ones bring salad.

6. Briefly *impart meaning to the announcements.* Why is it really important that everyone come to the alternative Christmas gift market?

7. *Create announcements that create the atmosphere you want to create.* If you are attempting to make your service welcoming to newcomers, avoid announcing lots of "insider" events and appealing to institutional structures or traditions. Beware of jokes and references that may be clear to long-time members but puzzling to new people. Don't assume people know how it's always done: Give quick, friendly and basic explanations.

8. *Now is not the time.* If you have a time designed for the fellowship to share "Joys and Concerns" or "Family News," do not use it— and do not allow it to be used—for announcements. "Tickets still available for the All-County Youth Bird Band Show and Elvis Impersonator Contest, see Clem after the service" does not count as a prayer request except in extremely unusual circumstances.

9. *Huh?* Arrange for appropriate sound reinforcement for announcers.

10. *Find and recruit the right people to make announcements.* Identify a few folks who communicate clearly and like to speak up, and help them grow and develop through consistent practice.

11. *Factor announcements into your overall worship plan.* Integrate announcements into the whole, lest they come off like chalk on a cheese sandwich. "Holy! Holy! Holy!" probably shouldn't be followed by announcing the new campaign to rid the church kitchen of rodents. If you know what I mean.

12. *Use some humor.* It will help people take in the information.

worship, music plays a supporting, not a central, role. In general, the liturgy takes care of many of the spoken transitions that a musical worship leader would normally supply. Because liturgies have been honed and practiced, often over centuries, they communicate very clearly on their own. Extra talking, especially poorly prepared chatter, undermines them. Be prepared simply to start a song without a verbal transition.

A good substitute for verbal transitions, however, is written transitions. The clarity of traditional liturgies is often obscured by poor instructions. In many churches the congregation has to juggle a service leaflet (filled with terms and abbreviations that are unintelligible to the uninitiated), a prayer book and two or more hymnals in the course of a service. This is fine for people who have been brought up in liturgical churches and have years of practice, but if you want newcomers to experience anything more than confusion, you will need to give them something more. Many liturgical churches print an all-inclusive service leaflet each week that contains the words of the liturgy, words for that week's service music and instructions for when to stand or kneel or whatever is required. Such leaflets can run eight or more pages and take time and paper to produce, but they are an invaluable investment in the worship experience of newcomers.

In a liturgical context the music leader will need to work closely with the other worship leaders—which may include the pastor, preacher and/or celebrant—to make sure that all the elements fit together and that you are each prepared to pick up where others leave off. This preparation is well worth the effort when you see a service come together with a richness that few traditional-only *or* contemporary-only services achieve.

A Modern Liturgical Worship Model

At a conference, I led the musical worship for a closing Eucharist service. We surrounded the traditional opening procession with twenty minutes of joyful, celebratory and anticipatory music. We sang a brief form of the creed with a well-known song. Its refrain, "We believe you're here now / standing in our midst / with the power to heal now / and the grace to forgive," led naturally into intercession and confession. After the confession and pardon, we sang a song thanking God for the power of his love to save us.

During the offertory, dancers brought the congregation's gifts, the bread and the wine to the table as we sang three songs of commitment. After the table had been set we allowed several minutes for silent contemplation before the Eucharistic liturgy began. During the Great Thanksgiving (the prayer over the elements) we sang the Sanctus ("Holy, holy, holy Lord") in a contemporary arrangement. As the bread and cup were distributed the whole congregation sang a series of songs, beginning with simple, meditative songs and culminating in joyful thanksgiving. We closed the service with an eighteenth-century hymn set to a familiar tune.

This service moved smoothly between ancient liturgical phrases, traditional forms that developed in the nineteenth century and music that was written in the past few years. It worked because every element had its own integrity and because all the worship leaders—musicians, clergy and dancers—understood where we were going: into the real presence of God in the body of Christ. When that goal is clear, language, ritual and music from every era blend together transparently into praise.

Cathedral or Parking Lot
The Setting for Worship

● ●

Alison Siewert

Some of the most beautiful buildings ever constructed are sanctuaries. Christians have used houses of worship to honor God and shelter the faithful since the first believers met in homes and caves. The architecture of buildings themselves, as well as stained glass windows, sculpture, gilding, textile art, paintings, banners and plants have all been used to create worship spaces.

Some of us still enjoy the use of well-designed and lavishly decorated church buildings. But many worship services take place in church basements, gyms, living rooms and warehouses. All kinds of nontraditional spaces house a huge variety of worship meetings. As our ancestors discovered, the visual environment for worship is important: it can either enhance or distract people's attention and receptivity in worship. Whether you meet in a Gothic cathedral or a parking lot, with some thought and creativity, you can use your space and place to draw your congregation to worship God. Here are some areas to examine and some possibilities to consider.

Your Aim
Architecture is more than simply designing buildings; it's also the applied study of human interaction with spaces and structures. You need to think about the architecture of your worship place and about what your congregation needs in order to be drawn into worship. The best-designed, highest-tech, most beautiful structures in the world are meaningless if they are hollow. People—not buildings—are what last forever, and it is the worship of God by his people that, in the end, makes a place meaningful.

Consider the needs of your congregation's worship. What kind of music will you use? A pipe organ needs a large and permanent space built around it, while rock music needs something to absorb the throbbing sound emitted from its portable sound system. Some congregations thrive in traditional sanctuaries, where the light is good for seeing a hymnal, the congregation sits in orderly pews and no one would think of eating a snack during the sermon. New churches are trying arrangements like auditorium seating, food courts and dusky coffeehouse-style services with the congregation around café tables, drinking and eating as they take in the Scripture lesson.

Our aim is to lead people into worship. Before you jump on the trend wagon of creative alternatives, spend some time considering what will actually help people focus on God and receive from him in worship. You must consider your group's ages, backgrounds, history, physical needs and style orientation. Figure out what your congregation needs in order to focus on God with minimal distraction. Believers in many places around the world stand for two hours at a time or sit on dirt floors in order to get around God in worship. Though we can hope our groups would be willing to do that, many are not. So if, for instance, reasonably comfortable seats help them focus for an hour in worship (this probably applies to most North Americans), you should consider arranging for comfortable seats.

The Building
Look carefully at your building. What does

it say about God and people? Some buildings inspire worship simply by their beauty and size. York Cathedral in England dominates the entire city. Its sheer size and heft make you aware that, at least when it was built, people worshiped a big God whose stature they attempted to express by the building. The chapel at my college always inspired me to worship by its clean, very modern and simple lines, and its cruciform shape; it is spare and invites the decoration of uttered praise. What does your building or space say to people? If it doesn't say much on its own, that's okay. You can think creatively about how your people, music, set-up and decoration speak of God. If the building was created to be a statement, as many sanctuaries were, you should examine this carefully. Some buildings, such as my college's beautiful but stark chapel, should be warmed up with color. Very large spaces may need to be pulled in by lighting, seating and other means in order not to feel cavernous. And tiny or cramped rooms can feel more open with the right lighting and good arrangement of seats.

Access

How accessible is your building? Can everyone, including people using wheelchairs and other special transportation, get in easily? Is it gracious and inviting or overwhelming and imposing? My home church invites people in by a quarter-mile drive that ends at the outside stairs to the sanctuary, in the center of a massive church campus. It's pretty, but intimidating, and a bit mysterious. The first time I visited, I couldn't figure out how to get into the sanctuary. My husband and I parked and walked toward the building. I'd seen the sanctuary stairs in front—at least I thought I had— but the parking was in back. There was not a single sign directing folks to the sanctuary section of the huge building, and no one welcomed or directed people at any door. We ended up following other people in, try-

ing to look nonchalant as we guessed which way to turn and hoped we weren't inadvertently headed for third-grade Sunday school! Several months into my tenure on staff there, I overheard one person explain that she'd always wanted to visit the church but just couldn't bring herself to make that long journey up the driveway. She said, "I didn't feel worthy, or something." (A wise outreach team has since added friendly and directive signs. Bravo!)

By contrast, another church I visited met in an unmarked warehouse. The only parking available was three blocks away. So members of the congregation, which is very large and very diverse, stood at twenty-yard intervals covering the entire walk from the parking lot to the sanctuary, greeting visitors and directing them toward the building. Several of the greeters were bikers with huge, burly, tattooed arms and black leather vests. They'd grab your hand to shake it, and in their gruff tones proclaim, "Praise the Lord! Good morning." It was a great way to get a feel for the church, and no one could claim a lack of welcome! Wherever you meet, you need to think through what your building does for people as they enter. How does your church look from the curb? And once people get from the curb to the door, can they find the worship service?

Seating

I was leading a service in a church basement one Sunday and walked in to find the chairs set up at a great distance from one another. The service usually drew about forty people, but seventy chairs were set up to fill a space for a hundred. The center aisle was a gap of about twelve feet. It felt like the wide Missouri had flowed between the two sides of the congregation, creating too much distance between people. Greeting was awkward because people had to travel so far to do it, and folks did the "Are you coming to me, or am I going to you?" dance. Singing was strained because people could hear only themselves and felt self-conscious and exposed by the lack of other voices around them.

People need some space but not too much, and this varies by culture and context. An urban congregation's "spacious" may qualify as a rural group's "crowded." You need to figure that out for your crowd. Also check for the safety of seating. Don't block aisles people may need in an emergency, and don't put chairs so close together that people get banged up just trying to sit down. (If you need advice, call your local fire department or public safety office.) Give people enough aisle space so they can get up to use restrooms, attend to children and leave early without being disruptive simply by trying to move. And make sure you can graciously accommodate worshipers in wheelchairs or with hearing impairments. Prepare space and necessary equipment for people with physical disabilities ahead of time so you avoid awkward shuffling and rearranging when someone shows up who has a special need.

Color and Decoration

God created a world of colors that can make places seem warm or cold, exciting or drab. Use color to enliven your space if its dull, or to focus and calm it if it's distracting. Think about using banners—not the 1970's burlap-and-felt-with-tassels variety but really creative, updated versions—to help define and decorate your worship area. One church I know meets in what used to be an indoor soccer stadium. The whole building is slate blue with gray trim and glaring gym-style lighting. There's no way to close in a worship space and make it really *warm,* so they put up half-wall dividers and used colorful banners to focus and draw in the visual field. You'd never know that just on the other side of the half-wall is a volleyball and basketball court where folks stay and play after worship! If you're inexperienced in this realm or aren't sure what to do with your space, see if you can find an interior designer or design student in your congregation. Enlist them to help think through how to use color and decoration to create a place for celebration in your building. (Check chapter 38 for more on this.)

Creating a Worshipful Environment

Decorations that fit your community's culture and the themes of worship can help people get ready to celebrate from the minute they walk in the door. We don't usually think of background music as decoration, but it is! Try playing some music (live or recorded) to set a mood and communicate warmth and worship as people enter.

We can learn from many traditional worship settings that are well decorated; from symbol-strewn banners and antependia (those things that are draped over the communion table and the pulpit) to organ preludes and incense, they invite worshipers into meeting God. If you don't know anything about liturgical seasons and colors, invest some time in learning. You may not follow the liturgical calendar or even have a place to put candles, but traditions, many of them ancient, will inform your use of new decorative ideas. They can help you to engage and communicate the beauty and depth of our faith.

One church celebrates the tradition of the communion table by surrounding the bread and wine with fruit and inviting worshipers to stay and enjoy it after the service. This honors the communion table as a meal table; its original is Jesus' final meal and the early church's agape feasts. Another congregation of university students and young adults worships in a darkened, candlelit sanctuary with Gregorian chant. Another group meets in the living room of someone's home, and another built its sanctuary with a huge window through which worshipers can take in the beauty of the High Sierra around them. Even a parking lot can function as a cathedral. (Unfortunately, if it does not hold meaningful worship, a cathedral can be as mundane as a parking lot!)

It's your challenge as a worship team to discover and uncover the unique beauty and benefit of the place God has provided for you. You can work with any space and any blend of traditions and new elements to create a beautiful, meaningful, well-focused environment that will help people out of the day's distractions and into worship.

51 Integration & Transitions in Worship

Alison Siewert

It's that moment of awkward silence: the singing has finished, and the music team makes way for the drama team to start the sketch. Nothing happens. So everyone's sitting there, craning necks to see what's happening, trying to figure out what to do next. It turns out the drama people just didn't know exactly when they were supposed to start. So while the worship leader was waiting for them, they were waiting for the worship leader. Oops.

It's happened to me! More than once I've neglected to think through what's next and left my congregation hanging out there . . . wondering.

How do you make worship times *smooth,* without coming off slick? The key is to work out transitions from each part of worship to the next. In the process of thinking out how things will move, you can also think about the relationships of worship segments to one another. For instance, how does *praise* lead us to *confession,* and how do these make us more ready to hear *God's Word* read, acted and preached?

Knowing *why* you make each transition will help you to choose your methods of getting there. It's not so unlike decisions you make daily: how to get to work, class, church. In worship planning you have many vehicles at your disposal. Music, silence, explanation, small-group discussion, prayer, drama—almost anything can help a congregation move from one part of worship to another if it's done well.

> *Transitions communicate and they organize.*

Transitions communicate and they organize. Use them to tell the congregation where you're going and how you'll get there. But also use them to communicate in the moment itself. For example, a shift from music to silence might communicate, "We've been talking to God, but now we're going to listen to him." A move from silence to music might say, "We've been quietly confessing our sin; now let's celebrate God's forgiveness through Christ."

More complex transitions, including "moments" in which the point or feeling really *fills,* or overwhelms the congregation, are harder to create but certainly possible in most settings. If you have more sophisticated lighting, sound, staging or visual-art capacities, you can employ them to create awesome transitions. A change in lighting, for example, can create warm, reflective space for meditation or shout, "We follow a resurrected Lord!"

Preachers can help make transitions. There's no rule that the sermon has to start abruptly or end with an amen. If preachers can sing, they might start or end with a song. You can include preachers in sketches if you're creative—just don't make them so goofy that people have difficulty taking them seriously as an expositor of Scripture! Spend some time with your preacher or preaching team, and get the preacher involved in planning the service. If you know each other and your gifts and strengths well, you can work to maximize your leadership of authentic and undistracted worship.

Putting It into Practice in a Service

I'll lay out a sample service I recently led at my church's contemporary-style worship meeting, noting each transition and how it was accomplished.

Gathering. Worshipers are welcomed into the meeting space by people around the lobby, music playing over loudspeakers; they make the *transition* from daily life to our meeting time through welcome. The worship team takes its place in the last minute of this time, ready to begin.

Opening. As recorded music stops, the

Choose Your Words Carefully

Alison Siewert

If you're a worship leader, you may never need to give a sermon, but you will still need to speak before a congregation on occasion. Try these four tips to get your point across smoothly and clearly.

1. Use accessible, friendly language. In most worship settings it's not necessary to use formal language for either people or God. If you can, try using contemporary translations of Scripture rather than the King James version to help people catch onto the meaning of the text. Praying from up front in familiar language instead of using thees and thous usually helps people to be more free in their own prayers. And when you direct the congregation, invite people to move and act as you would your friends: "Let's have a seat" is closer to our daily diction than "You may now be seated."

2. Think ahead. When you speak between songs to build transitions, you'll want to be open to the leadership of the Holy Spirit, but you should also think ahead of time about what you might say. Planning for worship does not by any means exclude God. It may seem like it really honors God to work only spontaneously, listening and responding to what you sense the Spirit is doing in the moment. Certainly we must listen and respond as we lead. However, the Holy Spirit is never spontaneous. He always has a plan, a direction, a way he is going. Planning ahead through prayer and disciplined reflection on the flow and direction of worship will help you listen better, not keep you from responding in the moment.

3. Take transitions seriously. Spoken transitions are just that: transitions. They should neither take the place of the sermon nor attempt to teach broad theological points. But they *are* teaching and direction, so don't take them lightly. Make sure your words square up with Scripture. Transitions should not repeat the sermon. It's best if you let the message stand on its own and do little talking—after all, people have just been sitting and listening for ten to forty minutes. Move them to respond to what they've already heard. When you talk in the midst of music or prayer, you are leading worship, and you need to keep in mind that your goal is to help people adore God, even as you adore him yourself. Evaluate your speaking on that basis.

4. Talk just enough. Think about how much you really need to say. Sometimes a song needs an introduction to be meaningful in the context. But sometimes the lyrics themselves are enough, and the guitar's introduction provides plenty of focus to move on. You usually don't need to talk about every song. When you do talk, try to limit yourself to *just enough.* It's unlikely, for instance, that people will be able to focus well on an entire chapter of Scripture, even a whole psalm. If verses two and three are really the ones that apply, read those. If you can tell a short story from your own experience to introduce a point, you don't necessarily have to follow up with Scripture too.

If doing this sort of speaking is new to you, ask a couple of people you trust to listen carefully to what you say, help you evaluate it and perhaps even assist you in thinking through next services.

worship team begins playing the introduction to an upbeat song, and people take their seats. Words come up on screen a few seconds before singing starts. (The lyrics are an invitation to worship.) People make the *transition* from being welcomed by the team to being welcomed by God in worship.

Greeting. Over the ringing of the last chord, the worship leader asks people to turn and meet the people standing near them. People make the *transition* from being a group of individuals to being a community of worshipers gathered around God.

Singing worship. A worship-team member interrupts the end of the greeting time by addressing God in prayer, thanking him for his presence with them and asking for help to worship fully. The next song, focusing on God's strength and power, begins at the end of the prayer. The congregation is still standing. Everyone sings two more songs, one in English and one in Spanish—the worship leader talks about their lyrical similarity—and another to end this set, inviting God to teach the congregation. Transitions between songs are worked out in rehearsal so that instrumentalists—even if the worship leader wants to introduce a song over their vamp—can be ready to move from tune to tune, keeping worship flowing.

Drama. As singing ends, the worship team sets aside instruments and microphones to perform a sketch based on Exodus 13—15, Moses and the people crossing the Red Sea. There is potential for disintegration here—it will take a full minute to get ready. So the worship leader will introduce the sketch with some humor (since it's a comedic piece) while the team gets set. This helps people make the *transition* from singing out to taking in. While the sketch is performed, the preacher adjusts his lavaliere microphone and makes sure he knows where the "on" switch is.

Message. Laughter and applause follow the sketch, creating a natural opportunity for the preacher to make his way to the front of the room and position himself, and for people to *transition* from focusing on humor to the implications of the text.

Reflection. The preacher offers a sermon on the text and ends with prayer. Next, to help the congregation to make the *connection* from hearing to doing the Word, he introduces an opportunity for the congregation to reflect silently, then to share briefly in small groups about a question he poses. The worship-team pianist plays softly in the background to create an easy atmosphere for quiet, individual processing, and only stops playing when the preacher refreshes the question and calls people to small groups.

Singing response. After a few minutes the pianist again plays, this time through a song the congregation will sing next in response to the Word. The worship team makes its own small group so that it can participate but then moves quickly into position to lead more singing worship. As the team gets ready, the pianist plays more distinctly and louder, notifying the congregation that they are about to *transition* to respond together in song.

The worship leader calls everyone to stand in response to what God is teaching them. This moves the congregation in *transition* from knowing what they need to do to asking God to help them do it. Everyone sings "Exodus 15," asking God to prepare their hearts for his work.

As the song ends, the worship leader remains quiet for a moment, allowing people to pray what they've been singing. The guitarists play the final song softly as the leader encourages people to remember that God does great things (referring back to the Red Sea) for those who trust him actively. The worshipers close by reminding themselves in song of how good God is and how able he is to come through for them. This helps make the *transition* to daily living.

Going out. The preacher comes to the front again as the song ends. He invites the congregation to stay for food and conversation, reminds them of an offering opportunity and offers a benediction, echoing the words of the Exodus text as a blessing for the week. The community time is designed to help the worshipers make the *transition* into living as a community not just at church but in day-to-day life as they leave. The music team plays as people move into conversations, toward coffee and to collect their children.

There's nothing particularly fancy in the outline of transition points I've just listed.

This is bread-and-butter stuff. But it requires careful thought and a little planning. If you want a smooth meeting, you need not only to think through transitions but also to communicate them to all the participants in the service. The preacher and actors and ushers all need to be aware of the goal of a particular moment. One unaware player can bungle a whole play! If you can meet to talk and walk through the worship time, you'll find it fairly easy to get everyone up to speed.

52 Rediscovering Communion

•••

Andy Crouch & Sundee Frazier

Quick! What form of worship have all Christians in every generation and every culture shared? With all the wild and wonderful diversity of Christian worship around the world, the one common practice is the meal we call communion, the Lord's Supper, the Mass or the Eucharist. Beginning with the Passover meal Jesus ate with his disciples on the night before his death, communion has been Christians' central expression of worship. In communion we remember with awe what Jesus has done for us, give thanks for his sacrifice and renew our participation in his death for us. The bread and wine, representing Jesus' body and blood, become tangible evidence that Jesus loved us in the most dramatic possible way and that it is possible to receive him into our lives, just as we receive food and drink into our bodies.

Among some Protestants, though, the communion table has historically been less important than the preacher's pulpit. Fearing that communion had become a ritual with little meaning, Protestant churches in-

creasingly restricted the celebration of communion to infrequent services, hoping that it would keep its special character. Over time, ironically, this often had the effect of simply making communion marginal to the "real" worship life of the church—a once-every-three-months interruption in the normal life of preaching, praise and prayer.

Today, however, communion is making a comeback, and this most ancient of forms of Christian worship is coming back most strongly in contemporary worship services! While more traditional congregations may attach little importance to their communion services, communion is unmistakably important in the lives of many contemporary worship communities. The frequency and form vary, but Christians are rediscovering the extraordinary power of an ordinary loaf of bread. and cup of wine (or grape juice!).

Making the Most of Communion
Like all forms of worship, communion is most valuable if both leaders and followers engage in it with understanding minds and

prepared hearts. So you have some homework to do if you want to make the most of communion in your worshiping community.

Creativity with Communion

Sundee Frazier

I spoke with a number of pastors of churches that are using communion to worship in new ways. Consider trying a few of their ideas in your worship setting.

☐ Add extended musical worship before communion, so the congregation is more fully aware of Jesus' presence before the meal.

☐ Occasionally celebrate communion in complete silence, allowing for individual prayer and a collective sense of awe.

☐ Provide prayer teams, located at the side or back of the church.

☐ Receive communion around a table to emphasize the communal nature of the meal.

☐ Encourage people to receive communion with someone else from the congregation with whom they have recently reconciled.

☐ Alternate between the congregation staying seated (to emphasize God's grace) and going forward (to emphasize their reponse to that grace).

☐ Ask people to say a simple phrase to one another as they pass the elements: "Jesus loves you," "Jesus loves you just as you are," "Don't forget."

☐ Offer both wine and grape juice (for congregations with recovering alcoholics present).

☐ Use a common cup (in a church that has traditionally used individual cups) to overcome the negative religious associations some have with traditional communion observances.

☐ Celebrate communion as a *celebration*, with upbeat music or other markers that signal a joyful occasion.

First, learn how your church understands the communion meal. While the practice of the Lord's Supper is universal among Christian churches, they understand its importance in different ways. Some see communion primarily as a sacrifice of thanksgiving in the tradition of Old Testament thank-offerings; others see it as a time for confession and forgiveness. Some emphasize the symbolic act of remembering Jesus' death; others emphasize the mystical experience of Christ in the communion elements themselves. While these different views of communion all have biblical roots (and, of course, they're not mutually exclusive), it is worthwhile to find out what your own worship tradition emphasizes, and why.

Second, once you understand it, explain it! Your community probably includes people from many different church backgrounds and people with no church background at all, and they all need instruction in how your community understands the meal. Take time during worship to explain communion's significance. Explanations need to be given for more basic questions too. Just as your family probably has some spoken or unspoken rules about family dinner, so there is etiquette for the communion meal. Give directions for these very practical questions: What do I do with the bread when it is handed to me? What do I do after eating and drinking the bread and cup? What if I don't want to receive communion—is there something special I should do?

Third, integrate communion into your worship planning. It's appropriate for the Lord's Supper to be the highlight of a worship service, but for that to happen, the other elements of worship need to prepare for and point toward communion. Otherwise it can seem like an uncomfortable add-on. Like a drama, song or reading of Scripture, communion has its own story and shape; all the methods you would use to integrate these elements into your worship service apply to communion as well.

One very effective way to integrate communion into worship is to have music while communion is served. While you need to avoid anything that is performance-like—nothing should take away from people's concentration on the meal itself—simple congregational songs can create a very rich atmosphere of worship. You may want to begin the music with soft instrumental music and then, toward the end of the communion time, move into congregational singing that emphasizes our thankfulness for Jesus' offering for us. Communion is also an excellent time to offer individual prayer for those who desire it, for healing or to respond to the message that was preached earlier in the service.

Fourth, create appropriate variety. Though your church may have certain expectations for how communion is celebrated (for example, what words are said over the bread and wine), there is great freedom, even in the most traditional ritual, for making the service fresh and accessible. Consider varying the way the congregation receives the elements: on a day when you want to emphasize God's individual love for each person, you might have people receive the

bread and wine individually at their seats, while at another time you might want to have members of the community serve one another or pray in small groups before coming up to receive communion together. (See the sidebar "Creativity with Communion" for more ideas.)

You may even want to vary the bread you use. But if you choose to use traditional communion wafers, don't underestimate their power to communicate the gospel too. One Sunday, Pastor Ken Fong of Evergreen Baptist Church held up the small cracker his congregation uses as the bread, saying to the congregation, "Jesus loves you this much." Some people, barely able to see the cracker, laughed at the implication that "Jesus loves you a little bit." But Pastor Fong responded, "Jesus loved you enough to be broken to bits."

Jesus loved us enough to be broken for us; that is the message of the gospel, and that is the message of communion. Make the most of this astonishing and marvelous meal.

53 Evaluating Your Leadership

Matt Frazier

As you lead worship, you'll grow in your ability to help others focus on God. To maximize that growth, take the time and energy to evaluate specific worship times alone and with your whole team. You'll be amazed at what you learn! There's no reason to be threatened by the idea of frankly discussing how a worship time went, since your security is in God's love for you and not in your performance. Frequently, in fact, evaluation times will be encouraging more than corrective. You'll especially want to take time to evaluate how you and your

team did if you're newly together, in a new situation or learning a lot of new music.

If you're the leader of the team, keep mental notes during worship times to share with your team when you meet. If you noticed God blessing the worship time, point that out and celebrate it together. If someone on the team did something particularly well, tell them. If something didn't go so well, talk about it as a team. How does the team feel about it? How can it be better next time? Are there parts of songs you need to practice? Are there arrangements that need to be clarified? If you're not sure how you did personally, ask for the team's reflections. Were your cues clear? Did you draw the congregation into worship well?

Discuss how the worship structure fit together as a whole. Was it well-organized? Did transitions between songs make sense to the congregation? Did transitions flow well musically? Did unintentional transitions prove pleasantly surprising? One time while leading worship at a student conference, we ran out of time and had to cut a few songs. As our team discussed it later, however, we realized that cutting those songs provided an unexpected but effective transition between two songs we had never planned on doing successively. In later worship times we often coupled these two songs together because it worked so well.

Another way to evaluate your worship times is by asking for input from those you respect outside your team. A pastor, staff worker, ministry partner or mature member of your congregation can give you good feedback about worship times. Don't be afraid to ask *and* listen.

After a worship service is over, you might be tired and have other things on your mind. You may want to talk to members of the congregation, pack up your equipment or just go home. A team evaluation may be the last thing you feel interested in; indeed, a break may be a good idea! But spending a few minutes together sooner rather than later will help you in many ways. You will not have to try to remember specific details for a long period of time. You may also be well served bycelebrating with your team what went well and how God blessed you. The short time you take to evaluate now may pay off with a great return later. Even the best worship leaders and teams have room to grow to become more complete worshipers of God.

54 Pearls in the Mud
Responding to Criticism

● ●

Alison Siewert

I once overheard a worship team discussing their congregation's response to learning several new songs (I think it was four) in a single worship service. Some members of their fellowship had felt the team introduced too much new material at one time, and the team heard about it from more than one person.

Hearing hard stuff can be annoying and even painful. And, unfortunately, because congregations tend to feel a high degree of ownership of worship, worship teams often hear lots of criticism. For many reasons people get emotionally attached to particular songs and certain ways of doing things.

The worship team I overheard responded defensively. By making fun of their congregation lagging behind the latest worship music trends ("They're so five-minutes-ago!"), by telling each other how tired they were of listening to complaints and by invoking insider jokes, they effectively kept criticism at bay. They never sought deeper insight by inviting conversation either with congregation members or other, more experienced, worship leaders. They missed an opportunity to learn and to serve.

If you're on a worship team, you're going

to get criticized. Here are some ways to deal with it.

1. Invite conversation, and listen carefully. Listening to people is a way to love them. So even if you dread a critical conversation, try to listen for anything useful, and look for ways to affirm the person's concern, even if you cannot agree with their itemized complaints. If people are awkward or difficult or really trying, give them the benefit of the doubt. If necessary, you can set a reasonable time limit (say, twenty minutes) for the conversation or ask them to write down their thoughts as a follow-up. You don't need to make any promises for change. You can close by thanking people for their input and agreeing to think it over.

2. Search for a pearl in the mud. My leadership mentor encouraged me to look through every heap of criticism—no matter how seemingly "muddy," unfair or even wrong—to see if there was a "pearl" of wisdom or insight that I could wash off and hold on to. Search for anything God might be offering you. This is how you make criticism constructive, even if it's not presented or intended that way. It's also an important way worship leaders maintain humility.

3. Consider the source. Without getting judgmental, ask whether the viewpoint presented is coming from an accurate perspective. If your critic is a first-time visitor, their input should be evaluated for what it tells you about the experience of a first-time visitor—which may be very helpful but doesn't tell you everything in depth. If you hear

from the guy who always sits in the back and every week can't understand why "you kids have to play that rock 'n' roll music so loud," well, you may need to lovingly encourage him to try the non-rock 'n' roll worship option.

4. Do regular evaluation, and don't be afraid to critique yourselves. Take time to discuss how things are going and to offer your own suggestions and feedback to yourselves as a group and to one another. When you're on a team together, it's important to be able humbly to trust one another for accurate, thoughtful input, whether it's praise or correction. This will give you a framework for processing other people's input as well.

5. Identify advocates. Get some help from a small number of people who care about you and who are wise and knowledgeable about worship and your congregation. Ask them to monitor how things are going and to give you feedback—both positive and constructively critical—on a regular basis. These people can help you balance the extremes you might hear elsewhere and set limits on how much and from whom you hear. They may even be able to advocate for you in the case of a particularly difficult conversation or inappropriate criticism.

6. Celebrate the ways you're growing. On your own and with your team, periodically review the things you've been learning, and celebrate how you've grown. Take time to worship together, to thank God for how he's taught you through experience, reflection, practice and, yes, constructive criticism.

Appendix 1

So You Wanna Start a Service

Alison Siewert

The current movement in "contemporary worship"—for lack of better title—began in the sixties when both Catholic and Protestant churches investigated new musical forms for their traditional liturgies. Christians saw their youth leaving churches for alternative communities and experiences. The cultural upheaval forced the church to reexamine its communication style and to recognize its inability to connect with its own children. "Contemporary" referred to music brought from the youth culture into churches—predominantly folk music—reworked and applied to worship.

From the sixties through the nineties a primary focus of the new worship movement has been relevance in communication. The thinking goes that if we want worship to continue being a significant life experience for young church members, and if we want not only to retain them but attract new followers, we must speak in language people can understand. After all, when Jesus called his disciples he did not say, "Come, follow me and I will make you become shepherds of people," but "I will make you fish for people" (Mark 1:17). They were fishermen. This made sense.

Scads of churches have begun zillions of contemporary services in response to a heartfelt desire to extend themselves in relevant and loving ways to the young and the unchurched. But many of the start-up services have been discontinued, and even more languish in frustration with poor attendance, lack of direction and waning zeal even in their leaders.

No one ever starts out saying, "Hey, let's create a new thing and make it real mediocre." But that's what we unwittingly are set up to do if we fail to begin by asking tough questions and building clear visions. What follows are some questions and suggestions to help you start thinking through important foundations on which to build a plan for contemporary worship in your setting.

I am assuming you are working with a team of people. If you are not working with a team, please stop here and go find one. You will have serious trouble exploring all this on your own, and even more serious trouble continuing the hard work—and it will be hard—once you start. If you are heading out to locate a team now, you should include someone who has pastoral authority in your fellowship, someone from the congregation who knows most of the people in the community, someone trained and up-to-date in music, someone who knows the intricacies and policies of the church and can work them for and with you. Some of these people may be one and the same, which is fine as long as they're not all you. But all the people on your team need to carry with them a heart for this ministry and the people group you're leading in worship. Here are some things to talk about together.

Why Do You Want to Create a New Service?

How is God calling you? Is it really a new service that's needed or simply some work applied to what you already have? What can you do with a new service that you can't do without it? You may be tempted to start fresh simply to circumvent old traditions and strong opinions. Sometimes that's a good reason to start over, but not always. In any case, you need a solid reason, or set of reasons, and a *calling from God* for a new service.

For Whom Is the New Service Being Created?

To whom is God calling you? There is a distinct difference between a *worship service* and what is popularly called a *seeker service.* The point of a worship service is to *worship God.* I have seen worship services be effectively evangelistic by remaining true to their focus of worship. For the nonbeliever to enter a sanctuary of any kind filled with people who really trust God with their lives, enough so that they have seen God work and have reason to worship him— that's a powerful witness. People who are interested in knowing God can be helped by spending time around folks who are intimately acquainted with him. Just as you would learn about a new friend by sitting in on a family slide show reviewing the person's life, people can learn a lot about God by sitting in on worship and seeing and hearing God's story told and celebrated by his children. For a generation jaded by marketing ploys for their attention, this is often a better and more authentic approach than making a direct appeal to them. What they get to see is spontaneous and immediate, not crafted to target them.

If you want to start a *seeker service,* you need to do plenty of thinking and research to define your audience. Many churches have attempted to replicate the ministries of megachurches like Willow Creek Community Church in Illinois without recognizing that these successes started not with a formula, really great resources and a cool building, but with a committed team doing door-to-door interviews with their unchurched neighbors, asking why church

was unattractive. These teams then worked diligently for years to innovate, experiment and ultimately build what they currently have. Willow Creek and its kin are responding to what God is doing in their particular context in this particular time among their particular people group. Before you decide you're going to create a Willow Creek-style service, you need to evaluate how much your community and people are like Willow Creek. It may be that you can, with some careful thinking, take some megachurch resources and adapt them for use in your community. But proceed with caution, and give yourself time and space to do honest reflection about who you are.

No matter the direction you take, you need to get an idea of who's going to come to a new service so you can create context and substance for worship that will actually help people know and adore God. You are probably already responding to this issue by seeing a need for a different sort of service than what you have: the traditional style is perhaps not so helpful for everyone in your fellowship. That's a good start. Try to identify what, exactly, distracts people from worship in your current setting. Is the music a problem? The lyrics? The style? Maybe folks are in need of a less formal atmosphere. In one church I worked with, families involved in the weekday urban ministry and a handful of men in residence at the downtown mission for substance-abuse recovery came to our service because we had specifically designed it not to require any particular sort of dress or formality. They felt comfortable entering the fellowship in whatever state they came—children in tow, dressed in jeans, inexperienced at Christian worship.

You might think of your service design in terms of "on-ramps" to the highway of faith. A good on-ramp is visible, well lit and clearly marked, and it gives safe and smooth access to the main road. By focusing on your community's people groups and knowing their needs, you will get educated about how to build appropriate on-ramps for them and to avoid creating something that looks beautiful but is too hard to reach, or that's hidden behind bushes and treacherous to find in the dark. Don't feel bad about taking plenty of time to do this part of the process. Jesus spent thirty years as a regular guy (well, more or less) before he began his ministry. What do you think he learned? If you can, get some people who represent the focus group you want to invite—in age, culture, social status—to join you in praying and planning for a new service.

What Costs Are You Willing to Pay?

Many churches spend big to start new services. They buy musical and technical equipment, hire a consultant or worship leader, develop support systems, decorate spaces. Then they figure they've spent, so it will work: it's the American way! But along the journey, other sorts of costs continue to present themselves. The worship team needs to use the music room, but the room is unavailable because it's being used by several choirs. So who gets priority? The church staff is accustomed to doing two services on Christmas Eve. Now the new service team wants staff to participate in an additional contemporary service, but the staff doesn't really want to spend another two hours at church on the holiday. So how do you negotiate? People resources and material resources—far beyond money—will be stretched if you start something new. What costs can you anticipate? Who will pay them?

When Will the Service Take Place?

Of all the "cost" questions, I've observed scheduling a new service to be most sensitive. Often churches attempt to replace a dwindling Sunday morning service with a contemporary format. Some insert the new service into an already packed hour between two traditional services, on top of Christian education or youth group activities. Other churches hold the new service during an evening, often Saturday or Sunday, hoping not to intrude on established programs and patterns, but creating the need for a whole new support system (child care, hospitality, custodial assistance, etc.). Whatever you choose, look carefully not only at your church's needs and preferences but also at the needs of the people you're hoping to invite. After all, if they can't come at the appointed time, the service won't be serving them.

Make certain that you have personnel available—worship-team members, pastors and support people—to lead the service. You need enthusiastic people who love God and want to worship to set a tone and welcome people. But remember that the worship team cannot hold the service all by itself; you need a congregation too. Especially if you are attempting to welcome new people, check to see that some core members of your church can and will commit to attending the new service. If you set the time of worship during the Sunday school hour, for instance, but all your worship-team and committed members are in or teaching classes, you will not be able to build much of a service. You want and need your committed members there on a regular basis if you want the service to succeed. These will be the people who create a framework for community within the new congregation; since they know each other, they'll be able to draw others into a network of relationships.

Finally, check your time for consistency. Saturday night might be good for people sometimes, but how many high-school youth-group retreats or football games at the local university will run smack into your service time? One church I know meets on Saturday nights and has a crowd of at least one hundred every week. But every week's one hundred is about 75 percent *different* from the last week's crowd. There are probably at least four hundred people who would say they regularly attend the Saturday-night service—but they are never there at the same time. The net result is that the service consistently feels like a special event. The people who attend never really get to know each other, and the pastoral-and-worship-team's efficacy is truncated because they can't really get to know the congregation as a whole—even *they* can't be there to lead consistently! I'm certain from watching them that if the whole worship team could lead together and could lead essentially the same fellowship week to week, they would improve and worship would grow much stronger.

Does the Whole Church Support the Service?

Many of the questions I've just posed will create tension and maybe even some pain for you and your team. They are not nearly so difficult, however, as what can happen in churches when new things are started without the agreement of the vast majority of members and all the leaders. Your whole congregation needs an opportunity to buy into the new service. Don't give in to the temptation to say, "They're old [or whatever they are], and they don't get it, so forget 'em!" You may not have absolutely everyone on your wagon by the time you pull onto the road, but you want as many on board as can possibly get ready for the trip. Give people a chance to ask their questions and to learn about this new thing. Some of the most supportive folks I've ever worked with have been those who say, "I don't like that rock 'n' roll stuff, but I understand you young people want to worship that way, and I'll support you in any way I can." Two nonagenarians were the first to arrive and sat in the front row at the very first contemporary service I led at my church. Give people a chance to grasp what you're doing and to become your allies in ministry. Explain the needs; identify the people group; meet with people individually and in groups—do what you can in order to interpret how God

is leading you, and invite people into partnership.

If you start with these questions, you'll probably find more you need to ask. That's the point. You don't have to have all the answers going in, but you do need to have a sense of the questions, and some of the answers, to get started. You need a beginning point, a clear vision for where you're trying to go and an idea of how you'll get there. You might find out in the first six months that on several counts you were wrong. That's okay. If you start off with a vision and with a team that will continue to work out the vision, you can continue to process, honing and adjusting as you go. If you start with nothing but good intentions and a vague idea of wanting hipper music than that in the sanctuary, you'll likely spin your wheels for a good long time before you ever—if you ever—really get the service moving.

A Model

One church I know did an exceptional job of developing a service. St. Michael-le-Belfry is a very old parish in the Church of England. The church building sits right next door to York Cathedral. St. Michael's has a long history of renewal (it was David Watson's church), and they have a vibrant arts ministry. They have several musical worship teams, all of them quite good. Their drama team, Riding Lights Players, produces everything from street theater to television. The banner team (yes, a banner team) works in prayer and Scripture study and art for six months at a time to create their gorgeous, unusual banners (neither felt nor burlap anywhere!). But one day a visiting American student asked a lay leader there, "So, what are you guys doing to connect with unchurched people in York?"

The leader thought about the question and shared it with friends. Soon, a small group of adults in their thirties and forties ventured out to York's night spots to explore what they could do to introduce the gospel to people who weren't much into banners and worship music and who had never seen the inside of St. Michael's. The group eventually focused their energy on young people who spent most nights hanging out in dance clubs. They learned how to dance. They made friends with club patrons. They began to dress like their new friends. Andrew, a guy in his forties, took to wearing tie-dyed Lycra running tights and long T-shirts . . . not exactly a "uniform" in England. Other church people identified him as, "Andrew—you know, the guy who wears the Lycra trousers."

After two years (years!) the group began to design a service that would welcome their new dancing friends. They arranged to use the church's office building, which was housed in another, unused church, for the new service. Once a month they draped all the inside walls with black fabric. Then they set up fourteen video and slide screens and projectors (borrowed, rented and bought). They set up a sound system and mounted speakers everywhere. They lit incense. They brought high-quality sodas and snack foods to serve. One team member, a professional musician, dubbed worship phrases into mostly instrumental house music. And the artists on the team created slides and video clips designed to provoke reflection about the meaning of life, who God is and why we like to dance. The whole design came together when they launched the Warehouse Worship service with an all-night dance party. It was holy. It was worshipful. It was evangelistic because the believers there gave themselves to God

in worship and gave themselves to their new friends in service.

The St. Michael's team produced warehouse services every month for several years. Sometimes they simply danced, inviting people to side rooms for conversation and food during breaks. Sometimes they had recorded music for dancing, then a live band for musical worship in the midst of the evening. Other times they included a short sermon by a speaker who could connect with the crowd, who knew the culture and could speak the language. They always had team members available to pray and talk with people as they responded to God. What made the St. Michael's effort a success, I think, wasn't even that their services were successful. The team succeeded because they spent the time and energy required to love people really well, to love them thoroughly, to love them in a way that made sense. They worshiped with their whole lives by laying them down for their friends: their worship was true because they put themselves in a position to depend on God, to have to "call on him in the day of trouble." They stepped out of all that was familiar and lived uncomfortably. They learned a new language so they could speak to a people who had never heard the gospel in their own language. They wore Lycra trousers in their own houses for the sake of bringing others to worship in the house of God. They worshiped God—they attributed him worth—by saying, "He's worth knowing." Then they extended themselves to demonstrate their point. May we so worship with our whole lives in new services and old ones, each day.

Appendix 2

Six Bible Studies for Worship Teams

●●

Study 1
Sing Out Loud, Sing Out Strong
Exodus 15:1-21   ■ Sundee Frazier

●●●

Purpose: To see that worship is a genuine and ecstatic response to how God has worked and is working in our lives.

Looking out into a group that we're leading in worship can be difficult at times. Expressionless faces, dull eyes and still bodies can be intimidating and discouraging to the worship leader who knows God is worthy of so much more praise. Worship is supposed to be thrilling, intense, fun—even good for us! It's a time to receive hope and healing from God, as well as to tell him how awesome we think he is. Yet we often look out and see reluctance, joylessness and what appears to be just plain old boredom. At the same time if we're honest, we frequently don't have to look beyond ourselves to see apathy and a lack of genuineness in worship. This can be an even harder reality to face when we're supposed to be the ones who are leading others in praise. What can we do about our own and others' lackluster approach to worship?

Introduction
1. Why do you worship?
2. Think of some times when you have worshiped God with genuine thanksgiving and joy. Why were these times meaningful for you? What made them meangingful?

Background
The Egyptians have pursued the Israelites, led by Moses, to the edge of the Red Sea. There the Israelites complain about Moses, saying they would rather have served the Egyptians than die in the wilderness. But Moses tells them not to be afraid, to stand firm and see the deliverance of the Lord: "The LORD will fight for you, and you have only to keep still" (Exodus 14:14). Of course, we've probably all heard how the story ends. Moses raises his staff, the sea parts, the Israelites pass through; when the Egyptians pursue, God has Moses raise his hand again, and the enemy is swallowed up by the sea. (Whoa!) "Thus the LORD saved Israel that day from the Egyptians . . . . Israel saw the great work that the LORD did against the Egyptians" (Exodus 14:30-31).

For Study

1. Imagine you are one of thousands of Israelites standing on the shore of the Red Sea after escaping the Egyptians' pursuit, and Moses begins to sing this song. What would the words mean to you? As you start to sing along, how do you feel? How would you sing the song?

2. What do you notice about the focus of Moses' song?

3. In verses 4-10 the Israelites recount what they have just experienced with the Egyptians. What do you notice about how they recount what happened?

4. How have you been rescued by God? Tell about an experience when he took care of you in a difficult or scary situation. How has this experience affected how you worship?

5. For what do the Israelites begin to praise him in verses 13-18? Why do you think they do this?

6. What's something God has promised to do but hasn't yet done, for which you could praise him now?

7. What is Miriam's role as a worship leader (vv. 20-21)? (Notice the change of perspective in her song.) What does the author hope for us to gain by telling us about her involvement in the worship time?

How Can This Passage Change Our Worship?

1. What are you usually thinking about before you go into a worship time?

2. Genuine worship for the Israelites came when they obeyed God in faith and saw him deliver them. How have you acted on God's Word recently in a way that caused you to need him to rescue or provide for you? What can you do in obedience to him that will put you in the position of needing him?

3. How can you help others to be aware of what God has done for them lately as you lead them into worship?

4. Write a song such as Moses' (with music or without) to describe some way God has rescued or provided for you. (Each person on your worship team can do this, and then share your songs, or you can write one together about how he's provided for you as a group.)

Study 2
Celebrating Before a Holy God
2 Samuel 6:1-15   ■ Alison Siewert

••

Purpose: To help us understand the right place of leadership within worship; to see that worship belongs, first and foremost, to a holy God who neither needs nor wants our human help—only our obedient, humble celebration.

It's tempting to objectify God, to think of him as a symbol or to treat him as a formula for curse or blessing (this is often called superstition). But God is a living person among us; he commands us with both the promise of blessing if we obey and the threat of being cut off if we fail to heed him. As worship leaders we bear responsibility to demonstrate both the seriousness and the joy of knowing God by letting him be responsible for his own worship—he doesn't need our help—and by giving ourselves to him in worship, trusting that he is good and will bless us.

Introduction
1. How do you deal with your anxiety about worship "going right"?
2. When have you had something go wrong during a worship time and had to figure out what to do to correct it? What did you do? How did this affect your experience of worshiping God?
3. Imagine a crowd of thirty thousand men who've just won a major battle because of God's intervention. What might be the challenges of leading worship in such a situation?

Background
David and his army won a great battle against a long-time foe when God went out before them "to strike down the army of the Philistines" in the valley of Rephaim (2 Samuel 5:24). Clearly, God was with David and his people. This narrative begins when David gathers his army of thirty thousand to celebrate God's victory. The ark was designed to be carried on poles by the specially designated sons of Kohath, but it is carried on "a new cart" instead. Many nations had national symbols such as arks, which they carried as impressively as possible in and out of battles. It is possible that in this instance, Israel saw the ark as more of a national symbol (leading to the events of the story) than as the locus of God's active presence.

For Study
1. David and thirty thousand men of Israel create a worship parade led by the ark of God (vv.1-5). What is the ark, and how is it described? (Look at Exodus 25 for details on the ark's construction.)
2. Compare the way Uzzah and Ahio carry the ark to the instructions given in Numbers 4:15, 19-20. What do you notice?
3. Why would Uzzah act in this way?
4. How does God respond to Uzzah? What do you think of this?
5. How does David respond (vv. 8-11)?
6. What convinces David to reclaim the ark (v. 12)?
7. How does David's treatment of the ark change when they pick it up from Obed-edom's place and move it?
8. How do you think the change in David affected Israel's view of the ark and of God himself? How did it change their worship?
(Note: The author uses "God" (Elohim) in the first half of the story but shifts to using "LORD" (Yahweh) for the second half. Elohim is the more general word for God, used also to describe gods, while Yahweh is the formal name of the Hebrew God, the "self-existent One.")
9. How do we keep our hands "off the ark" in worship?

How Can This Passage Change Our Worship?
1. It's easy to objectify God as either a malevolent force, striking at random, or as an easygoing, slap-on-the-back, casual friend—when in fact, God is neither. What can you do to know God better? How might your team work together to clarify a picture of God for yourselves and your congregation?

2. Think of some ways you can celebrate God as holy (which means "set apart"). Do this together as a team, and then choose at least one way to incorporate what you've learned in your next worship service.

3. What's one thing that you tend to get anxious about, that you can give over to God this week? Ask your team to help you by praying for you and coaching you to do this.

Study 3
Safety in God Alone
2 Chronicles 20:1-30   ■ Sundee Frazier

● ●

Purpose: To understand the importance of worshiping God when we face danger and crisis.

Safety is not found in the absence of danger but in the presence of God. Nothing helps us stay in his presence more than worshiping him with genuine hearts and remembering at all times that "his love endures forever." When we face crisis situations (the failing health or faith of a friend, persecution from nonbelievers, physical or spiritual danger to ourselves) there is no better way we can respond than to praise God. The battles are not ours but God's, and he will fight them if we let him. This is one of the most significant and frequent lessons taught throughout all Scripture—one that every believer must learn, and one that we, as worship leaders, can teach those we lead.

Introduction
1. How do you respond in crisis situations?
2. How do you respond when you've been faithful and yet bad things start happening to you?

Background
King Jehoshaphat of Judah has worked hard to bring the people back to the Lord, the God of their ancestors, from whom they had strayed. He has demolished idols and reestablished an infrastructure of judges who rule not by human standards but by God's. He has really turned Judah around. Suddenly, an insurmountable army of three nations is discovered to be upon his country, and the people of Judah are not prepared. They've been focusing on domestic issues, not defense! It would be enough to cause anyone to question where God was and why he would allow something like this to happen, especially to a king who's been doing all the right things.

For Study
1. What do you notice about how Jehoshaphat responds to the crisis situation he faces (vv. 3-13)? (What does he do? What does he not do?)
2. What does his prayer (vv. 6-12) reveal about his knowledge of God? What does his prayer reveal about his relationship with God?
3. Jahaziel is a descendant of worship leaders (v. 14). What stands out to you from the instructions Jahaziel is given by God?

4. Why do the king and the Levites worship God in verses 18 and 19?

5. Why would Jehoshaphat have the worshipers on the front lines sing of God's love and not something else, like his power, or his wrath against the wicked (v. 21)?

6. What is the effect of the people's faithfulness to God and God's deliverance of them on surrounding kingdoms?

7. What roles does worship play throughout this passage?

8. How have you seen worship be a powerful experience in times of trouble?

How Can This Passage Change Our Worship?

1. In your setting, where are the battles occurring and what are they over? How might you put worshipers on the front lines of those battles?

2. Consider the role of crises in producing authentic and meaningful worship. How do you try to protect yourself from crisis, danger and evil? How might worshiping God help you face these things head on?

3. What do you think the "splendor of his holiness" is (v. 21)? How could you incorporate this into your worship as a central focus?

Study 4
God's Word Like You've Never Heard
Nehemiah 7:73—8:12   ■ Sundee Frazier

●●●

Purpose: To see that leading people in worship includes helping them to understand the words they are hearing and to respond to these words appropriately.

As worship leaders we share in the responsibility to help a congregation understand and accept the Word. Through music, drama and teaching we can assist people in allowing God to captivate their minds and hearts, and in letting go of the lies, worries and empty diversions that held them captive when they arrived. We are there to help people know how to respond, individually and corporately, to what they are hearing from God. How will we ever accomplish such a weighty task? The Bible gives us excellent models to emulate.

Introduction

1. Imagine that you've never heard any of the stories in the Bible. You know nothing of God's character, miracles or relationship to his people. How do you think you would respond to hearing Genesis and Exodus read aloud?

2. How have you seen worship leaders direct groups to a particular response to God and his Word? (Or how have you done this yourself?) Explain.

Background

God worked through Nehemiah and Ezra to bring many of the Israelites who had been taken captive by the Babylonians back to Jerusalem. For years the Israelites had been living among people who didn't know or fear God. During that time they stopped passing on the stories of God's faithfulness. They no longer knew the commands that he had given them to obey—commands that made them his people and him their God. Through Ezra the people learned about the God they had forgotten (Ezra 7:1-10).

For Study

1. What evidence is there in the text that these people want to hear the Book of the Law (most likely the Pentateuch)?

2. How do they respond to hearing the words of the Lord (vv. 3, 5-6, 9, 12)?

3. Why do you think they respond the way they do?

4. How does your desire to hear God's Word compare to theirs? How does your typical response to God's Word compare to theirs?

5. The Levites were set apart for "the service of the LORD" (Exodus 32:29) and could be likened to pastors and worship leaders today. They were responsible for helping priests carry out worship duties in the tabernacle and temple (see 2 Chronicles 29:20-30, for example). What role do the Levites (along with Ezra and Nehemiah) play in the reading of the Law of God?

6. In verses 9-11 what do you notice about how the "pastors" and "worship leaders" redirect the peoples' response?

7. Why did the people go and obey what they had been told to do by their leaders?

8. Think of a time when you clearly understood what God was saying to you through his Word spoken in a corporate worship setting. How did the worship and/or the worship leader contribute to your understanding of how God wanted you to respond to him?

How Can This Passage Change Our Worship?

1. As a worship leader how do you understand your role in helping people understand what God is saying to them?

2. What are the different methods you can use as a worship team to help people grasp the significance of God's words for their lives?

3. Have you ever read through an entire book of the Bible with a group of people (not including Philemon!)? People can take turns reading out loud, and at various points you can stop and let people respond to what they've heard so far. If you really want to get into it, come into the reading as if you are the original group of people to whom the book is written. Talk about how you might help people worship God when you are finished with the reading.

Study 5
The Truth About God & You
John 4:4-42   ■ Alison Siewert

● ●

Purpose: To look carefully at Jesus' definition of true worship and to apply it to our lives.

As worship leaders we must worship in spirit and in truth. We need to give attention to our own hearts and come to God in true worship before we can help our congregation. We can understand only as much of God as we understand of ourselves. To know God truly is to see ourselves for who we really are: broken, sinful, desperate creatures in need of a loving, healing Savior. When we encounter God as he really is—as does the woman in this passage when she meets Jesus—we face the opportunity to deal with who we really are. Being truthful about ourselves leads us into further opportunity to grasp and enjoy the truth about God. And grasping this truth, we are, like the woman, prepared to invite others to see themselves and Jesus clearly.

Introduction

1. How would you feel if everyone on your team found out about something you've done that makes you feel ashamed? What kind of measures would you, or have you, taken to ensure that no one does find this out about you?

2. Imagine yourself talking to Jesus. And then he brings *it* up—the thing you're most ashamed of. What do you do?

3. Have you ever confessed shame to another person or to God? What happened?

Background

Jesus didn't have to pass through Samaria; in fact, most "good Jews" avoided it by taking a longer route. Samaritans were descended from Israelites (left in the area after the fall of the Northern Kingdom in 722 B.C.E.) and other people groups relocated there by the Assyrians. The Samaritans were despised by the Jews because they were considered impure not only because of lineage but also because, along with their stance opposing the rebuilding of Jerusalem's walls under Ezra and Nehemiah, they developed an adulterated form of Judaism that included a separate temple at Mt. Gerizim (probably "this mountain" to which the woman referred in this passage). It would be highly unusual for a Jew to stop in Samaritan territory, but it is unimaginably inappropriate for a rabbi such as Jesus to speak with a woman—and a Samaritan woman of ill repute, at that—especially in public. (Note the disciples reaction in v. 27.)

For Study

1. What do you notice about the circumstances of this interaction? What do the circumstances tell us about the woman? (What's the time, place and position of the characters? Note: The "sixth hour" would be noon, as hours were counted from 6:00 a.m., or approximately sunrise.)

2. Look carefully at the conversation between Jesus and the woman. You might want to have a couple of your team members read it out loud to help you get a feel for the conversation. How would you characterize the woman's response to Jesus?

3. The two talk about water. What is Jesus offering? How does the woman understand the offer? How does Jesus help her grasp what he's saying?

4. Why does Jesus insist on bringing up a shameful subject?

5. If you were the woman, how would you react? How does she react?

6. What does Jesus do when the woman changes the direction of the conversation to controversy surrounding worship (vv. 21-24)?

7. What allows the woman to see who Jesus is?

8. What does she do with her new picture of the world (vv. 28-30)?

9. The woman carried a water jar in the heat of the day in order to avoid being seen and further shamed. John makes a point of telling us that she leaves the jar. What does this reveal about how she has changed? What are the results (vv. 39-42)?

10. What does this passage teach you about true worship?

How Can This Passage Change Our Worship?

1. Worship requires seeing and admitting the truth about who we really are, which allows us to see and celebrate the truth about who God really is. How do you need to see or admit the truth about yourself?

2. Once the woman grasps Jesus' identity, she responds by dropping her old stuff and going into the city (the most populated place) to tell everyone the news—really, to invite them to worship Jesus with her. How will you invite people from your "city" (or campus, or neighborhood) into worship? How will you encourage them to see themselves and Jesus clearly?

3. The woman is enticed by Jesus' offer of water. What would be like "water at the sixth hour" to you?

Pray together, asking Jesus to give you what you need. Look and listen to see if, like with the woman, he offers you something better than what you asked for.

Study 6
When Worship Leaders Are Hurting
Psalm 42   ■ Alison Siewert

● ●

Purpose: To see how God works with us in times of pain, trouble and depletion.

Worship leaders have bad days, rough weeks, troublesome months, just like everyone else. But worship leaders are supposed to be able to get up front and seem glad about God, right? We always have to be excited to see people in the congregation, don't we? And we need to put our "stuff" on the back burner in order to look happy and get others into worship. Usually, but not always. Sure, sometimes we need to be able, in faith, to give trouble over to God and trust that even if we can't figure things out in the moment, the Lord will help us work through things in due time. Occasionally worship leaders need breaks in the action, some time for repentance and rest (Isaiah 30:15). And we may occasionally be responsible to lead worship even when we don't feel all that excited. (See chapter 18 for an example.) We are not alone. Throughout history people have led worship when they were tired, depleted, anxious, troubled and overwhelmed. Psalm 46:10 says God is "abundantly available for help in tight places." We know God is able because we've needed him to be. Let's look at the experience of the psalmist, imagining his situation-in-life as he wrote this song to God.

Introduction
1. How do you usually feel about leading worship?
2. Have you ever had to lead at a time you were stressed or unhappy or tired? What did you do? What happened in worship?

For Study
1. Think about the image of a deer heading for a flowing stream. Why do you think the psalmist chose this? What image(s) describes your soul in times of difficulty?
2. What is the psalmist looking for in verses 1-3?

3. How does the writer feel about his past experiences of leading worship (v. 4)? How does he compare them to his current state of heart (vv. 5-6)?

4. What does the psalmist command himself to do in verse 5? What does this mean?

5. How does the author "remember" God (v. 6)? (Note: "the land of Jordan and of Hermon" is a wide expanse of territory. Check a Bible map to get a sense of this.)

6. What resources does the psalmist draw on in verse 8?

7. How does he handle his complaints about God?

8. How does the psalmist resolve his situation?

9. How do you feel about the ending?

10. This is a psalm written to be performed or used in worship. How does this fact affect your understanding of it?

How Can This Passage Change Our Worship?

1. What do you usually do when you feel down but need to lead worship? How does your response differ from the psalmist's?

2. What can you do differently—perhaps taking a cue from Psalm 42—when you hit a point of fatigue or trouble?

3. How can you work together as a team to bless and encourage one another?

Index